30 YEARS AT
Ballymaloe

30 YEARS AT Ballymaloe

DARINA ALLEN

A celebration of the world-renowned cookery school with over 100 new recipes

Photography by Laura Edwards

Kyle Books

Dedication

To Ivan and Myrtle Allen, who had the vision to start it all at
Ballymaloe, and to the next generation, Isaac, Toby, Lydia and
Emily, who will continue on the journey

First published in Great Britain in 2013 by
Kyle Books, an imprint of Kyle Cathie Limited
67–69 Whitfield Street, London W1T 4HF
general.enquiries@kylebooks.com
www.kylebooks.com

10 9 8 7 6 5 4 3 2 1

ISBN: 978 0 85783 207 8

A CIP catalogue record for this title is available
from the British Library.

Darina Allen is hereby identified as the author
of this work in accordance with Section 77
of the Copyright, Designs and Patents Act 1988.

Text © Darina Allen 2013
Photographs © Laura Edwards 2013,
except for those listed on page 319
Design © Kyle Books 2013

'Other Worlds', from *Amarcord* by Marcella Hazan
and Victor Hazan, copyright © 2008 by Marcella
Hazan and Victor Hazan. Used by permission of
Gotham Books, an imprint of Penguin Group
(USA) LLC appears on pages 110–111.

Editor: Vicky Orchard
Design: Louise Leffler
Food Photography: Laura Edwards
Food Styling: Linda Tubby
Props Styling: Polly Webb-Wilson
Production: Nic Jones and David Hearn

Colour reproduction by ALTA London
Printed and bound in China by 1010 printing Ltd.

Contents

Foreword by Alice Waters

Darina invited me for my first visit to Ballymaloe in her characteristic expansive fashion: 'Come any time!' she told me. 'Celebrate your birthday here!' I had, of course, heard of the Cookery School and knew about the groundbreaking work that Darina was doing with Irish food – but even so, I was not prepared for the full attraction of the place. The first time I came, I stayed in the hotel that Myrtle Allen, Darina's mother-in-law, had created, and it was magical: windows that opened right onto the garden, freshly picked flowers brought into your room every day. They always had a big buffet on Sundays and invited all their family and friends, with Myrtle and her husband Ivan there at the end of the table. I was so touched by those dinners, and the fact that I was so effortlessly included in them. The message was always 'come as you are, bring your friends, and join us on Sunday night'. It was such a loving, lively scene every Sunday: the kids in the family would come in still dripping from the sea and have this beautiful meal around the table with their parents, aunts and uncles, cousins and grandparents. Sometimes one daughter would sing, or another would play music for the hotel guests. This is how Ballymaloe is: you are instantly made to feel completely at home – you are included, no matter what.

Darina took me out to see the Cookery School, and we did everything: we went out to the lobster boats in Ballycotton and saw the daily catch, visited the fat, happy pigs that rooted through the fields, gathered herbs from the garden and eggs from the henhouse. The School at that time was already a bustling, well-established institution, but was ever-evolving: they were developing their greenhouse, making cheese from the milk of their Jersey cows, inviting renowned chefs from all over the world to teach classes, and, of course, teaching all the fine forgotten traditions of Irish cooking. I remember Darina's brother Rory, a chef and teacher himself, cooked up a soup for me with wild garlic, which remains one of the best things I've ever had. I learned about the sweet, milky pudding they make that's so delicious, thickened with foraged carrageen moss, that my daughter Fanny now loves; and

Darina's husband Tim taught me to make the Irish soda bread I now make every Christmas. Almost every year since that first visit I have found myself back there, celebrating my birthday with friends it seems I have known forever.

As I have returned over the years, I have watched the School change and grow as Darina has become one of the most prominent voices in Irish food politics, and a vital leader in the Slow Food movement. Last year, at Ballymaloe's first ever Literary Festival of Food and Wine, she invited the greatest chefs, authors, and voices in food to gather and exchange ideas, from Stephanie Alexander to Madhur Jaffrey, Claudia Roden, David Thompson, David Tanis and so many more. Darina is interested in the big picture of culture, forever challenging herself and others to expand the conversation about food into something deeper and more meaningful.

I think of Ballymaloe Cookery School as the very best sort of cooking school, and I send as many people to it as I possibly can. It is so exquisitely beautiful – you are always close to nature, digging your hands into the dirt, smelling the salt air. This is the sort of hands-on, immersive experience of cooking that is so important to impress upon people right now in order for them to understand the broader context of sustainability. I love how Darina takes her family and friends to have breakfast on the rocks down by the sea – bringing rashers of bacon, eggs, jam and marmalade she's made and freshly baked bread – and everyone sits down on the big, soft grass by the side of the ocean and eats together. How can a young person – or an older one, for that matter! – not be seduced by that vision? I believe almost everyone who visits Ballymaloe Cookery School comes to think of it as a home away from home, much as I have – it is impossible not to fall in love with the way of life there. Ballymaloe's great and powerful message is not just about bringing back an appreciation of food and taste, but an understanding of the culture of food, and of Ireland: a culture of stewardship of the land, tradition, hospitality, and, above all, beauty.

Introduction

The Ballymaloe Cookery School opened on 5 September 1983 in converted farm buildings in the courtyard behind our house on the farm in Kinoith. I co-founded the School with my brother Rory O'Connell and it was the culmination of several years of planning and soul-searching.

I first came to work in the kitchens at Ballymaloe House fresh from the School of Hospitality Management and Tourism on Cathal Brugha Street, Dublin, on 16 June 1968. I had heard about Myrtle Allen, a farmer's wife down in East Cork, who had opened a restaurant in her rambling old country house in the midst of a farm in Shanagarry, close to the little fishing village of Ballycotton. The menu was written every day depending on what was in season and available on the farm and in the gardens. Fish and shellfish came from Ballycotton and were added to the menu when the fresh catch was landed in the late afternoon. This was extraordinary at a time when most restaurants wrote their menu when they opened and it remained the same ten years later.

The food at Ballymaloe House was made from scratch every day. We shelled broad beans and peas and made ice cream from the fresh Jersey milk and cream. Veal, or rather baby beef, came from the male calves, fresh pork from the pigs in the farmyard, freshly laid eggs from the hens who fed on the food scraps from the restaurant, watercress from local streams. Local children foraged for blackberries, damsons, sloes and wild mushrooms and brought them to the kitchen door; Myrtle paid them generously and incorporated the fruits of their efforts into the menu. An older generation brought wild bilberries from the Knockmealdown Mountains and harvested carrageen moss from the little rocks in Ballyandreen after the spring tides. Berries and fruit came from the walled garden; tomatoes, cucumbers and lettuce came from the greenhouses in Shanagarry. In autumn over 15 varieties of apple came from the orchards around Kinoith and in May baskets full of asparagus came from the sandy field near the beach in Ballynamona.

I worked side by side with Myrtle and soaked up everything she said like a sponge; she was a gentle and patient teacher with an unerring belief in the importance of good raw materials. I soon realised that if you start off with fresh, naturally produced local food in season, then it is easy to create something utterly delicious, whereas mass-produced, denatured ingredients require a magician to make them taste good – that's where those fancy sauces and twiddles on top are needed to compensate for the flavour that is not there originally.

In October 1970 I became a member of the Allen family by the simple expedient of marrying Myrtle's eldest son Tim. We inherited Kinoith, the beautiful Regency house we now live in, and the surrounding farm and thriving horticultural enterprise, which included five acres of greenhouse, a mushroom farm and 65 acres of apple orchards. Since 1968 Myrtle had been giving cookery classes at Ballymaloe House to help to fill the bedrooms during the winter. She sweetly asked me to help; I weighed the ingredients and gave my opinion when asked. In 1981 she decided to take over the management of a restaurant in Paris to showcase Irish food: La Ferme Irlandaise. Her involvement in this restaurant meant that she was too busy to give classes at Ballymaloe House, but people continued to enquire, so she encouraged me to go ahead on my own. I thought no one would come to my classes because my name was totally unknown. But we really needed the money, so I plucked up the courage to put an advert in *The Cork Examiner* (now the *Irish Examiner*) for a series of eight Saturday morning courses. I taught them in the kitchen of the White Cottage, which had been converted into a self-catering unit for summer holiday lets. A local carpenter built a little dais for chairs, which I put in front of the window so guests could have a clear view of proceedings. My mischievous children used to come along to the window and put out their tongues and make funny faces behind people's backs, which I had to pretend not to see.

For me the first class was the most scary. People arrived in their little fur jackets and BMWs. We hid our rusty old Renault

Right: In the vegetable garden at the Ballymaloe Cookery School.

4L around the back of the house and welcomed them with freshly ground coffee and homemade biscuits. The response to the class was overwhelmingly positive – I suddenly realised that this was something I could actually do. Some things that I found easy and imagined everybody must know how to do, others seemed to find difficult and were really impressed by! I started to think about more classes and my dear friend Pauline O'Kennedy suggested starting a residential cooking school, like the Cordon Bleu in London or Paris. Irish people were sending their children abroad to learn to cook, so why not open a cookery school here? I thought about it off and on, but all the while I was cooking at home and occasionally at Ballymaloe House, as well as looking after a young family.

At the same time I longed to learn more about Italian food and, as luck would have it, Jane Montant, then editor-in-chief of *Gourmet* magazine in New York, came to stay at Ballymaloe House. Myrtle introduced us and Jane told me about an Italian cook, Marcella Hazan, who gave classes in Bologna, which included trips to markets, local bakeries, cheesemakers, vineyards and restaurants. I wrote away for details – it cost £650, a fortune in those days. I longed to go, so Tim went to the bank, took out the last money we had and enrolled me on the course as a present. It proved to be the best investment he ever made. It was a wonderful week. The group were all American and I was the only Irish student they had ever had; they were intrigued that an Irish farmer's wife had signed up.

When we visited the markets the produce was beautiful and fresh but I realised that it was no better than that at home in our garden and greenhouses. The week passed in a happy blur. On the last evening there was to be a celebration farewell dinner in a seafood restaurant in Cesenatico, the town where Marcella was born. The restaurant, La Gambara, was right on the beach and supposedly had the freshest, most wonderful seafood one could imagine. The fish dishes were indeed delicious, but no more so than the stunning fresh fish landed by our local fishermen in Ballycotton. Suddenly I truly, deeply understood what Myrtle had known all along – that fresh Irish produce is unsurpassed anywhere. I realised that the answer to my dilemma was staring me straight in the face. The solution was under my feet, a cooking school in the middle of our farm, close to the sea in Ireland – what could be more obvious? I came home with renewed determination to start a cookery school.

From the beginning we operated all year, coinciding with the school terms; I still had small children and so had many of my teachers, so I needed to be free during the school holidays. We offered two 12-week courses a year (this has now increased to

Left (top): The Cookery School, which was converted from an old apple barn designed by Henry Hill, Myrtle's father, who was one of a long line of renowned Hill architects in Cork City.
Left (bottom): The interior of the Pink Cottage, which was originally a cow byre with stalls for milking the cows. We converted it in the late 1970s, first into simple accommodation for a local potter, then a Farm Shop and subsequently a self-catering holiday cottage. It has been used as student accommodation from the start of the School. Originally furnished with traditional old dressers and settles, which we begged, borrowed and swapped, it is now rather more luxurious.
Above: The Pink Wash laundry, which overlooks Lydia's Garden, and which the students use to do their laundry during the 12-week course; a skill some students learn for the first time, much to their parents' delight!

three) intended to teach students a wide range of skills to equip them for a career in food, plus a whole series of short courses covering entertaining, vegetarian food, pub grub and cooking with fresh herbs, which were still unfamiliar to many. I also taught a new trends course every year, which had a loyal following. During the nouvelle cuisine era I included a series of classes covering that topic as well as a course entitled a Taste of Italy, France, Spain, Mexico or Morocco, depending on where I travelled.

The School has expanded over the years and on 11 September 1989, we found ourselves expecting 36 students from all over the world for the 12-week course, including five different nationalities: Irish, English, Scottish, American and Australian. Our numbers had doubled from 18 to 36 students between June and September so we needed to expand the School buildings to accommodate them. Our local builders were beyond heroic; they literally worked through the night for the last 3–4 days. I ran up and down the

ladders with freshly baked scones, topped with raspberry jam and cream, to keep them going. It really was a race against time. When the first students arrived on Saturday and Sunday, the School still wasn't finished, so we brought them into the conservatory in our house and welcomed them with homemade cakes and biscuits in the midst of the red geraniums, summer jasmine and plumbago.

We gave them a tour of the gardens, greenhouses and the farm, but we had to keep them well away from the School or they would probably have bolted, convinced that it couldn't possibly be ready by 10a.m. the next morning. They would have reckoned without Will Kenneally and his ace gang of builders, carpenters, electricians, plumbers and painters, plus a whole team of cleaners who whipped the place into shape the moment the tradesmen finished. I remember the quarry-tiled floor in the hall was still damp as we brought the students into the newly expanded School on Monday morning. The heating in the dining room wasn't connected for another week but fortunately the early September weather that year wasn't too cold!

The School has grown in size from a small kitchen adjacent to our house, to a beautifully converted apple store complete with demonstration kitchens, four hands-on student kitchens, dining rooms, prep rooms and a shop. The Cookery School Shop sells preserves, chutneys, breads, cakes, raw milk from our Jersey cows and cookery-related items and gifts. Each year has lead to a new venture and we have developed the gardens one after the other over the past 30 years, adding a berry and currant garden to the original fruit garden and expanding the herb and vegetable gardens. In 1997 we even started the ambitious planting of a Celtic Maze in yew over a ¾-acre site (a costly enterprise which was conceived in 1991, the Year of the Maze). Then 1998 saw the completion of a colourful, airy new restaurant called the Garden Café next to the Cookery School, equipped with furniture made by our nephew Sacha Whelan and hand-painted by Nicky Krussman.

We grow most of our own fruit, vegetables and herbs for both Ballymaloe House and the Cookery School. When we started the School we didn't have anything like the range of vegetables and fruit we have today. Tomatoes, cucumbers, lettuces, courgettes, peppers and the like were abundant in season but in the winter months we relied on the produce from the walled garden at Ballymaloe House – leeks, sprouting broccoli, Brussels sprouts and parsnips, all grown

Far left: Antony Worrall Thompson has been a guest chef at the School on several occasions since the early 1990s. The students have always loved his eclectic food, self-deprecating wit and the mischievous twinkle in his eye! He used to regularly propose to my teachers and he eventually married Jay, one of our past students, who assisted him at a demonstration at the Cookery School.

Left: Jane Grigson was always a food hero of mine and one of my greatest pleasures was when Jane was able to teach a guest chef course at the School. Her daughter Sophie came with Jane on further occasions and also to teach a course of her own in 1993.

Above: Students enjoying a hands-on cooking session in Kitchen Two. The photographer gathered all the students together from Kitchens One and Two (the main kitchens) for this busy picture, but we would usually have fewer students. There are four hands-on kitchens in total, which vary in size from 4–6 students in two, to 18 and 20 in the others. In each kitchen we have at least one teacher to every six students.

by Mick Cullinane, who produced superb winter vegetables and herbs for over 60 years. We now grow over 80 different different crops on the farm, in the garden and greenhouses, albeit in small quantities. It is just possible that our 100-acre farm now has a more diverse range of crops than any other farm in Ireland.

In the mid-1980s, when we could no longer get the sweet, juicy pork I remembered as a child, I decided to get pigs and bought two weanlings from a smallholder in West Cork while I was filming one of my *Simply Delicious* TV series. When our local butcher Michael Cuddigan retired in 2000, we decided to rear a few cattle to have our own beef. I got advice from Michael on what to buy in terms of traditional breeds and we now have Dexter, Angus, Shorthorn, Kerry and Jersey cows. The rest of our meat is supplied by local farmers and fish is bought directly from the boats in Ballycotton, a stone's throw from the School. Where possible we try to source organic, local produce. The five Jersey cows provide milk and cream for the School from which the students learn to make butter, cheese and yogurt. Eggs come from our own chickens and

Ballymaloe House in Shanagarry.

Festive delights along Ireland's south coast

By Joan Scobey
Special to The Globe

A lot more than potatoes and Irish stew are cooking along the southern coast of Ireland. Inventive chefs are turning the natural bounty of seafood and fresh farm produce into a new light Irish cuisine; an international cooking school affiliated with one of Ireland's best-loved inns has been established; Ireland's only wine-producing vineyard has celebrated its first vintage; and the annual Gourmet Festival always adds a dollop of Gaelic hilarity to the newly-serious business of food.

This is an enticing menu for visitors to the area around Cork, who come to swim, sail and fish at coastal resorts, canoe and hike the river valleys, and explore old and new Cork, whose history goes back to the Vikings. The Republic's second city is celebrating the 800th anniversary of its charter, and the Irish will be celebrating through the year. What visitors might not expect is some of the best eating in Ireland.

At Kinsale, for instance, the picturesque resort and fishing village 18 miles south of Cork, a remarkable number of small chef-owned restaurants offer distinctive cuisines, most of them utilizing the superb local seafood. "Fish swim in the front door," says Brian Cronin, the tall, red-haired, genial proprietor and chef of The Blue Haven, a lively seafood restaurant.

Cronin is also the spokesman for the Good Food Circle, an informal group of 10 young restaurateurs that sponsors the Kinsale Gourmet Festival, a 4-day gastronomic extravaganza the first weekend in October.

"The Festival is fun, not at all serious," says Cronin. It opens with a champagne reception where you can sample fare from the participating restaurants and, after demonstrations by chefs and food and wine receptions on any pretext whatever, it ends with a special contest. One tried recently, for example, was a cocktail-shaking competition in which the winner used 27 ingredients.

Harbor view at Kinsale

If you get to Kinsale and need help with this culinary bonanza, head for the Harbour Bar in Scilly. Sit on the patio overlooking the harbor and study the menus of Kinsale over a drink; the proprietor will call your order in to the restaurant of choice.

Between meals, Kinsale, an international sailing and angling center, offers a variety of diversions. You can fish the wreck of the Lusitania lying 20 miles off shore, visit the 17th-century fortifications that guard the harbor, wander the cobbled streets past the quays, the ramparts and well-tended Georgian homes. You can visit the museum (formerly the courthouse where the Lusitania inquest was held). Or you can browse the picturesque shops of Market Street that supply fish, produce and meat to Kinsale's restaurants.

If you want to play country ladies and gentlemen, settle in at Longueville, a Georgian mansion in the beautiful Blackwater River Valley in Mallow, 22 miles north of Cork. Longueville is known for its cuisine, its setting along the "Irish Rhine," and its romantic past that includes its forfeit to Cromwell and its rescue, 300 years later, by the original landowners.

The 500-acre estate furnishes virtually all provisions, from garden vegetables, salmon and trout (you can fish for your own), to the hundred sheep that graze on the front lawn under towering oaks.

Darina Allen of the cookery school.

A lot more than potatoes and Irish stew are cooking along the southern coast of Ireland. Inventive chefs are turning the natural bounty of seafood and fresh farm produce into a new light Irish cuisine.

Even the vintner is in danger of being replaced because proprietor Michael O'Callaghan recently uncorked the first vintage of "Longueville," a sweet Riesling grown and bottled on the estate.

A French-style cuisine

The kitchen is supervised by O'Callaghan's wife, Jane, who periodically goes to France to refresh her imaginative and elegant country French-style cuisine. In keeping with manorial life, you'll dine in front of a white marble Adams fireplace under the portraits of the presidents of Ireland. The typical fare will be Longueville lamb, or Blackwater salmon and trout, always garnished with vegetables fresh from the garden.

Longueville has a fine wine cellar, but you won't be discouraged from trying the house wine. After a sweet from the trolley, you'll retire to the gracious high-ceilinged drawing room for coffee, truffles and perhaps a brandy. The fixed-price dinner is $18.

O'Callaghan claims the only vineyard in Ireland. In 1978, he planted his former rose garden with a variety of German Riesling, which thrives in a climate similar to Ireland's and hung "Vineyard" on the iron fence. How now cultivates 3 acres.

Vinification at Longueville has a certain insouciance. The whole family, including his 90-year-old mother, picked the grapes, crushed them in a motorized laundry mangle, then pressed them into oak barrels imported from France.

The Longueville label claims a particularly inventive wine review: "Every night I gave my pregnant wife, Jane, a glass of Longueville, but it didn't agree with her at all," said Michael. "I thought, 'Oh, dear, what did I get wrong?' and took her to the obstetrician. He gave her a Medoc, and everything was fine. He gave her a Burgundy, no problem. Then he gave her a glass of Longueville, and the

rumbling started again. He sent her to X-ray – and there was the baby clapping!"

If life at Longueville and Kinsale has a continental air, Ballymaloe is all Irish, and celebrated for the special style of Myrtle Allen. "It's the tradition of Irish country house food with local ingredients of high quality – prime, fresh, simply cooked," she said.

Surrounded by acres of serene farmland and grazing sheep, Ballymaloe is the pastoral country house-hotel of Myrtle and Ivan Allen in Shanagarry, 23 miles southeast of Cork. Here, her cooking is served up with easygoing hospitality in the Yeats Room, named for its paintings by Jack Yeats, brother of poet William Butler Yeats.

The Sunday evening buffet is the best time to sample some of the specialties that have won Myrtle Allen culinary recognition from Michelin, Egon Ronay, and Gault-Millau: fish soups, pates, sea urchin, fresh oysters and mussels, spiced beef and rib roasts, Ballymaloe's famous brown bread, and sweets that are likely to include caramel mousse and gooseberry fool. The fixed-price meals are $19.

Life at Ballymaloe is unhurried. You might stroll down to the nearby fishing village of Ballycotton and watch the day's catch unloaded, or drive to Waterford. Perhaps play tennis or swim, or read on the front lawn. You'll feel like family, waiting for the next meal.

Truly a family enterprise

Ballymaloe is very much a family enterprise. Myrtle Allen developed her recipes over the years, testing them with her husband and six children. One son runs the surrounding 400-acre farm that provides the dairy products, lamb, pork and bacon for the kitchen; another supplies vegetables and fruit from his 100-acre neighboring produce market; their wives help run the kitchen and the hotel. Ivan Allen buys the wine for the outstanding cellar, and one son-in-law manages the Allens' Paris restaurant, La Ferme Irlandaise.

In 1983, daughter-in-law Darina started The Ballymaloe Cookery School, which teaches Myrtle Allen's "Ballymaloe style." Darina describes it as "using the natural produce of the area, which combines rich farmland and an abundance of seafood." The school, set in a lovely Regency House in the middle of orchards and gardens, offers several 1-week courses, 3- and 4-day sessions, and afternoon demonstrations, in addition to the 12-week certificate course. The school is open from September to mid-May; for details, write to Darina Allen, The Ballymaloe Cookery School, Kinoith, Shanagarry, Co. Cork, Ireland (021-646785).

Joan Scobey is a free-lance writer from New York.

---

are collected every morning by the students on a rota basis.

Over the years I've noticed students becoming more and more detached from the reality of how food is produced, so I decided to begin each 12-week course by introducing the gardeners and farm manager to the students. On the first morning we start with a welcoming cup of coffee and then I introduce the students to Haulie Walsh and Eileen O'Donovan. We then make our way to the fruit garden, where I have a wheelbarrow full of compost ready. This has been made from the food scraps and organic matter from the 12-week course a year earlier. I talk to the students about the importance of sourcing good ingredients, how all good food comes from good earth and that we all depend on the few inches of topsoil around the globe for our survival. I discuss the emerging food security concerns and remind them that there is no more than 90 days of food available in the world at any one time. I run my hands through the soil and tell them about the extraordinary bacteria, enzymes, minerals, trace elements and magic earthworms in the soil. Without rich, fertile soil we won't have clean water or good food. All of this gets a rather baffled and confused response as they stand around in a polite circle, clearly thinking, 'Crazy, aged hippy! It didn't say anything about this is the brochure!' – but by the end of the course they are every bit as passionate as I am.

Then we wander through the gardens, past the herbs, vegetables and fruits, through the wildflower meadow and down to the greenhouses, where Susan Turner, our consultant head gardener, is waiting to show them how to sow a seed. For me this is a very important first lesson of the course, because for many people food is something that comes wrapped in plastic off a supermarket shelf. In their busy lives they have little time to think about where it comes from or how it is produced, not to mention the breed or the variety. I know of no better way to give people a respect for food and those who produce it than to show them how to sow a seed and for them to watch it grow. We give each student a vegetable – it could be broccoli, spring onions or even lettuce, depending on the season – to put into the ground. They write their name on a lollipop stick and watch their vegetable's progress over the three months of the course. The responsibility for caring for their plant is a real revelation, as is the understanding that it can take the full 12 weeks of the course for their sweetcorn or broccoli to be

Left: An early article about the School, which appeared in The Boston Globe *on 16 June 1985.*

ready to eat. This also brings home the precariousness of our food system, as they begin to realise that you can't just plant a vegetable and expect it to be ready to eat next week. Students suddenly appreciate the sheer work and dedication that goes into producing delicious ingredients, and realise that plants have to be regularly watered and animals need to be fed and cared for every day. It also ensures that they treat produce with more care and respect in the kitchen. Students are so excited when they harvest and cook the vegetables that they have grown and want to share this with the rest of their class.

Students on the 12-week course come from all over the world. There is a teacher for every six students and the day is structured so that everyone gets an opportunity to cook several of the dishes they have watched being demonstrated the previous afternoon. The afternoon demonstrations often cover as many as 25 recipes illustrating variations on the same techniques, ingredients and themes. By the end of the course, these recipes are a comprehensive anthology of everything the course has covered. These sessions are open to the public as well as the 12-week students.

The day officially starts at 9a.m. but many students begin at 8a.m. or earlier if they want to learn how to milk the cows. Duties are split by rotas and include picking salad and vegetables, making butter, preparing stock, weighing ingredients and general kitchen tasks that need to be done before the pressure of the morning starts. Students work in pairs, although everyone cooks their own dishes. Once they have completed their dishes, we have a tutor tasting, where the teachers mark each recipe. Continual assessment gives us the chance to gauge progress. Halfway through the course there is a mid-term test. At the end, there is a full examination, which together with the assessment marks, goes towards the 12-week course certificate.

The age range is as diverse as the nationalities and backgrounds of the students. There are a number of gap year students, 30-year-olds embarking on a career change, mothers whose children have left home, people working in the food business who want training and a qualification, B&B owners, food writers and food lovers from all walks of life.

When I joined the International Association of Culinary Professionals (IACP) in 1986 I met many iconic cooks, chefs, food writers and teachers and invited them to teach at the School. One of the earliest guest teachers in 1985 was Ada Parasiliti from Milan and Anne Willan, who ran the highly regarded Ecole de Cuisine La Varenne in Paris, came in 1991. John Desmond, who has worked in many three-starred Michelin restaurants, came annually for many years – an excellent teacher, he and his wife Ellmary own Island Cottage Restaurant on Hare (or Heir) Island off Baltimore. Each chef has added to our knowledge and their recipes have become favourites in our repertoire over the years.

Ever hungry and curious for knowledge and new ideas, I also incorporated what I learned from my travels into the courses. Fortunately food and agriculture are my passions, so each trip I had was a delicious experience, with a perfect excuse to eat for Ireland, all in the name of research. I introduced Mexican recipes after my trips to Oaxaca, Michoacán and Teotitlán del Valle; Asia provided further inspiration as dishes from Thailand, Singapore, Malaysia and Cambodia have been added to our curriculum. These experiences bring my classes to life as I paint word pictures of Vietnam, India, Laos, Europe and the US and their food for the students. After my first visit to California I was so excited that I have tried to return to the West coast at least bi-annually. The IACP Conference is held somewhere on the North American continent every year, which has given me the opportunity to visit many US cities including Denver, San Francisco, Dallas, Houston, Seattle, Chicago and New York. Slow Food has brought me to Salone del Gusto and Terra Madre in Turin, a life-changing experience.

When I first visited Galle in Sri Lanka in 2010, everyone was agog with excitement about the Galle Literary Festival. We caught the end of it and had fun with Louis de Bernières, author of *Captain Corelli's Mandolin*, Skye Gyngell, Nick Lander and Jancis Robinson, all participants in the festival, who had stayed on for a few days to enjoy beautiful Sri Lanka. The festival's wildly creative director Geoffrey Dobbs suggested that we think about having a literary festival at Ballymaloe and so the concept was born.

It took three years for The Ballymaloe Literary Festival of Food and Wine (or LitFest) to become reality. With the Ballymaloe connection it seemed natural to celebrate the work of iconic food and wine writers from around the world. When the decision was made to go ahead, I picked up the phone and invited friends from all over the world to come to Ballymaloe on the May Bank holiday weekend and all, apart from two people who were already committed, said yes. Alice Waters and Stephanie Alexander, who are both committed to edible food education, were top of my list. Grand dames of the food world Madhur Jaffrey and Claudia Roden, guest chefs in earlier years, agreed to return. David Thompson came from Bangkok to talk about Thai and Asian street food. Claus Meyer, co-founder of Noma, agreed to talk about the Nordic

Above (clockwise, from top left): Matthew Fort moderates a panel of Donal Skehan, Rachel Allen, Stevie Parle and Thomasina Miers giving a talk on New Voices in Food; my nephew, Sacha Whelan, expertly hand-carving a pata negra at the LitFest – in real life he makes beautiful bespoke wooden furniture and the hardwood chopping boards we use at the School; iced biscuits sold at the LitFest by past student Gail Porter;

me and Madhur Jaffrey giving a cookery demonstration from her book Curry Nation; our line-up of 42 speakers at the LitFest included Sandor Katz, who drew people from all over the world, including a fan from Japan, and David Thompson, who gave a riveting demonstration on Asian street food; Rosie Campbell and Dennis McCarthy demonstrate falconry with the birds from their Animal Magic Wildlife Rescue Centre.

food revolution. David Tanis, prominent American chef from Chez Panisse, and David Prior, journalist for various publications including *The New York Times*, both said an enthusiastic yes, as did 'King of Fermentation' Sandor Ellix Katz. Thomasina Miers, Stevie Parle, Claire Ptak, Donal Skehan, Rachel Allen (all past students) and Skye Gyngell represented the new young voices in food. Joanna Blythman, Suzanne Campbell and Ella McSweeney gave a workshop on Digesting Unsavoury Truths. Bill Yosses, the White House pastry chef, came to tell us about Michelle Obama's vegetable garden.

There were food historians, bloggers, foragers and restaurant critics attending literary dinners and readings, question and answer sessions and talks covering topics such as food writing for the digital generation. There was a strong Irish presence and a huge wine element organised by Colm McCan, sommelier at Ballymaloe House, who also teaches a number of wine courses at the School. People travelled from around the world to hear Jancis Robinson, MW, speak on wine grapes and her husband Nick Lander, restaurant correspondent for the *Financial Times*, speak on the Art of the Restaurateur.

The LitFest took place at Ballymaloe House, the Grainstore at Ballymaloe and the Ballymaloe Cookery School. There were back-to-back cookery demonstrations at the School plus Saturday Pizzas and Sunday Roasts from the wood-burning oven in the Garden Café. The huge fringe festival in the Big Shed at Ballymaloe took on a life of its own. It had a makeover with recycled furniture made from lots of pallets and was decorated with graffiti and a chandelier made from old whiskey barrels.

We had hoped for 2,500–3,000 people over the weekend; instead more than 8,000 visitors poured in, creating a continuous bustle of people roaming around the farmers' market stalls and enjoying the many free fringe events. The festival received write-ups in *The New York Times*, *International Herald Tribune*, *The Malaysian Times* as well as the *Guardian* and over 100 other publications. It trended several times on Twitter in Ireland and Europe over the weekend; an amazing achievement. Plans have started for the festival in 2014 and it looks like it may be an annual, or at least biannual, event over the next few years.

When Rory and I started the school in 1983, I was aware of only one other cookery school in Ireland, Alix Gardner's school in Ballsbridge, Dublin. Now there are around 40-plus, many of which are very successfully run by my ex-students. So we have created our own competition, which is great because it not only keeps us

Above (top): Skye Gyngell has returned to teach at the School on many occasions. Here she is making a green salad and adding her own twist by grating lemon zest and Parmesan over it at the last minute before tossing. She loves to fill the salad bowl with freshly picked greens grown here at Ballymaloe.
Above (middle): Sam Clark from Moro taught at the School in 2002, sharing the food that has made Moro and, more recently, Morito famous.
Above (bottom): Jacob Kenedy of Bocca di Lupo, another of my food heroes, visited the School in 2013 and showed us how to make artichokes a la giudia and a shaved radish salad, among other delicious dishes.

on our toes but also spreads the word and teaches more and more people to cook – a skill badly needed in a society, which, like many in the Western world, has placed greater emphasis on the value of academic rather than practical skills for the past two or three generations. Consequently, a high percentage of the population are no longer equipped with the basic skills needed to feed themselves properly. For many, anything more than slitting the top of a packet or reheating a pre-cooked meal in a microwave is a mystery. I love teaching people how to cook and feel fortunate that food is my subject. The look of pride on a student's face when they take their first loaf of bread out of the oven gives me a feeling of excitement every time.

Over the past few years I've become more and more concerned about the quality of the food we eat. Food is the fuel for our bodies; if you don't put good petrol in the tank, the 'car' won't perform properly. It's ironic that so many of us care for our cars and motorbikes much better than ourselves. We wouldn't dream of putting inferior oil or petrol in them, yet we shovel any kind of old rubbish into our bodies and then wonder why we are low in energy, sluggish or lacking in concentration. For most people the only criteria when choosing food is price; never before have we spent so small a percentage of our income on food. The truth is that very few people connect the food they eat with how they feel. If we did, we would make it a greater priority.

At this point in time I have no intention of retiring and plan to keep teaching as long as I have the energy and strength. I am eternally curious and love learning as much as my students. Food, wine and farming give me the opportunity to add to my knowledge and meet fascinating, inspirational people – both here at Ballymaloe and on my travels across the globe – who are every bit as passionate as I am about delicious, nourishing food, sustainable farming and looking after the soil that nourishes us all. Ballymaloe Cookery School students now work all over the world cooking and teaching and are involved in food in a myriad of ways, from manning stalls at farmers' markets to running farm shops and their own cookery schools, writing cookbooks and blogs to cooking on yachts, oil rigs, in the Outback or in pubs, cafés and food trucks. They work in food manufacturing, artisan food production, cake shops, delicatessens, bakeries and at food camps. Some give pop-up dinners, teach kids' cooking classes, run dining clubs and make homemade chocolates. Others have careers as cooks and chefs, TV presenters, cheesemakers or organise food conferences and symposiums. They use their skills foraging, preserving, pickling, brewing, butchering and making charcuterie. It doesn't matter where in the world I go now, from Asian airports to Sri Lankan beaches, gastropubs to cafés and food fairs, an ex-student will pop up, calling my name.

I love what I do and feel blessed to be teaching a subject that not only excites people but gives them the skills and confidence that will enhance the quality of their day to day lives.

Above (left): Jeremy Lee from Quo Vadis in London is a wildly entertaining teacher – this image captures a serious moment amongst the usual hilarity. When the students taste the food of our guest chefs they immediately add the chef's restaurant to their 'London list' and plan to book a table and taste more when in town.
Above (right): Rory O'Connell teaching in the newly renovated demonstration kitchen in the summer of 2013.

Art around the School

The collection of art around the School is eclectic to say the least; a mixture of contemporary paintings, mixed media pieces, oils, etchings and watercolours of the gardens, plus some early portraits painted by our daughter Lydia while she was at art school in Florence. Poetry by Seamus Heaney and the 'Deer's Cry' (also known as 'St. Patrick's Breastplate'), a beautiful piece from the late 7th or early 8th century, adorn the walls in the reception area close to the blackboard where the 'Food from the Farm Today' is written.

In 1987 the boxwood hedges in the herb garden were becoming more established. Rory and I had been working very hard setting up the Cookery School, so our caring GP Dr. Derry McCarthy ordered a rest and I spent a lovely two weeks with Mummy up in Cullohill. When I arrived back at the Cookery School I was met by Tim in a suit and I knew something was afoot. I was led out to the garden blindfolded and up the rickety steps of the viewing platform made of recycled greenhouse timber and old apple stakes. Suddenly down below people burst into a rousing 'Happy Birthday!' The herb garden was packed with friends gathered from all over the country and abroad – a surprise birthday party.

The family presented me with a beautiful stone sundial carved by Tanya Mosse, one of the multitalented Mosse family from Bennettsbridge in County Kilkenny. We have been collecting the drawings and paintings of her brother Paul since the mid-1990s; Nicholas Mosse's pottery has been a part our lives since he first opened his studio in 1976, and his brother Keith is a woodturner extraordinaire. The huge timber bowl, which holds the green salad in the Blue Dining Room at the Cookery School every day, was turned by Keith from Irish elm in 1988. Oliver, the youngest member of this extraordinary Mosse family, is a horticulturalist and recently gave me a present of a truffle oak, which we hope will bear fruit in the not too distant future. Tanya's sundial, carved in Kilkenny limestone, incorporated four cherubs on the panels of the pedestal (representing our four children) bearing gifts of fruit, vegetables, flowers and herbs. Owen Deignan, a member of the Royal National Lifeboat Institution (RNLI), made the actual sundial from brass. The piece embedded in the gravel in the boxwood semicircle on the northeast side of the herb garden, close to the old potting shed and remains of Lydia Strangman's fernery.

In 1991, I commissioned sculptor Ken Thompson, of Ballytrasna, near Ballycotton, to made a bird bath for Tim for Christmas. It's a beautiful piece, also carved from a chunk of Kilkenny limestone,

large enough to be a tabletop – 1.4m (4½ft) in diameter and 9cm (3½in) deep, but with a shallow water bath in the centre. The inscription is a William Blake quote, which reads 'He who binds to himself a joy/ Does the winged life destroy;/ But he who kisses the joy as it flies/ Lives in eternity's sunrise'. On the inner circle is written 'A Christmas gift from Darina to Tim 1991'. It sits outside the main entrance to the Cookery School surrounded by seats for the students to sit and chat around it every day in nice weather.

The Ballymaloe Baker (pictured above) is the newest addition to the grounds. This beautiful sculpture of a baker proudly taking a loaf of bread out of the oven on a paddle was also carved by Ken Thompson. Its inscription, in Latin, reads 'T*D MMX mefieri fecit' and translated means 'Tim and Darina caused me to be made in 2012'. The students quickly christened it the 'feck it' statue, an irreverent play on the Latin word *fecit*.

The First 12-week Course

When my brother Rory O'Connell and I started the Cookery School in 1983, I was aware of only one other in Ireland: Alix Gardner's school in Ballsbridge, Dublin. However, in the 30 years since then, over 40 cookery schools have opened across the country, many of which are very successfully run by my ex-students.

When we decided to open a residential cookery school, I decided to visit those with the best reputation and, wherever possible, enrol in an afternoon class. I was quite open with everyone about my own plans and was greeted warmly and generously by each and every school I visited.

Alix generously welcomed me at Ballsbridge to see how she operated her classes. Caroline Waldegrave and Sally Proctor showed me around Prue Leith's and generously shared their experience with me, as did John and Beryl Childs at Tante Marie in Woking (now co-owned by Lyndy Redding, Andrew Maxwell, a past Ballymaloe student, and Gordon Ramsay). I went to see Sabine de Mirbeck's cookery school in Sussex, where I had a lovely convivial day, lunch with the students and teachers and a tour of the school's facilities and gardens. I also loved La Petite Cuisine in

Richmond run by another superb chef and teacher, Lyn Hall. After the cookery demonstration I introduced myself to Lyn and I always remember her words as I enthusiastically told her about my plans: 'Well, be prepared to work 11 hours a day and then it'll be great!' She wasn't far off the mark.

The bank manager had turned down our original application for a loan to open a cookery school – in fact he was quite amused by the idea. My parents-in-law Ivan and Myrtle Allen generously acted as guarantors for us. So, as soon as Tim and I received the bank loan that we needed, we started the process of converting some farm buildings into a school and extra accommodation. The builders and carpenters worked non-stop for several months to get the kitchen-cum-demonstration area and dining room into shape. (The latter had been the children's playroom plus an extra bedroom where we took overflow from Ballymaloe House on a B&B basis during the summer months.) The new kitchen was 6.4m x 6.7m (21ft x 22ft) with an A roof. We decided to put a long, narrow casement window along the front, overlooking the orchard, and inserted some skylights into the roof. The walls of the building were about 0.6m (2ft) thick, so we were able to have a wide windowsill for pots of herbs and edible flowers, including sweet geranium, and of course space to cool bread. I've always loved the image of a loaf of soda bread cooling on a wire rack by an open window in the traditional way.

The kitchen cupboards and shelves were made from white deal. Barry O'Keeffe, our local carpenter, made them and fortunately unpainted wood was just becoming fashionable. The counter and shelves were easy-to-clean white formica – I had always liked the look of it. The original plan had been to use hardwood, but that proved to be outside our budget.

We framed a couple of Tessa Traeger's *Vogue* food posters and hung them on the walls. A couple of red wire grids to hang utensils completed the country chic look. The floor was tiled with beautiful terracotta quarry tiles imported from Spain by Stephen Pearce, our potter friend from the village of Shanagarry. The softly plastered

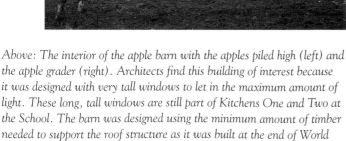

Above: The interior of the apple barn with the apples piled high (left) and the apple grader (right). Architects find this building of interest because it was designed with very tall windows to let in the maximum amount of light. These long, tall windows are still part of Kitchens One and Two at the School. The barn was designed using the minimum amount of timber needed to support the roof structure as it was built at the end of World War II when timber was scarce. These images show the farm buildings before their conversion into the Cookery School, with the Pink Cottage in its original state as a cow byre. It had a galvanised roof, which we later replaced with hand-cut slates and timber windows and doors. The White Cottage (bottom right) was where the original School was and this was where the students were taught for the first classes in 1983.

Left: A very much younger version of my brother Rory and me demonstrating together in the early days of the Cookery School. Right: Very intense pictures of me from the early days of School, looking like I could do with a hearty steak and good night's sleep! From the beginning we used the gardens at the School to provide fresh produce for the students' cooking. In the image on the top right I can be seen slathering butter onto chicken liver pâté – very of its time.

walls were white-washed with burnt lime in the traditional way. A little corridor between the kitchen and dining room with a worktop and shelves on each side was our weigh-up area, where the preparation of ingredients for the cookery demonstrations was done. At the other side there was a washroom and store and an office-cum-library on the balcony overhead. This busy little office overlooking the dining room was where my secretary, Rosalie Dunne, worked when she joined us in February 1984. The phone was answered, enquiries and bookings dealt with, and recipes typed and printed. Anyone visiting the School was greeted from up here and immediately looked after. My cookbook collection was housed on shelves up under the eaves and the students were allowed to browse and borrow. Over the years the cookbook collection grew and grew and is now in the region of 3,000 copies and still expanding!

The dining room had a couple of round tables, just over 2m (6.5ft) in diameter, with a large wooden revolving lazy Susan (sometimes called a dumb waiter) in the centre, from which the dishes were accessible. I love round tables; they seem very welcoming and somehow there's always room for another person. We used blue and white gingham tablecloths, beautifully laid with a little vase of flowers from the garden, small bowls of sea salt and pepper mills, unusual in 1983. From the beginning the students and teachers sat down together to relax, enjoy and discuss the results of the morning's cooking, always a very convivial time. This interaction between students and teachers and sharing the results of the students' labours is not a common feature in all cooking schools but something we really value at Ballymaloe. The students and teachers are often joined by a few guests, perhaps friends or family of the students who are always welcome to join us.

While the building was taking shape, Tim, Rory and I were grappling with another decision – what should we call the school? Shanagarry Cooking School? Darina Allen Cooking School? At that stage my name was totally unknown. However, the name Ballymaloe already stood for integrity and quality; Ivan and Myrtle Allen's hotel and restaurant, Ballymaloe House, was highly regarded, with top ratings in the *Good Food Guide* and *Egon Ronay Guides* for the quality of its food. We didn't dare propose it, but my parents-in-law suggested we call it Ballymaloe Cookery School. This was an incredible boost and a show of faith in us. A friend who had been in advertising helped us design a simple brochure. We put an advert in the national newspaper *The Irish Times* and the local *Cork Examiner*, and waited for the postman to come and the phone to ring. By now we were deeply in debt – it simply had to work, so we decided to operate all year round during the normal school terms.

There was NO money for extra advertising. We decided to charge similar fees to the Cordon Bleu and Prue Leith Cooking Schools in London – I was determined that if we were going to run a cookery school it would be as good as, if not better than anywhere else in the world. So we needed to charge enough to do it really well with a margin for generosity. If someone burnt their bread or made a mess of something I wanted to be able to give them more ingredients without feeling resentful. I was determined that everyone who came should feel that they had at least got value for money and, preferably, much, much more.

As I planned the menus for the first 12-week course in 1983,

Above (top): Rory and me with the students of one of the first 12-week classes.
(middle): The mirror we had above the demonstration area from the beginning provided a view directly into the saucepans for the students, which intrigued people when they first came but is now a common sight at many cookery schools.
(bottom): This was initially a dual-purpose room; in the morning the students cooked in a hands-on session and in the afternoons we brought chairs into the centre of the room to create a demonstration area.

it suddenly occurred to me that I needed to incorporate a wine element into the course. It was almost unthinkable to enjoy a good meal without a glass or two of wine. In the early 1980s many people's knowledge of wine was very limited. Most houses would have had a little sherry and whiskey, maybe a bottle of port wine in the sideboard in the drawing room or parlour, but it was another decade at least before one could buy wine in virtually every supermarket and garage forecourt. Consequently, many found wine an intimidating subject – they felt they ought to know a bit more about it but weren't sure how to go about learning. There weren't all that many books on wine and few off-licences.

I decided to incorporate some wine lectures into our first 12-week course, and from then on I took every opportunity to learn as much as I could about the subject. I was very anxious to take the mystery out of wine, to equip the students with enough knowledge to make them comfortable about the subject in any social situation and to give them the necessary confidence, know-how and contacts to assemble a wine list in a restaurant.

My father-in-law, Ivan Allen, also came to my rescue, giving the wine lectures for the first couple of years, and since then we've had a series of wonderful wine lecturers, including the late John O'Connell, Kevin Parsons, Tom Doorley, Sacha Whelan and Colm McCan (head sommelier at Ballymaloe House for many years).

Tim and I swapped roles; he looked after the children, getting them to school and cooking for them, so that I could concentrate on getting the School up and running. We started on 5 September 1983 with 11 students on a 12-week certificate course that aimed to equip them with the basic culinary knowledge and skills to earn their living from their cooking. My brother, Rory O'Connell (who had been a chef at Ballymaloe House) and I did absolutely everything – wrote the recipes, which were then typed with an electric typewriter onto stencils and printed off on a Gestetner printing machine (this was before the days of word processors, computers and laser jet printers), demonstrated, taught hands-on classes, washed up and answered queries.

On the first 12-week certificate course we had ten girls and one lucky chap – all Irish. Several came from their own family-run businesses, either hotels or restaurants, and a couple of others were anxious to do the course so that they could cook and entertain with confidence and panache. Caroline Casey from Blackrock in Cork had always had a great interest in cooking. Her ambition was to start her own catering business doing lunches, private dinner parties, etc. She intended to go to London to do a course in cookery, but

when she heard about the new diploma course at Ballymaloe she decided to enrol. Susan Cummins from Dublin wanted to concentrate on getting into the catering business in Ireland. Mary Cotter from Co. Cork already worked in the hotel trade locally and enrolled on the course to further her knowledge of cooking. Clodagh McAlinden worked in the Adam and Eve Restaurant in Cork but wanted to gain experience in cooking and to get new ideas for her job. Anna Sheehan, of Charleville, was also involved in the hotel business. She worked in her family hotel and, like Clodagh, wanted to gain the experience and confidence to cope with staff and the running of a hotel kitchen. Tim Rooney from Sligo had spent several years at sea, fishing. He had also done a business course, but discovered that his real love was cooking and that he yearned to work in a kitchen. Several of our first batch of students have continued in the restaurant business.

We taught an extensive range of cooking techniques: butchery, fish filleting, preserving, freezing, ethnic cooking and so on. There were lectures on menu-planning, food costing, food hygiene and career advice. We still cover all these topics and, over the years, have added in more information and expanded students' learning opportunities.

Gradually, news of Ballymaloe Cookery School spread, mainly through word of mouth. Once we had settled in and things were up and running smoothly, we decided to have an official opening on 14 November 1983. We chose that date because we wanted to have the opening before the current class came up to their exams, and before Ballymaloe House was getting busy for the Christmas season. It was also a good way of generating publicity for the next course, which was to start in January 1984. We invited Michael MacNulty, Chief Executive of Bord Fáilte (Irish Tourist Board); Minister for Agriculture Paddy Hegarty; Pat McDonagh of Bord Bainne (Dairy Board); Maeve Bracken of CBF (The Irish Meat Board) and many friends and members of the press. Ever generous, my parents-in-law invited them all to Ballymaloe House. The new students cooked and proudly served a delicious afternoon tea at the Cookery School: little scones with homemade jam and cream, raspberry and almond tartlets, praline cake, gingerbread and a traditional Irish fruit cake called a barmbrack. There were speeches and much well wishing – I remember being amused and a little overwhelmed when I heard my friend Pauline O'Kennedy, who had always encouraged me, remark to my mother: 'History is being made today.'

Above: Teaching a class in the original Cookery School, wearing what became my trademark red glasses.

Equipping the School

When I started the School, I was determined to equip the kitchens with the best and most beautiful equipment. For me that was Le Pentole ICM saucepans, which I had bought one by one over the years for my own house from David Mellor's lovely shop in Sloane Square, London. Simply designed, beautiful stainless-steel saucepans, they have solid three-layer bases in each (copper, steel and alloy) to conduct the heat. It was a big investment, but one that has proved to be worth every penny. I also chose David Mellor's range of Provençale cutlery for the dining room, which we still use and enjoy.

Rory and I made a trip to Dehillerin in Paris, an old-fashioned kitchen shop on the corner of Rue Coquillière and Rue Jean-Jacques Rousseau. It is a cook's heaven. Dehillerin has been owned by the same family for over 200 years and is known for selecting items for quality not just price. Kitchen utensils are piled high from floor to ceiling on (sometimes dusty) timber shelves. It is primarily for the professional chef, but you are just as likely to see American and Japanese tourists rummaging through the cramped and crowded aisles of this unique and historic store to find obscure utensils – all are welcome. I bought a nest of stainless steel bowls for every section in the School's kitchen and they are still in use 30 years later. I also bought some madeleine and genoise tins and a couple of rum baba moulds, which would have been difficult to find in Ireland at the time.

❧

French Peasant Soup

This is a very substantial soup – it has 'eating and drinking' in it and would certainly be a meal in itself, particularly if some grated Cheddar cheese was scattered over the top. We have added different variations to the soup over the years, sometimes including cooked beans, such as haricot, to the soup to make a more substantial meal, or a drizzle of kale pesto during the winter. When Myrtle Allen ran La Ferme Irlandaise in Paris serving Irish country food, she changed the name of this soup to Connemara Broth – the French loved it.

Serves 6

175g (6oz) unsmoked streaky bacon (in the piece)
1 tablespoon olive or sunflower oil
150g (5oz) potatoes, peeled and cut into 5mm (¼in) dice
50g (2oz) onions, finely chopped
1 small garlic clove, peeled and crushed (optional)
450g (1lb) very ripe tomatoes, peeled and diced or
½–1 x 400g (14oz) can of tomatoes and their juice
½–1 teaspoon sugar
700ml (1¼ pints) homemade chicken or vegetable stock
50g (2oz) cabbage (Savoy is best), finely chopped
sea salt and freshly ground black pepper

To serve
flat-leaf parsley, coarsely chopped

Remove the rind from the bacon if necessary and cut the bacon into approx. 5mm (¼in) strips. Blanch the lardons of bacon in cold water by bringing it to the boil over a high heat to remove some of the salt and nitrates, if present. Drain off the frothy water and dry the bacon lardons on kitchen paper.

In a frying pan, sauté the bacon in the olive or sunflower oil until the fat runs and the bacon is crisp and golden. Add the potatoes, onions and crushed garlic, if using, sweat for 10 minutes, and then add the diced tomatoes along with any juice. Season with salt, pepper and sugar. Pour in the stock, bring to the boil and simmer for 5 minutes. Add the finely chopped cabbage and continue to simmer just until the cabbage is cooked. Taste and correct the seasoning, if necessary. Sprinkle with lots of chopped parsley and serve.

This basic soup has been a Ballymaloe staple since the beginning of the School. It teaches students how to slice and dice and how to blanch and refresh, as well as how to extract salt from the bacon.

Glazed Loin of Bacon

❧

We sometimes serve the bacon with spiced plums or Peperonata; in the earlier days the usual accompaniments were tomato fondue and champ. We use loin of bacon off the bone.

Serves 12–15

1.8–2.25kg (4–5lb) loin of bacon, either smoked or unsmoked
approx. 20–30 whole cloves
350g (12oz) demerara sugar (not soft brown sugar)
approx. 3–4 tablespoons pineapple juice (from a 400g (14oz) can of pineapple)

Put the bacon in a large saucepan, cover with cold water and bring slowly to the boil. If the bacon is very salty, there will be a white froth on top of the water and, if this is the case, it is preferable to discard this water. It may be necessary to change the water several times, depending on the saltiness of the bacon. Finally cover with hot water and simmer until almost cooked, allowing 45 minutes to the kg (approx. 20 minutes to the lb).

Preheat the oven to 240°C/475°F/gas 9. Remove the bacon from the pan and cut off the rind. Cut the fat into a diamond pattern and stud with cloves. Blend the brown sugar to a thick paste with a little pineapple juice, being careful not to make it too liquid. Spread this over the bacon. Bake in the preheated oven for approx. 20–30 minutes or until the top has caramelised. Remove from the oven and put on a carving dish. Carve in thick slices lengthways so each slice includes some of the eye of the loin and streaky bacon.

Fork Biscuits

❧

We've been making these simple biscuits since the beginning; originally they were plain, but we now have fun doing many variations on the theme. Try Jette Virdi's Cumin Biscuits (see Variations); the spice proved to be a really good addition.

Makes approx. 45–50

225g (8oz) butter, softened
110g (4oz) caster sugar
275g (10oz) self-raising flour, sifted
grated zest of 1 lemon or orange
vanilla sugar, to sprinkle

Preheat the oven to 180°C/350°F/gas 4 and line two baking trays with baking parchment.

Cream the butter and add in the caster sugar, sifted flour and grated lemon or orange zest and mix until it all comes together. Alternatively, put all four ingredients in the bowl of a food processor and mix slowly until all the ingredients come together. (At this stage, the dough can be put in the freezer or kept in the fridge for up to a week.)

When required, bring up to room temperature and form into small balls the size of a walnut. Flatten them out onto the prepared baking trays using the back of a fork dipped in cold water. Allow plenty of room for expansion.

Bake in the preheated oven for approx. 10 minutes. Sprinkle with the vanilla sugar and leave to cool. When cold, store in an airtight container.

Variations

For Jette Virdi's Cumin Biscuits, add 2 teaspoons of freshly roasted and ground cumin seeds and the freshly squeezed juice of 2 lemons to the basic mixture.

For cinnamon, ginger or chocolate biscuits, add 2 teaspoons ground cinnamon or ginger or 50–75g (2–3oz) chopped chocolate to the basic mixture.

Almond Tart or Tartlets with Raspberries or Loganberries

These little tarts are still made at Ballymaloe House and are also a favourite here at the Cookery School. Students can't believe how easy they are to make and how many variations they can explore with seasonal toppings – kumquats, rhubarb, raspberries, strawberries, blueberries… I have a particular soft spot for this recipe, apart from the fact that it is super-delicious. Years ago, when I was a student at Cathal Brugha Street College in Dublin, I went to an afternoon tea party with my boyfriend. Among the dainties on offer were little almond tartlets with homemade raspberry jam and a blob of cream. I loved them and ventured to ask for the recipe. The hostess was flattered but flatly refused; it was her secret. When I arrived at Ballymaloe a few weeks later, Myrtle had these little tartlets on the dessert trolley and she not only shared the recipe but showed me exactly how to make them.

Preheat the oven to 180°C/350°F/gas 4. To make the pastry, cream the butter really well and then stir in the sugar and ground almonds. (Don't overbeat the mixture or the oil will leak out of the ground almonds as the pastry cooks.) Divide the mixture between 24 shallow 6.5cm (2½in) tartlet tins or 2 x 17.5cm (7in) sandwich tins. Bake in the preheated oven until golden brown – approx. 10–12 minutes for the tartlets or 20–30 minutes for the tarts.

Meanwhile, make the redcurrant glaze. Melt the redcurrant jelly with the water in a small stainless steel saucepan. Stir gently, but do not whisk or it will become cloudy. Simmer for 1–2 minutes, no longer or the jelly will darken.

Remove the tartlets or tarts from the oven and set aside to cool in their tins for 5 minutes before turning them out. Do not allow them to set hard or the butter will solidify and the pastry will stick to the tins. If this happens, pop the tins back into the oven for a few minutes so the butter melts and then they will come out easily. Set aside to cool.

Just before serving, arrange the whole raspberries or loganberries on the base. Briefly reheat the redcurrant glaze and brush over the fruit. Decorate with rosettes of cream and tiny mint or sweet cicely leaves.

Serves 12 (Makes 24 tartlets, 2 medium tarts or 1 tart and 12 tartlets)

For the pastry
110g (4oz) unsalted butter, softened
110g (4oz) caster sugar
110g (4oz) ground almonds

For the redcurrant glaze (makes 300ml)
350g (12oz) redcurrant jelly
approx. 1 tablespoon water (if necessary)

For the filling
450g (1lb) fresh raspberries or loganberries
300ml (10fl oz) whipped cream

To serve
mint or sweet cicely leaves

Redcurrant Jelly

900g (2lb) redcurrants
900g (2lb) granulated sugar

Remove the strings from the redcurrants either by hand or with a fork. Put the currants and sugar into a wide, stainless-steel saucepan. Heat and stir continuously until they come to the boil. Boil for exactly 8 minutes, stirring only if they appear to be sticking to the base. Skim carefully. Turn into a nylon sieve and leave to drip through – do not push the pulp through or the jelly will be cloudy. You can stir gently once or twice just to free the bottom of the sieve of pulp.

Pour the jelly into sterilised pots immediately. Cover and store in a cool, dry place. Redcurrants are very high in pectin, so the jelly will begin to set just as soon as it begins to cool.

Local Artisan Producers

I recently heard a new term for a type of food sadly on the increase: 'catalogue cooking'. Not exactly a complimentary term, it refers to an ever-increasing number of establishments where the chef picks up the phone and orders virtually everything from a catering catalogue. Much of it is pre-prepared, portioned and already garnished. At the Cookery School we seem to be the polar opposite of that; we source our produce from well over 150 food suppliers, mostly Irish. Some are tiny, others slightly larger, but the majority are local artisans, small farmers, fishermen, farmhouse cheesemakers and foragers; we know them all and the list continues to grow. I was lucky that Myrtle had built up a loyal network of suppliers at Ballymaloe House so that when I started the School I was able to tap into her contacts list and gradually add to it. This is a vitally important element of the Ballymaloe Cookery School and the restaurant at Ballymaloe House. It is not an exaggeration to say that we are totally indebted to all these passionate people who produce the beautiful raw materials that make it possible for us to make delicious food. We have a 'Wall of Fame' in the Blue Dining Room with photos of many of our food heroes, framed for all to see.

Many of our producers have been supplying us since the day we opened, some have retired, others have come on stream. Nora Aherne has been sending tasty, plump Aylesbury ducks to both Ballymaloe House and the School for many years. Ballycotton Seafood has for a long time been a source of fresh fish, and one of our more recent suppliers, Brenda O'Riordan, sells the fresh catch from the boats in our local fishing village Ballycotton, directly from her Love Fish van. Patrick and Mary Walsh from the farm across the road grow rhubarb, floury potatoes, juicy strawberries and other soft fruit. Jane Murphy makes several goat's cheeses, including the mild and gentle Ardsallagh, and like many other farmhouse cheesemakers, comes to talk to the students and tell her story. Michael Woulfe from Midleton supplied us with honey from the early days and helped us set up hives in the apple orchard for our own bees. He still gives us advice on all 'bee matters', and supports our new young beekeeper, Gary O'Keeffe.

Left: Geese grazing.
Above: The humble mackerel, discounted by many, is my favourite sea fish, but it has to be super fresh. In coastal communities there is a saying that the sun should never set on a mackerel, so it is best eaten within hours of being caught. We get fresh mackerel from Ballycotton in the summer. Word spreads around the village when the mackerel arrive in shoals. Anyone with a rod and line runs down to the pier and the fishermen take to their boats to take advantage of their presence.

Left: Michael Cuddigan's butcher's shop in the shadow of St Colman's Cathedral in Cloyne, Co. Cork, with Michael working at his beautiful timber butcher's block and meat hanging at ambient temperature from the meat hooks in the background. Michael originally wrapped his meat in time-honoured fashion in greaseproof and brown paper, tied with butcher's string. Here he is explaining different cuts of beef and the importance of hanging and dry-ageing.

A local butcher, Michael Cuddigan, supplied the Cookery School with superb beef and lamb for 17 years until he retired in 2000. He had been supplying meat to Ivan and Myrtle Allen at Ballymaloe House since 1948, initially to the family and then to the Yeats Room restaurant when they opened in 1964.

Michael, a third-generation craft butcher, always bought his meat 'on the hoof' (live cattle) directly from the local farmers he knew and trusted. He kept the animals on his own farm until such time as he judged them in prime condition for slaughter. Some of his land had never been tilled in living memory – virgin soil, full of wild flowers and a wide variety of grasses and herbs for the cattle to feast on. He knew all the farmers who reared the animals and what they had been fed on; this is real traceability, local food for local people.

Michael (and I completely agree with him) favoured the traditional breeds, like Aberdeen Angus, or Aberdeen Angus crossed with Shorthorn or Pol Angus, Strawberry Roan Shorthorn, or Hereford. They are suited to our terrain and can be completely fattened on grass rather than grain for premium flavour. Recently, several farmers have started to rear Dexter cattle again. Dexter are a small, hardy breed of cattle that originated in the South West of Ireland; they are good dual-purpose cattle, suitable for producing both beef and milk. The joints of meat from this breed are small but the flavour is superb. Ireland's climate is ideally suited to grass-growing, and the cattle may be kept outdoors for much of the year.

Buying this meat keeps the traditional breeds thriving, and I was heartened to hear that the Irish Rare Breeds Society, which had become dormant due to the Foot and Mouth outbreak in 2001, is being reactivated by people interested in supporting our traditional native breeds. Sadly, many of the heritage breeds can be difficult to find nowadays because of the general shift towards continental breeds, such as Belgian Blue, Simmental, Charolais and Limousin. They have a larger, leaner carcass, which makes them popular in a market that is increasingly paranoid about fat. At the School we love the fat and I stress over and over again to the students that without the fat, the meat would not be juicy and succulent. I emphasise that only two vitamins are water soluble; all the rest are fat soluble, so unless we eat some fat we cannot absorb all the nutrients from our food – yet another reason why a low-fat diet is not necessarily the healthiest choice. If you really would rather not eat the fat, leave it on the edge of your plate, but the flavour of the meat will be infinitely better if it is cooked with the fat on.

Like many other local butchers, Michael killed maiden heifer grass-fed beef and hung it for about 14 days. These younger animals produce more tender meat and hanging greatly enhances the flavour and texture. Meat loses weight while hanging and therefore costs a bit more, but the result, worth every penny, was tender, with a rich, beefy flavour – delicious. His simple butcher's shop was in the village of Cloyne, Co. Cork, close to St Colman's 13th-century cathedral and the 11th-century Round Tower. Like many family butchers, he knew his customers and their needs, and sometimes even what they wanted for dinner. Once when I was in the shop, a little local lad ran in and just asked for chops 'for the dinner'. Michael didn't even hesitate; he took down a loin of lamb from the

hook and cut the chops on the ancient wooden butcher's block. He seemed to know exactly how many would need dinner in that house and exactly what type of chop they'd expect – now that's service for you!

Now that Michael has retired, we buy from several other local butchers, including Frank Murphy, a third-generation butcher on the Main Street in Midleton, who also has his own abattoir. His son Brian has now come into the business, proudly continuing the legacy of his father, grandfather and great-grandfather before him. We are fortunate in Ireland to have over 550 craft butchers around the country; many of these are family-run businesses where the skills have been passed down from generation to generation. There's a growing realisation of the importance of tradition and the value of having small abattoirs. These butchers buy their animals from the local mart or from farmers with whom they have built up relationships over many years. They know how the animals are reared, the quality of the feed, the breed and the values of the farmer. Some, like Michael, have their own farms and bring the animals to the stage where they are ready for butchering (known as finishing) on their own pasture – this is the ultimate standard. We introduce our butchers to the students and encourage them to seek out and build up a relationship with their local butcher and to highlight the provenance of the meat on their menus when they have restaurants of their own.

In 2001 we introduced the 'Producer of the Week' concept to the 12-week course, inviting a farmer or food producer to come to the School to join us for lunch and afterwards to tell the students their story. For example, when we are using bacon, we might invite pig farmers Martin and Noreen Conroy from Woodside Farm in Ballincurrig, East Cork, who rear and cure the heritage saddleback pigs. The students love to be able to put a face to the name and they certainly handle the produce with more care and respect after they have heard the story of how it is produced. We have a network of suppliers, local and small producers, whom we buy from throughout the year. We encourage students to link in with local farmers and to establish a similar network when they set up their own businesses. We emphasise that buying everything locally ticks all the desirable boxes: you build up a good relationship and a bond of trust with your producer, with the added bonus that the fresh seasonal produce invariably tastes better. Buying locally also keeps the money in the local economy, which helps everyone. Also, if you run out of some vital supplies at a weekend, it's always easier to ring someone you know to come to the rescue!

Right: I've always loved offal and 'variety meats', as they are known in the US, and loved the succulent dishes that you can tease from the slow cooking of lesser cuts. Frank Murphy, our local craft butcher, brought a range of inexpensive cuts and offal including sweetbreads, hearts, liver, kidneys, oxtail and tripe to a Slow Food event we held at the School for students and members of the public. He explained the cuts and I then provided recipes and lots of suggestions for how to cook them.

The Farm Shop

We first started a farm shop in June 1982 after we decided, for economic reasons, to stop growing tomatoes commercially. The idea developed from selling apples directly from the farm; we thought that we could expand on that kind of thing, so both Tim and I travelled to England to get an idea of how they went about it, as farm shops were a more established tradition there.

On our return we converted the old mushroom-packing shed into a farm shop. Our Ballymaloe carpenter Danny Power made some sloping stands to hold the traditional wicker baskets. We filled them with fresh vegetables and we also sold homemade jams, marmalade, chutneys and a beautiful collection of cakes and biscuits, free-range chickens and salamis, and beans and pulses. I went down to the end of the road and put up a sandwich board with a chalk sign for Shanagarry Farm Shop and Garden Café, and waited for the curious passers-by to come up the lane. We put little ads in the *Cork Examiner* and later put some proper signs up in the village.

Within a few weeks of opening we took on three extra people to work in the Farm Shop. We employed a highly skilled organic gardener called Jill Gairdner to help us set up a pick-your-own fruit and vegetable area to complement the Farm Shop. Jill joined us in May 1982, having replied to an advertisement for a Head Gardener in *The Grower* magazine.

The Farm Shop, probably the first in the country, was much-loved by local people, summer residents of the nearby caravan parks and other visitors, and the Corkonians, who drove out from the city to buy fresh vegetables and fruit, and to eat at the little Garden Café behind the shop. All day long we baked to replenish the selection of our cakes and biscuits. I remember one day Florrie Bolger (now Florrie Cullinane and a senior tutor at the Ballymaloe Cookery School), who had come from Co. Wexford to work with us that summer, and I baked six batches of scones during the day. Imagine – we sold 120 scones from a galvanised shed, albeit a very pretty one, with long window boxes full of geraniums. The bases of the tables in the little café were made from Singer sewing machine bases, the chairs a motley borrowed collection, blue and white gingham cloths here and there – all very retro chic, but this was out of necessity, long before the term was coined. Those were the days when you could decide to get up and do something and just do it. There was far less regulation and red tape involved in getting an enterprise off the ground.

We charged a price halfway between wholesale and retail costs. We also gave away unfamiliar vegetables for free – courgettes, aubergines, peppers, globe artichokes – plus simple but delicious recipes for people to experiment with. By the end of the summer, many of our customers had become much more adventurous in their cooking habits.

The Farm Shop operated for three years, seven days a week, but we realised by the end of summer 1984 that our energies would be better spent concentrating on the Cookery School. This was getting much busier, generating quite a bit of interest and beginning to attract students from abroad.

Smoked Gubbeen Cheese and Pearl Barley Salad with Toasted Almonds, Apple and Pomegranate Seeds

The Ferguson family at Gubbeen in West Cork make the famous Gubbeen washed rind cheese. Their smoked Gubbeen is not so well known, but it is equally delicious. Their son Fingal makes an ever-increasing range of charcuterie, and their lovely daughter Clovisse has created a garden of Eden from whence she sells salad leaves and organic vegetables to local restaurants and friends.

Recently there's been a tremendous revival of interest in cheap and cheerful pearl barley, an almost forgotten grain with lots of flavour and a rich complement of vitamins and minerals, including iron and some calcium. It's also a source of protein and natural fibre.

Put the pearl barley and water into a saucepan and add the salt. Bring to the boil and simmer gently for approx. 20 minutes. Drain well.

To make the dressing, whisk the extra virgin olive oil, vinegar and crushed garlic together. Season to taste with salt and pepper.

Place the drained pearl barley in a mixing bowl, spoon over half the dressing and toss while still warm. Spread out to cool.

Meanwhile, quarter and dice the apple. Put in a mixing bowl, squeeze over a little lemon juice and add the pomegranate seeds, toasted almonds and diced smoked Gubbeen cheese. Add the remainder of the dressing. Toss gently and combine with the pearl barley. Taste and correct the seasoning if necessary. Transfer to a serving dish and allow the flavours to meld for an hour or so. Scatter with parsley leaves and serve.

Serves 4 as a main course or 8 as a starter

185g (6½oz) pearl barley
1.5 litres (2½ pints) water
1 teaspoon salt
2 dessert apples, Cox's Orange Pippin or Gala, cored
freshly squeezed lemon juice
seeds from ½–1 pomegranate, depending on size
60g (2½oz) toasted almonds, coarsely chopped
110–175g (4–6oz) Smoked Gubbeen cheese, diced
flat-leaf parsley leaves, to serve

For the dressing
125ml (4fl oz) extra virgin olive oil
3 tablespoons Forum Chardonnay vinegar
1 garlic clove, peeled and crushed
sea salt and freshly ground black pepper

Salad of Lamb, Green Beans and Fennel with Tomato and Chilli Jam

Our local butcher for many years, Michael Cuddigan, had his own fields of pasture, some of which had never been turned in living memory. The texture and the flavour of the meat reflected the variety of grasses and wildflowers in the pasture where the lambs grazed. Irish lamb in general has a sweet flavour, which varies from one area to another and changes whether it comes from the hills or lowlands. It's fun to experiment – look out for Wicklow, Connemara, Kerry and Mayo lamb; each has its own unique flavour.

This salad may be served in a wide serving bowl, family style, or in individual portions for a summer lunch.

Bring a saucepan of water to the boil. Add the green beans and the salt, and blanch for 2 minutes. Drain, refresh under cold running water, drain again and set aside. (If the beans are large, cut them on an angle and blanch for a little longer.)

Slice the fennel very finely with a sharp knife or Japanese mandolin and put into a bowl of cold water. Add the lemon juice to prevent discolouration.

Preheat a griddle pan over a medium heat. Season the meat generously with sea salt and freshly ground black pepper, and then drizzle with extra virgin olive oil. Put the lamb onto the hot pan and cook for 4–5 minutes on one side without moving. Then turn and cook for a further 4–5 minutes on the other side. Remove from the heat, transfer to a hot plate, cover loosely with foil and allow to rest for 15 minutes. The lamb should still be pink in the centre but not too rare.

Meanwhile, wash and dry the salad leaves.

To make the dressing, put the lemon zest into a bowl. Add the freshly squeezed lemon juice and whisk in the extra virgin olive oil. Season to taste with a little sea salt and some freshly ground black pepper.

Just before serving, drain the fennel and dry on kitchen paper. Put the salad leaves in a bowl, whisk the dressing once again and drizzle over the leaves. Sprinkle with the grated Parmesan (or Desmond or Gabriel cheese) and toss gently. Carve the lamb on the diagonal into slices, approx. 1cm (½in) thick.

To serve, arrange the salad on individual plates and layer with the fennel slices, beans and warm lamb. Drizzle a spoonful of Tomato and Chilli Jam on top. Scatter with some tiny olives and a few cubes of ewe's milk cheese (if using). Serve immediately.

Serves 6

225g (8oz) fine green beans, topped and tailed
3 teaspoons salt
1 large or 2 small fennel bulbs, tough outer layer removed
freshly squeezed juice of ½ lemon
2 boned, short racks of lamb, we use eye of the loin
   (total weight approx. 900g (2lb))
extra virgin olive oil, for drizzling
6 handfuls of mixed salad leaves
2 tablespoons freshly grated Parmesan or Desmond or Gabriel cheese
sea salt and freshly ground black pepper

For the dressing
freshly squeezed juice of ½ lemon, plus 1 teaspoon finely grated zest
125ml (4fl oz) extra virgin olive oil
sea salt and freshly ground black pepper

To serve
4 tablespoons Tomato and Chilli Jam (see page 266)
18 tiny black Niçoise olives (optional)
110g (4oz) Feta or Knockalara Sheep's Cheese (optional)

Watercress, Blood Orange and Toons Bridge Mozzarella Salad

~ఎోఎ~

We are overjoyed to have Irish mozzarella at last, made from the milk of happy grass-fed buffalo. The rich West Cork pasture that the buffalo feed on gives the Toons Bridge mozzarella its quintessentially Irish taste. In this salad, a few beautiful, fresh ingredients put together simply make an irresistible starter. If watercress is not an option, rocket works well also.

Serves 4

a bunch of fresh watercress
2–3 balls of fresh Toons Bridge mozzarella
2 blood oranges
2–3 tablespoons local honey
a good drizzle of extra virgin olive oil
coarsely ground black pepper
8–10 toasted almonds (optional)

Scatter a few watercress leaves over the base of each plate, and slice or tear some buffalo mozzarella over the top. Using a sharp knife, remove the peel and pith from the blood oranges and cut them into slices, 5mm (¼in) thick. Tuck the orange slices here and there in between the watercress and mozzarella. Drizzle with honey and really good extra virgin olive oil. Sprinkle with a little coarsely ground fresh black pepper and serve.

I love a few slivers of toasted almonds over the top as an extra treat.

Claudia Roden

" When Darina called me, almost thirty years ago, to ask me to do a course on Middle Eastern food at Ballymaloe Cookery School, I was intrigued. Ireland was hardly known for its cuisine or interest in food, and neither was Britain at that time. Although 'nouvelle cuisine' had created excitement about the new French approach to cooking and presentation, going out to restaurants was still a rare activity, reserved for events like birthdays. Chefs had no status and cookery schools catered for well-to-do girls waiting to be married. They, like hotel and catering schools for professionals, taught only French classic cuisine according to the rules set by Auguste Escoffier.

Middle Eastern cooking was thought of as strange and the ingredients were hard to find. I wondered whether Irish people would be interested in what I had to offer. I made out a very long list of recipes I could demonstrate for Darina to choose a few from. When she came to see me in London, I was impressed by the intense, fast-talking, serious young woman – she looked at the list, asked me to describe the dishes and said we could do a lot more. I was used to schools demonstrating at most six dishes a day but she said 'Don't worry, I'll be there cooking with you' and that she would be getting all the ingredients – the filo and kadaif, the bulgur and couscous, the tamarind, pomegranate syrup and tahini, and the spices.

I was entirely charmed by Ballymaloe – the house, the Allen family, Myrtle, the landscape, the way the School operated, the way Darina and Rory taught. We cooked a dazzling number of dishes – tagines and pilaffs, spicy mezzes, cool yogurt salads, puddings scented with rose and orange blossom water. During a break, Darina suddenly said, 'Let's do another fish' and we went off to Ballycotton and bought a monkfish from a fisherman, which we skinned and cooked with a Moroccan chermoula sauce. The smells and tastes in the demonstration theatre and the methods of cooking were entirely strange to the students, but Darina's enthusiasm was contagious and they were enchanted. I could see I was with a live wire with boundless energy and an extraordinary

passion for food, who had a hunger for discovering everything that was good to eat and a desire to pass it on. The School was serious and very professional, but what made it unique was the special enthusiasm and affectionate warm spirit that radiated from Darina, Rory, Tim and the extended Allen family. I stayed at Myrtle and Ivan's Ballymaloe House. The idyllic setting and Myrtle's cooking made it a memorable experience.

It has been a joy over the years to see the School and its organic farm expand into a formidable centre of gastronomy that attracts people from all over Ireland and all over the world. It has trained chefs in classic French cuisine and given them a real knowledge of Italian, Indian, Thai, Middle Eastern and North African, among other cuisines, and the chefs have gone on to cook all over the world. By honouring Irish products and cuisine, by supporting local farmers, fishermen and artisans, by inspiring home cooks and restaurateurs, Myrtle, Darina and now also Rachel have transformed Ireland from a food wasteland into a vibrant and exciting destination for food lovers. You can see their influence in the splendid English Market in Cork, at the farmers' markets and on restaurant menus all over Ireland. At one farmers' market I was thrilled to find people selling their home-cooked Middle Eastern foods. One said she used recipes I had demonstrated at Ballymaloe.

I brought my family over for my seventieth birthday lunch. They were enthralled by the ducks and geese, the pigs and cattle, and the fabulous greenhouse and market garden. The School, with its organic farm, holistic approach and outreaching activities, is a utopian food empire whose example and influence is felt well beyond Ireland. It is an international phenomenon. The spirit and the magic was still there at the Ballymaloe Literary Festival of Food and Wine in April 2013, which attracted gastronomic luminaries from all over the world. It was unique among festivals in the way it examined the problems of food in the world as it celebrated the pleasures of cooking and eating and the joy of bonding over food. **"**

Left: I had long admired Claudia Roden and pored over her book on Middle Eastern food, so was thrilled to be able to invite her as a guest chef. Her first course introduced us to Middle Eastern cooking – at that time even hummus and tabbouleh were unusual and exotic recipes. Many of the ingredients Claudia used would have been unfamiliar to the majority of students, although I was fortunately able to source most of what she needed from Mr Bell's stall at the English Market in Cork City.

Moroccan Lamb Pitta Wrap with Hummus

We offer one, and sometimes several, barbecue or grilling courses every summer. The first was in 1991 when over eighty people turned up, predominantly chaps. Since then Irish people have really taken to grilling, and there's scarcely a household that doesn't have one, or in some cases several, types of barbecue. Everyone has become much more adventurous and are having fun with flavours from Mexico, Asia, India, the Middle East, the Mediterranean…

Serves 4

500g (18oz) boneless lamb (shoulder or leg), cut into
    4cm (1½in) cubes

For the Hummus
170g (6oz) chickpeas, soaked in cold water overnight
freshly squeezed juice of 2–3 lemons, or to taste
2–3 garlic cloves, peeled and crushed
150ml (5fl oz) tahini paste
1 teaspoon ground cumin
salt

For the pitta bread
25g (1oz) fresh yeast
325ml (11fl oz) lukewarm water
450g (1lb) strong flour, plus extra for dusting
1 teaspoon salt
sunflower oil, for greasing

For the marinade
1½ teaspoons roasted and ground coriander seeds
½ teaspoon roasted and ground cumin seeds
¼ teaspoon ground allspice
¼ teaspoon ground cinnamon
2 tablespoons freshly squeezed lemon juice
4 tablespoons extra virgin olive oil
½ medium onion, finely chopped
2 garlic cloves, peeled and crushed

To serve
4 handfuls of shredded Baby Gem or Cos lettuce
4 ripe tomatoes, cut into wedges and seasoned
16 fresh mint leaves

Start with the hummus. Drain the soaked chickpeas, cover with fresh water and cook until tender, approx. 30–60 minutes, depending on the quality.

Meanwhile, make the pitta bread. Crumble the yeast into 125ml (4fl oz) of the water and set aside for 10 minutes until the yeast has dissolved.

Sift the flour and salt into a large mixing bowl. Add the yeast along with the rest of the water and mix well – the dough should not be too dry. Turn out onto a lightly floured work surface and knead until smooth and elastic, approx. 5–6 minutes. If the dough is a bit sticky, add a little extra flour while kneading.

Transfer the dough to a lightly oiled bowl and turn the dough so that the whole surface is oiled. Cover with clingfilm and set aside in a warm place to rise for 1–1½ hours or until the dough has at least doubled in volume.

Meanwhile, whisk all the ingredients for the marinade together in a large bowl to make a purée. Add the cubed lamb and toss well to coat evenly. Cover and set aside to marinate in the fridge for 1 hour.

Turn the dough out onto a floured work surface and knead again until smooth, approx. 2 minutes. Roll into a thick log and divide into 8–10 equal-sized pieces. Roll each piece into a smooth ball. Put on a floured surface, cover with a tea towel and set aside to rise for approx. 30 minutes or until doubled in size again.

Preheat the oven to 230°C/450°F/gas 8 and heat two baking trays.

Light the barbecue and finish the hummus. Drain the chickpeas, reserving the cooking liquor. Whizz up the cooked chickpeas in a food processor with the freshly squeezed lemon juice and a little of the reserved cooking liquor if necessary. Add the garlic, tahini paste, cumin and salt to taste. Blend to a soft creamy paste. Taste and continue to add lemon juice and salt until you are happy with the flavour.

Roll out the dough balls into circles, approx. 15cm (6in) in diameter and 5mm (¼in) thick. Bake two at a time on a hot baking tray for approx. 3 minutes or until just brown and puffed. If not using immediately, leave to cool on wire racks.

Thread the lamb onto wooden skewers, which have been soaked in water for 30 minutes, and grill over medium-hot embers, turning every couple of minutes until well browned but still juicy and slightly pink inside, approx. 7–8 minutes. Alternatively, cook on a hot grill pan – but make sure you open the windows, it creates quite a bit of smoke! Split each pitta into two pieces and put directly onto the grill to warm through.

To serve, fill the pitta bread with the grilled lamb, top with the shredded lettuce and tomato wedges and scatter with the mint leaves. Drizzle with the hummus, sprinkle with sea salt and freshly ground black pepper and serve immediately while the lamb is still warm.

Claudia Roden's Flan de Naranja – Orange Flan

Claudia Roden came back to teach at the Ballymaloe Litfest of Food and Wine in May 2013. She cooked for three hours and every recipe had a story – she had the audience transfixed. Claudia suggests that this refreshing, creamy, slightly sharp flan is just what you need to end a rich meal. You must use the freshly squeezed juice of oranges or clementines – it's best if you squeeze the fruit yourself.

Serves 8

600ml (1 pint) freshly squeezed orange or clementine juice
125g (4½oz) caster sugar
2 large organic eggs plus 10 yolks

To serve
oranges, clementines, fresh mint leaves and orange blossom water

Preheat the oven to 150°C/300°F/gas 2.
   Heat the citrus juice with the sugar over a low heat and stir to dissolve the sugar.
   Beat the egg yolks and the whole eggs lightly with a fork in a large bowl, then gradually beat in the citrus juice. Ladle the mixture into the ramekins. Put them in a shallow roasting tray and pour in enough boiling water to come halfway up the sides of 8 x 175ml (6fl oz) ramekins (it is called a bain-marie). Bake in the preheated oven for 30 minutes or until the custard sets. It needs to be cooked at a low temperature to get a perfectly smooth texture without bubbles.
   Take the ramekins out of the pan and allow to cool. Cover with clingfilm and transfer to the fridge to chill. Serve chilled on its own, or with a little citrus salad of oranges, clementines and perhaps a few fresh mint leaves and a couple of drops of orange blossom water.

Syrian Laymoun bi-na na Fresh Lemonade with Mint

We had a memorable holiday in Syria in 2009. The food was wonderful and the people were friendly and welcoming. Freshly squeezed juices were widely available everywhere in Damascus and Aleppo, in restaurants and on street stalls (lots of orange and pomegranate of course), but we particularly enjoyed this refreshing lemon and mint drink. It's a brilliant way to use up an abundance of fresh mint.

Serves 6

juice of 6 lemons
300ml (10fl oz) stock syrup (see below)
300ml (10fl oz) chilled water
2 handfuls of fresh mint leaves

Squeeze the lemons and pour the juice into a liquidiser. Add the syrup, chilled water and fresh mint leaves, and whizz until the mint is finely chopped and the drink is frothy. Pour into tall glasses and drink through a straw while still fresh – divine.

Stock Syrup

Makes 850ml (1½ pints)

450g (1lb) sugar
600ml (1 pint) water

Dissolve the sugar in the water and bring to the boil. Boil for 2 minutes, then allow to cool. Store in the fridge until needed.

The Herb Garden

Fresh herbs have excited cooks for not just hundreds but thousands of years, even as far back as the late 4th and early 5th centuries, when *Apicius*, a collection of Roman cookery recipes, also known as *De re coquinaria* ('On the Subject of Cooking') was compiled, containing numerous recipes for dishes flavoured with herbs. Notwithstanding that, I would hazard a guess that never at any period during history has there been such a universal interest in herbs as in recent times, both for healing and culinary purposes. I don't know what we would do without herbs; our cooking at Ballymaloe is laced with them and big bunches come from the garden and greenhouses every day.

When the Ballymaloe Cookery School opened in 1983, for most people, fresh herbs other than parsley, chives, thyme and mint were exotic – it was five or six years before basil was widely available. In the early years of the School I ran several courses on how to use

fresh herbs to add magic to your cooking; I introduced students to new flavours and demonstrated how familiar dishes could be made more exciting by adding a variety of fresh herbs. The first course, entitled Cooking with Herbs, was held in July 1991. The students loved the Onion and Thyme Leaf Soup, Roast Chicken with Summer Herbs, Cod with Cream and Bay Leaves, Lemon Sorbet with Borage Flowers, Lavender and Honey Ice Cream and Summer Fruit Salad with Rose Geranium leaves. I chose about 15 fresh herbs, some reasonably common, e.g. mint, sage and rosemary, and others, like angelica, lovage and hyssop, less well known, and gave recipes to showcase each one, mostly in culinary terms, but also mentioning medicinal uses.

My abundant use of herbs led to the construction of our very own formal herb garden with boxwood-edged beds, inspired by a visit to the potager vegetable gardens at Villandry in the Loire Valley.

Left: Lavender and fennel growing in the herb garden in the early morning light. We crystallise lavender at the bud stage to decorate cakes and also use it to flavour honey and make lavender ice cream and syrups.
Right (above): A view of the formal herb garden and potting shed from the treehouse, which overlooks them. The beech hedge, one plant deep, is estimated to be about 180 years old and considered by many gardeners to be the most remarkable in Ireland.
Right (below): The herb garden in winter. Because of the formal structure of the garden with its boxwood hedges it looks lovely even in the snow. In the centre is the Myrtus ugni, which I planted as the axis of the garden as a homage to my mother-in-law, Myrtle Allen.

In 1986 we found a perfect site in the middle of the old gardens in Kinoith, enclosed by 6m (20ft) beech hedges and overlooked by the old potting shed. The initial plans were drawn, as every inspired design should be, on the back of an envelope! Over 70 different herbs are now to be found in this garden, including lemon balm, bronze fennel, purple sage, lovage, summer savory, sweet cicely, parsley, garlic, chives, angelica and 6–8 types of mint and thyme, planted in sculpted beds. These are laid out parterre style in a formal pattern of beds, edged with boxwood and set in gravel paths. We like to grow from organic seed whenever possible as we find that the plants are invariably hardier and healthier. Organic seeds come from plants that have been grown organically and have not been treated with chemicals during their life cycle, and have therefore built up their own resistance to disease.

Each bed is planted with three or four herbs, to provide a contrast of texture, leaf shape, colour and height – for example, a bed may be edged with chives, then golden marjoram, with angelica or fennel planted in the centre for height. We try to ensure that we choose herbs that flower at different times in the same bed to provide a

Above: An early picture of me in the herb garden.

variety of textures and continuity of colour and perfume in the garden. Some herbs, for example green or bronze fennel, grow into a glorious feathery clump about 1.5m (5ft) high, while others, such as parsley, are scarcely 15cm (6in) tall.

Bees, so vital for pollination, love borage, both white and blue, so it attracts them into the garden. We use the pretty flowers to decorate cakes and to scatter into salads. Bees also love comfrey, another important medicinal herb useful for drawing out infection; it's the main ingredient in comfrey cream and we use the leaves for fritters. One can also make 'comfrey tea', a potent plant food and fertiliser. It is a valuable addition to the compost heap and the pigs love it. Sweet cicely is a lesser-known perennial, with a feathery fern-like leaf, which we use in fruit compotes to reduce the sugar and frequently for garnishing sweet dishes. The young leaves of salad burnet are delicious in salads and hyssop is particularly tasty when dried; few are aware that this is the same as the herb used to make the Middle Eastern herb mix za'atar, which has become so popular over recent years.

We grow both curly and flat-leaf parsley and chives. Chives are brilliant because they are perennial and are 'cut and come again'. Parsley plants will usually last for a year or more, so I like to have lots. More recently I've also introduced the flat-leaved garlic chive. Over the years we've expanded the thyme bed with five varieties: common, creeping, lemon, lavender, orange and pizza. (Not a misprint, this last variety is low-growing with rich, deep purple flowers, pity about the name!)

There are about a dozen varieties of mint, including ginger, mojito, after eight (tastes just like the chocolates), lemon, banana, basil, orange, limette, strawberry, Kentucky Colonel, spearmint and peppermint – spearmint or Bowles's mint are best for general use. We also grow French tarragon, not to be confused with Russian tarragon; the French have here, as in most things, the gastronomic edge as far as flavour is concerned. I started with one sage – the common green variety – to jazz up stuffings and combine with pasta, but we now grow purple sage, pineapple sage and Russian sage. Lemon verbena is grown alongside lemon balm plants, both of which we add to herb butter or float in jugs of iced water at lunchtime. A lovely refreshing flavour instead of the hackneyed lemon wedge.

All these are perennial but there are a few annuals that are essential basics in my kitchen, which I urge students to grow if space permits. My absolute favourite annual is marjoram or oregano; there are several varieties here, but the annual variety is by far the most

fragrant. I also love to have golden marjoram to include in green salad; plant in the shade as direct sunlight can burn the edges of the leaves. A few dill and chervil plants are also a must. Dill is essential for gravlax and chervil just goes with everything and deserves to be better known. Basil plants need plenty of rich soil and sunshine to nourish them. When they start to run to flower, we pinch off the growing point so they will throw out more shoots and produce a lusher plant. Finally, we are all hooked on coriander – it can be a bit of an acquired taste but quickly becomes quite addictive – and it is essential for all Asian, Middle Eastern, Mexican and South American food. All parts of the coriander plant are edible and each has a different flavour. We use the roots for Thai curry pastes, the stalks can be added to salads, stews and tagines, and of course the leaves are an invaluable addition to so many dishes – in fact coriander is by far the most widely used herb in the world, much more so than parsley. We use the delicate white flowers in salads and starters and then the seeds are dried to provide the coriander spice, which we use on its own or in conjunction with cumin and other spices in a myriad of delicious ways.

We tend to use fresh herbs all year round, but a couple of herbs are worth drying, e.g. annual marjoram or oregano and perhaps thyme. In 2012 we bought a dehydrator, which lives in the larder of the School and is brilliant for drying herbs, mushrooms and chillies.

Two other wonderfully robust and gutsy herbs, which are hardier than any of those I have mentioned so far, are rosemary and bay. Both need space but are tremendously useful herbs for stews, pasta sauces and roast vegetables. Bay grows easily, but for a real treasure try to plant a standard bay outside your kitchen door in a pot or as the axis of your new herb garden. We have six standard bays in the herb garden, which add height to the scheme, and because they are evergreen, as are the boxwood hedges, the herb garden looks brilliant both in winter and summer.

Most culinary herbs are perennial, so once you plant them they will re-emerge each year in early spring in nice fat clumps ready for picking. Each herb has several uses; the leaves can of course be chopped and used to flavour a huge variety of dishes in various combinations, but the flowers are also edible. Some are inconspicuous and not worth bothering with, but others, e.g. sage, make glorious garnishes and are quite delicious, and some are particularly good eaten raw in salads, for example chives, coriander, chervil, mint and tiny sprigs of tarragon and lovage. One can also collect and dry the seeds to use as a spice; fennel, dill and coriander seeds are especially worthwhile. Fennel pollen, particularly magical,

Above: We have constant requests for internships at the School and organic farm gardens because of the range of experiences they have to offer. Here one of our interns, Sonya McGee, is holding a recycled can containing clary.

is one of the must-have cheffy ingredients right now. In August we show the students how to shake the pollen onto parchment paper and how to collect it. When the poppy and nigella seed heads dry in early autumn, the students collect them and learn how to shake out the seeds. They then use them to flavour cakes and sprinkle on breads.

Fresh herbs are so easy to grow, I feel everyone should have a herb garden – if not an actual garden, at least a few pots or tubs, or even a window box, brimming with parsley, thyme and chives. It's not just the fact that a little sprinkling of fresh herbs can add magic to your cooking, there's also the buzz you get when you make a little foray into the garden to snip a few sprigs of rosemary, lemon balm, sweet cicely or whatever it is you need. It is an easy and inexpensive way to garnish and add flavour to your food, and ring the changes with basic ingredients like potatoes and beans, which are greatly enhanced by a sprig of savory in the cooking water. It is this that I try to teach the students, especially those on the 12-week course who are able to watch the herbs grow and appreciate what is available seasonally. The reality is that, after spending a few days, not to mention 12 weeks at Ballymaloe, they can scarcely imagine cooking without fresh herbs. On the May 12-week course, the students have the option to have a raised bed area or a patch of ground to plant herbs or vegetables, to create an edible garden while they are with us. It doesn't press everyone's buttons, but for those who are interested it is sheer magic and can trigger a lifetime passion for growing one's own food. Students go out on a rota basis with the gardeners every morning to pick herbs for the cooking and it is a great resource for them, a cook's paradise. Residential students can help themselves to herbs for their cooking, enjoy the herb garden in the evening or at weekends and just sit and listen to the birds in the surrounding trees.

When we were designing the herb garden in 1986 I had a thought. I decided to plant a myrtle tree in the centre bed as a tribute to Myrtle Allen, who has been an inspiration and constant support throughout the years. I ordered a *Myrtus luma* and planted it within a boxwood circle, then got on with planting the other beds with a mixture of contrasting herbs. As the year passed it grew, but rather oddly; eventually in June it was covered with pale pink flowers, as opposed to the pretty white flowers of *Myrtus luma*. My good friend and renowned gardener, Jim Reynolds, inspected it and pronounced it to be a different cultivar, *Myrtus ugni*. He predicted that it would be covered with wine-coloured myrtle berries in autumn, and so it was. I was thrilled; I had inadvertently planted a variety that produced delicious berries, what a quirk of fate. We look forward to nibbling them in the autumn, and scatter them into salads; they are also delicious with game.

Shrimp or Prawn Salad with Rice Noodles and Prawn Crackers

The whole world of noodles was quite a revelation to me – nothing beats slithery fresh rice noodles in Thai or Vietnamese dishes, but noodles of all types are a must-have for my store cupboard. There are a million delicious noodle salads you can make, but they are also great added to soup or as an extra something in spring rolls.

Although we have become more familiar with coriander over the past 30 years, some people are determined it is a herb that they don't like. I try hard to convince them to change their minds, as it is a key ingredient in so many Asian, South American and Middle Eastern dishes.

Note: We use Ballycotton shrimps, which vary in size but are roughly one-third of the size of an Asian prawn. If using king prawns, these may need to be cut into 2–3 pieces, depending on size. We don't use Asian prawns unless we can source sustainable organic prawns.

First deep-fry the prawn crackers. Heat some oil in a deep-fat fryer or frying pan and fry the prawn crackers, two or three at a time, for approx. 30 seconds until puffed up and golden. Drain the crackers on kitchen paper.

Put the noodles into a bowl. Cover with boiling water and set aside for 4–5 minutes until just tender but still a little al dente.

Meanwhile, make the dressing. Combine all the ingredients in a bowl and stir until the sugar has dissolved.

Tip the softened noodles into a colander, rinse briefly under cold running water and drain well. Transfer the noodles to a serving bowl and toss lightly in the dressing while still warm.

Cut the cucumber in half lengthways, scoop out the seeds with a melon baller or a sharp spoon and discard (or feed to your hens). Cut the cucumber into 5mm (¼in) slices at a long angle. Add the cucumber to the noodles along with the shrimps or prawns, spring onions, coriander and mint leaves. Toss well, taste and correct the seasoning if necessary. Scatter with the peanuts or cashew nuts and serve with lime wedges and lots of fresh coriander. Accompany with the prawn crackers.

Serves 8

225g (8oz) thin flat rice noodles
1 small organic cucumber
48 shrimps or 32 prawns (see note), cooked and peeled
8 spring onions, finely sliced at a long angle into 2cm (¾in) lengths
10g (½oz) fresh coriander leaves
10g (½oz) fresh mint leaves
110g (4oz) chopped peanuts or cashew nuts, roasted
sea salt and freshly ground black pepper

For the Prawn Crackers
approx. 24 prawn crackers, uncooked
sunflower oil, for deep-frying

For the dressing
125ml (4fl oz) soy sauce
50ml (2fl oz) rice or cider vinegar
50ml (2fl oz) extra virgin olive oil
1 red chilli, thinly sliced
1 teaspoon freshly grated root ginger
2 tablespoons brown sugar or palm sugar

To serve
lime wedges
fresh coriander leaves

Pickled Carrots with Star Anise

Scott Walsh, a talented chef from Ballymaloe House, came up with this recipe. We serve it as part of the selection of salads on the Sunday night Ballymaloe buffet, but you can imagine how delicious it is in other salad combinations.

Serves 10–15, depending on how it is served

10 carrots (approx. 1kg (2¼lb)), peeled and sliced thinly lengthways on a mandolin
600ml (1 pint) unsweetened carrot juice
100g (3½oz) caster sugar
200ml (7fl oz) white wine
200ml (7fl oz) white wine vinegar
200ml (7fl oz) water
250ml (9fl oz) extra virgin olive oil
bunch each of tarragon and thyme
8 star anise
2 tablespoons coriander seeds
10 black peppercorns

Put all the ingredients into a wide, stainless steel sauté pan. Bring to the boil, and then simmer gently for 10 minutes until the carrots are soft. Set aside to cool before serving. Serve with some of the spiced liquid.

I can't imagine cooking without fresh herbs and spices. It doesn't matter where you are, all you need to grow your own herbs are a few containers, water and light. You won't believe it until you grow your own, but the flavour is vastly superior to anything you can buy.

Spatchcock Chicken with Rosemary and Chilli Oil

Spatchcocking enables the bird to cook much faster; there will be lots of crispy skin and it will be really easy to carve. All poultry can be cooked in this way – you can vary the seasoning and spices if you wish to give Mexican, Moroccan or Asian flavours.

First spatchcock the chicken. Remove the wishbone from the neck end (keep it for the stockpot). Insert a heavy chopping knife into the cavity of the chicken from the back end to the neck. Press down sharply to cut through the backbone. Alternatively, put the chicken breast-side down on a chopping board and use poultry shears to cut along the entire length of the backbone as close to the centre as possible. Open out the bird.

Preheat the oven to 180°C/350°F/gas 4 or light the barbecue. To make the marinade, combine the rosemary, garlic, pepper, chilli flakes, lemon juice and extra virgin olive oil in a bowl. Just before cooking, brush the chicken – both inside and out – with the marinade. Sprinkle with the Maldon sea salt.

If cooking in the oven, lay the chicken skin-side up on a rack inside a roasting tin and roast in the hot oven for 40 minutes. Alternatively barbecue for approx. 40 minutes, 20cm (8–9in) from the coals, turning halfway. Make sure the chicken is fully cooked through before serving.

Accompany with a good green salad and wedges of avocado.

Serves 6 or more

1 x 1.8–2.25kg (4–5lb) organic chicken
1 teaspoon Maldon sea salt

For the marinade
1 tablespoon freshly chopped rosemary
4 garlic cloves, peeled and crushed
1 teaspoon freshly ground black pepper
½ teaspoon chilli flakes
1 tablespoon freshly squeezed lemon juice
4 tablespoons extra virgin olive oil

To serve
2–3 avocados, cut into wedges
fresh green salad

Variation

Spatchcock Quail with Rosemary and Chilli Oil
Spatchcock the quail as above and brush with the marinade. Cook under a moderately hot grill or on the barbecue for approx. 8 minutes on the bone-side and then approx. 5 minutes on the skin-side. Quail vary a lot in size; the birds we get tend to be quite small, approx. 150g (5oz) in weight.

Fresh Herb Tisanes

❦

We've just planted a tisane garden outside the Garden Café with our favourite fresh herbs. Herb teas and tisanes are best made with freshly snipped herbs, so plant them close to your kitchen door.

All you need to do is pop a few leaves into a teapot and pour on the boiling water – the result is infinitely more delicious than using dried herb teabags.

I'm very wary about ordering herb tea in a restaurant, but a Paris restaurant I dined in recently served herb infusions in the most delightful way. The waiter came to the table with several china bowls of fresh herbs on a silver salver. With tiny silver tongs he put the guest's chosen herb into a little china teapot, poured on boiling water and served it with a flourish. Exquisite.

We use fresh leaves from the garden to make herb teas and infusions, both in the Cookery School and at Ballymaloe House. The leaves can also be put directly into a cup if you just want to make one infusion. Students and friends are sometimes surprised at first when they are served a virtually colourless liquid that is so clear and fresh tasting. They are often amazed at how easy it is to make.

Use lemon verbena, rosemary, sweet geranium, lemon balm, spearmint, peppermint… the choice is endless.

Bring fresh cold water to the boil. Scald a china teapot, take a handful of fresh herb leaves and crush them gently. The quantity will depend on the strength of the herb and how intense an infusion you enjoy. Put them into the scalded teapot. Pour boiling water over the leaves, cover the teapot and set aside to infuse for 3–4 minutes. Serve immediately in china teacups rather than mugs.

Ginger Tea

Put 3–4 slices of fresh root ginger (each approx. 4mm/¼in thick) into a cup. Cover with boiling water and infuse for 3–4 minutes. Sip after dinner for a calming effect and to aid digestion.

Lemon Posset with Rose Geranium

❦

This lemon posset recipe has done the rounds – it is always lip-smackingly good, but it was Skye Gyngell who introduced us to this version scented with sweet geranium leaves (*Pelargonium graveolens*). She in turn attributed it to Jeremy Lee, so on it goes… Anyway, it is sublime, so thank you all.

Serves 4

400ml (14fl oz) double cream
100g (3½oz) caster sugar
5 rose- or sweet-scented geranium leaves
50ml (2fl oz) lemon juice

To garnish
tiny rose- or sweet-scented geranium leaves

Place the cream, sugar and geranium leaves in a heavy-bottomed saucepan and bring to a simmer. Reduce the heat to low and cook, stirring often, for 5 minutes. Remove the pan from the heat, squeeze in the lemon juice, strain and allow to cool, discarding the leaves. Pour the posset into small, tall glasses, cover with clingfilm and chill overnight.

Serve garnished with a tiny scented geranium leaf.

Game

Dealing with game can certainly seem intimidating when you are faced with a brace of pheasant in the feather for the first time – where to start? We've been offering game courses here at the School consistently for the past 30 years and it's been so much fun demystifying the subject. The first game course was started in 1987 by George Gossip from Ballinderry Park in Co. Galway. George is a family friend and the best game cook I know and, 30 years later, he still teaches the occasional class. George has been shooting since he was a child and has a great love and respect for, as well understanding of, the countryside and the harmonious balance of nature. He is a brilliantly entertaining teacher with lots of stories – told in a booming baritone and interspersed with colourful language – everyone loves his lessons. Over the years he has built up a wonderful repertoire of game recipes; we especially love the Game Pie, Game Terrine, Roast Loin of Venison, Roast Wild Mallard with Jerusalem Artichokes and the Carpaccio of Rabbit.

When George introduced the first game course at the School, people thought it was normal to be taught how to pluck, skin and gut poultry or game. However, by the mid-to-late 1990s, attitudes had changed. Students on the 12-week course would turn their noses up in disgust and ask me in incredulous tones: 'You can't seriously expect me to clean out this chicken?' People obviously expected to be presented with an oven-ready bird and were not interested in learning how to gut a chicken or skin and prepare game.

However, in recent years there's been a huge revival of interest in game and, surprise, surprise, it's become trendy again. I think it must partly be the Hugh Fearnley-Whittingstall effect. Hugh has done a series of television programmes from River Cottage, extolling the virtues of self-sufficiency and showing people how to use and cook game. These have proved extremely popular and have encouraged many people to take an interest and even give it a try for themselves.

In my opinion, game is fantastic to cook with. It's all natural, for a start, and free-range and organic. None of it is endangered; in fact you're often doing farmers a huge favour by saving their precious crops from rabbits and deer. Furthermore, it's cheap and nutritious

Left: A brace of pheasant hanging by the neck in the feather. It is best to hang them in a cool larder, ideally individually, especially in humid weather. Most people, even if they aren't very keen on game, will have tasted pheasant. I like a rich, gamey flavour, which is achieved by hanging the birds for longer.
Above: George Gossip with two of his faithful gun dogs, Badger and Treacle, hunting at Birr, County Offaly. He has taught game courses at the School since its beginning, covering all aspects of game and introducing us to his favourite recipes.

and a much healthier alternative to red meat. Wild game tends to be very lean due to the animal's active lifestyle and natural diet. Their meat is lower in saturated fat than red meat and contains a higher proportion of polyunsaturated fatty acids, so they are naturally low in fat, but with just as much texture and flavour as red meat – a very attractive prospect for many people.

It's gratifying to see how the times are changing. These days, our 12-week students almost always want to learn about game, and not just how to cook a mallard or a pheasant, but how to pluck, eviscerate and remove the sinews. Furthermore, this isn't just a job for the boys – the girls too want to learn how to skin a rabbit or truss a woodcock or snipe with its beak in the traditional way.

At Ballymaloe, we're fortunate to have a local game enthusiast, Tom Duane, who supplies us with a wide selection of game. From late autumn through to Christmas, he brings us birds, rabbits and pigeons, and an occasional hare, which I love as they make a fantastic stew or jugged hare and also the best sauce for pasta. In the summer, out of game season, Tom brings in his beautiful collection of stuffed birds to show the 12-week students, plus a few frozen birds so he can demonstrate how to pluck and prepare them.

Tom shares his in-depth knowledge with the students. There are about ten varieties of pheasant in Ireland and he points out the subtle differences between each one. He shows how you can distinguish the age of a pheasant by the length of its spur and also how to tell the difference between wild birds and those from a driven shoot.

Students learn the different types of wild duck: mallard, teal, widgeon, shoveler and the rarer pintail. They hear that grouse, now so rare in Ireland, was the only indigenous game bird and that the large red deer is native to Ireland, unlike the sika and fallow deer. Fallow deer were introduced into game parks in Ireland around 1169. However, sika deer were not introduced into the Powerscourt Estate in Co. Wicklow until 1860. Tom also teaches students about the game season and about hanging times and techniques – such as the fact that game birds are best hung in the feather by the head and furred game by the back legs.

Learning about game connects the students with the countryside in a very direct way. Some who live in cities or big towns don't necessarily feel a connection to the place where they live, or to their neighbours or local community, nor to the earth, trees and birds. They are living their own lives in their own space, independently of everyone and everything around them. Spending time at Ballymaloe therefore often opens them up to the countryside around them and our essential interdependence with our environment.

Deh-Ta Hsiung

Deh-Ta Hsiung, author of (among other books) *Chinese Regional Cooking* and *The Chinese Kitchen*, was the first guest chef to come to the School in 1984 and returned again a couple of years later. Several friends, including local potter Stephen Pearce and Declan Ryan, chef/owner at that time of Arbutus Lodge Restaurant in Cork and now a renowned artisan baker and owner of Arbutus Breads, had a wish list of guest chefs and topics and Chinese food was high on the list. Ken Hom had a television series at the time and they wanted to learn the secrets of some simple dishes such as fish with bean sauce, Jiaozi (Peking dumplings), chow mein, wontons and special fried rice. I did some research and friends from London heartily recommended Deh-Ta Hsiung, who had just written the first book on Chinese cooking for Marks & Spencer.

Deh-Ta is pint-sized with a wonderful chuckle. A few weeks before the course, I arranged to meet him in London so that together we could buy the right cooking utensils and ingredients. Our shopping expedition was a wonderful experience: Deh-Ta took me into huge, strange-smelling Chinese supermarkets in Soho where we bought woks, steamers, chopsticks, ladles and huge spiders (perforated wire spoons) and lots of then-unfamiliar ingredients, such as wood ear and shiitake mushrooms, Chinese brown rice vinegar, Shaoxing rice wine, sesame oil, black bean paste and different types of soy sauce.

When we were finished, Deh-Ta took me to one of his favourite Chinese restaurants and ordered all kinds of weird and wonderful dumplings, steamed buns, tofu and crispy duck and showed me how to assemble a Peking duck pancake. I ordered chicken's feet and the waiter was so impressed that I was given my lunch for free – he said I was the first Westerner ever to order chicken's feet! I love them – they are soft and gelatinous with lots of little bones to be elegantly disposed of.

Deh-Ta and his lovely wife Paula came to Ballymaloe on several occasions and fell totally in love with Irish produce. Deh-Ta was so impressed by the superb grey sea mullet from Ballycotton that he almost moved to Ireland! In return, he took the mystery out of Chinese food for us and delighted the class participants.

Deh-Ta is a mere five foot two, so we provided him with a platform to stand on so he could be seen behind the counter. His courses were always great fun as not only is he a brilliant teacher but also a scholar. He explained that what distinguishes Chinese food from other cultures lies not only in the preparation and cooking,

but also the way the food is eaten. A Chinese meal doesn't follow the conventional Western sequence of soup, fish, meat, cheese and dessert. An everyday Chinese meal, served at home or in a restaurant, is like a buffet, with all the dishes (including soup) arranged together in the centre of the table. Each person is given a bowl of rice and everyone must help themselves to whatever else they like, though not from every dish on the table, but from one or two at a time. Only on formal occasions are the dishes served course by course and even then, they will appear in groups rather than singly, with soup the only course to be served in an individual dish.

Left: Tom Duane and Frank Mansell with their Springer Spaniels, in pursuit of pheasant for dinner.
Above: Deh-Ta Hsiung teaching a class at the School. He was a real gentleman and introduced us to authentic Chinese cooking as well as Chinese history, culture and traditions.

Rabbit and Prune Terrine with Celeriac Remoulade

The students love rabbit. They get even more excited when we get a wild rabbit so they can skin, gut and prepare it themselves. This terrine, like many coarse-textured pâtés, improves after a day or two.

Preheat the oven to 180°C/350°F/gas 4. Line a 20 x 13cm (8 x 5in) terrine or bread tin with most of the streaky bacon, setting aside 75g (3oz) for the terrine.

Chop the reserved bacon into cubes and put with the chopped livers in a large bowl, add the brandy and port and season with lots of black pepper. Set aside to marinate while you prepare the other ingredients.

Heat the oil in a sauté pan, add the chopped onion and garlic and sweat until soft but not coloured. Set aside to cool.

Add the rabbit and pork to the marinated liver and stir in the fresh herbs. Add the beaten egg and pistachio nuts, and season with salt and freshly ground pepper. Mix really well. Finally stir in the cooled onion mixture. Fry off a small amount and correct the seasoning if necessary.

Put half the mixture into the lined terrine, arrange a line of prunes down the centre and cover with the remaining mixture. Fold over the ends of the streaky bacon, lay a bay leaf and a sprig of thyme on top and cover with the lid. Seal the lid with luting paste – white flour and water mixed to a loose paste like play dough – if necessary.

Transfer the terrine to a roasting tin and pour in enough boiling water to come halfway up the sides. Bake in the preheated oven for 1¾–2 hours or until a skewer inserted into the mixture for 30 seconds feels hot to the touch when taken out. If you are still in doubt, remove the lid and check: the pâté should have shrunk away from the sides of the tin and the juices should run clear.

Transfer the terrine to a large plate, remove the lid and weigh down the pâté with a scrubbed piece of timber or similar weight to form a compress. Alternatively weigh down with the upturned lid and some weights. Set aside to cool, and then transfer to the fridge to mature overnight.

To make the Celeriac Remoulade, trim the celeriac with a knife, peel off the skin and coarsely grate the flesh into a bowl. Stir the Dijon mustard into the mayonnaise and add some to the celeriac (keep back a little in case not all is needed). The remoulade should be saucy but not too sloppy. Add freshly squeezed lemon juice to taste and a little more seasoning if necessary.

To serve, turn the terrine out onto a board and cut into slices, 1cm (½in) thick. Accompany with a little celeriac remoulade, a salad of organic leaves and herbs and some crusty bread.

Serves 10

For the terrine
450g (1lb) rashers of smoked streaky bacon
150g (5oz) rabbit and chicken livers, trimmed and chopped into small pieces
2 tablespoons brandy
2 tablespoons port
2–3 tablespoons extra virgin olive oil
175g (6oz) onion, finely chopped
2 garlic cloves, peeled and crushed
350g (12oz) rabbit meat, coarsely minced
400g (14oz) fat streaky pork, chopped into small pieces
2 teaspoons freshly chopped thyme leaves
2 teaspoons freshly chopped marjoram
2 teaspoons freshly chopped oregano
1 organic egg, beaten
75g (3oz) pistachio nuts
8 soaked prunes, stones removed
1 bay leaf, to decorate
a sprig of thyme, to decorate
Maldon sea salt and freshly ground black pepper

For the Celeriac Remoulade
700g (1½lb) celeriac
1 tablespoon Dijon mustard
350ml (12fl oz) homemade mayonnaise (see page 72)
freshly squeezed lemon juice
sea salt and freshly ground black pepper

To serve
a salad of organic leaves and fresh herbs
crusty bread

Pheasant or Partridge with Savoy Cabbage, Cream and Bacon

Partridge are pretty scarce in Ireland, but a fine plump pheasant also works well here. George Gossip loves Madeira and quite rightly thinks it should make a more regular appearance in our kitchens!

Serves 2

1 whole pheasant or 2 whole partridges
1–2 knobs of salted butter (optional)
110g (4oz) smoked streaky bacon or pancetta, cut in cubes
½ Savoy cabbage, finely shredded
125ml (4fl oz) double cream
a good splash of red wine or Madeira
sea salt and freshly ground black pepper

Preheat the oven to 230°C/450°F/gas 8. Season and truss the pheasant and roast in the preheated oven for 35 minutes according to taste. Alternatively roast two partridges, stuffed with a small knob of butter, for 15–20 minutes.

Meanwhile, fry the bacon or pancetta in a heavy saucepan until crisp, throw in the cabbage and stir-fry for 1 minute. Add a glass of water, cover with a lid and turn down the heat. Cook for 5–6 minutes until the cabbage has softened.

Once the cabbage has softened, remove the lid and boil away the remaining water in the pan. Add the cream and boil rapidly until it forms a thick sauce. Season with a little salt (you may not need much if the bacon is salty) and plenty of black pepper.

Remove the bird(s) from the oven and transfer them to a warm plate to rest while you deglaze the pan. Put the roasting tin over a high heat, pour in the wine or Madeira and bubble away to form a rich sauce. Season to taste with salt and pepper.

To serve, cut the birds in half and arrange on a bed of cabbage. Pour over the juices from the pan.

George Gossip's Venison Sausages with Colcannon

George likes a very coarse, meaty sausage with no extraneous ingredients: 'We do not use oatmeal or rusk, and the addition of diced bananas or cranberries is definitely not for us. That said, we do like plenty of good Dijon mustard, and venison sausages are the perfect foil for spicy or fruity sauces and chutneys.' They are a really delicious way to use shoulder or scraps of flank. Venison sausages make good sausage rolls and they are also great served cold for picnics.

Note: These sausages do not contain a preservative and should be eaten within 4–5 days unless you possess a vacpac machine, which will allow you to keep them a little longer. They freeze very well and are an ideal lunch or supper dish.

Makes approx. 8 large sausages per 450g (1lb) meat, 128 sausages in total

approx. 1.8m (6ft) natural sausage casings
5.4kg (12lb) chopped venison (we used shoulder)
900g (2lb) pork fat (from a free-range heritage breed)
900g (2lb) lean pork meat (from a free-range heritage breed)
100g (3½oz) salt
7g (¼oz) ground black pepper
7g (¼oz) ground nutmeg
slightly more than 7g (¼oz) ground ginger
slightly more than 7g (¼oz) ground cloves
olive oil, for frying

For the Colcannon (Serves 6–8)
1.3kg (3lb) 'old' potatoes, e.g. Golden Wonders or Kerr's Pink
450g (1lb) kale, Savoy or spring cabbage
approx. 50g (2oz) salted butter
approx. 250ml (9fl oz) milk
25g (1oz) spring onion, finely sliced (optional)
sea salt and freshly ground black pepper

Soak the sausage casings in cold water overnight.

Next day, chop the meats, mix together and mince in a mincer. Add the seasonings gradually and fry up a small amount of the mixture to check that the flavouring is to your liking. Take great care not to over-salt. Keep everything very cool.

When you are happy with the taste, add sufficient water to make the mixture malleable. Fill the casings, twist and link the sausages, and hang them up in hanks to dry in a cold place overnight.

To cook the sausages, heat a little olive oil in a frying pan over a moderate heat. Cook the sausages for 3–4 minutes on each side, depending on the size. They should be golden in colour and cooked through to the centre.

To make the Colcannon, scrub the potatoes but leave them whole. Put them in a saucepan of cold water, add a good pinch of salt and bring to the boil. Parboil for approx. 15 minutes, and then strain off two-thirds of the water. Replace the lid and 'steam' over a gentle heat until fully cooked.

Meanwhile, remove the dark outer leaves from the kale or cabbage. Wash the rest and cut into quarters, remove the core and cut finely across the grain. If using kale, remove the central rib. Cook the kale or cabbage in a little boiling salted water until tender. Drain, season with salt and freshly ground pepper and beat in a small knob of the butter.

Once the potatoes are just cooked, tip them into a colander and set aside until they are cool enough to handle. Meanwhile, put the milk and spring onions into a clean saucepan and bring to the boil. Pull the skins off the potatoes and discard. Mash the flesh quickly while it is still warm and beat in enough boiling milk to make a fluffy purée. Finally stir in the cooked cabbage and taste for seasoning. For perfection, serve immediately in a hot dish with a lump of butter melting in the centre, and the sausages on the side.

Colcannon may be prepared ahead and reheated later in a moderate oven at 180°C/350°F/gas mark 4 for 20–25 minutes. Cover while reheating so it doesn't get too crusty on top.

Irish Food

In 1986 I heard about and became a member of the International Association of Culinary Professionals (IACP), a hugely influential international organisation for cookery school teachers and food writers. Many of the most prominent food people from all over the world were members, including Julia Child, Stephanie Alexander, Alice Waters, Ann Yonkers, Marion Cunningham, Nathalie Dupree, Francois Dionot and Nancy Kirby Harris. It was a brilliant networking tool and through it I met and exchanged ideas with people from the global culinary scene. The Annual Conference in the US was unmissable and earlier presidents like Lauraine Jacobs from New Zealand, who was then editor of *Cuisine* magazine, Anne Willan, of Ecole de Cuisine La Varenne in France, and Paula Lambert ensured that the international viewpoint was well represented. It was at IACP that I had my first workshop on how to cook for the camera, several years after I started making television programmes!

The Annual Conference is held in a different US city every year and I have been invited as a speaker on many occasions. A series of smaller regional conferences were later initiated and this is a brilliant way to discover the culinary landscape of the host country. In October 1993 we attended a Regional Conference in Mexico organised by Marilyn Tausend, where I met Diana Kennedy, Rick Bayless, Mark Miller and Maria Dolores Torres Yzabal, all recognised authorities on Mexican food. The event was based in Oaxaca and this began my lifelong love affair with Mexico its food. In winter 2012, I visited Diana Kennedy on her farm in Michoacán and had a memorable couple of days with this extraordinary woman who has dedicated a great part of her lifetime to collecting and recording recipes from around Mexico. Diana was born in the UK but has lived in her adopted home since she moved there in 1957.

Other memorable regional meetings were in Norway with Ingrid Espelid Hovig (the Julia Child of Norway), and in Sicily with Anna Tasca Lanza of Regaleali. I ate spleen sandwiches and tucked into soft buns with Parmesan in Palermo, watched hand-rolled couscous being made in Erice and enjoyed some of the most delicious food I've ever eaten. I still make the semifreddo di mandorle from the recipes I was given in Erice. I also remember eating a timballo with macaroni as described in *The Leopard* by Giuseppe Tomasi di Lampedusa.

In June 1985 we offered the first Cook's Holiday in Ireland, intended to promote Irish produce and change people's perceptions of the country's cuisine. This was a holiday programme for people like myself who love to combine travel with an opportunity to learn about the food and produce of another land. The week-long schedule included cooking classes at the School, visits to markets, bakeries, farmhouse cheesemakers, a fish smoker, a visit to Cork's English Market, dinner in private houses and a talk on Irish food history. We met the fishing boats coming into Ballycotton, foraged for shellfish on Shanagarry strand and listened to traditional Irish music in the pub. I realised that we could offer a truly wonderful Irish experience and help to change people's image of Ireland. We ran these courses every summer from 1985–1989.

In 1988 we hosted an IACP regional conference at Ballymaloe. Delegates came to Shanagarry from Italy, France, Holland, the US and UK for four days. I was anxious to change the image of Ireland as the land of corned beef and cabbage. The delegates loved Myrtle's cooking at Ballymaloe House and the cooking class at the Cookery School. They were delighted by the emerging food movement and particularly loved the Irish farmhouse cheeses that had begun to earn international recognition for their quality.

On the Friday of the visit they walked with me through the English Market in Cork, where they were mightily impressed at the selection of fruit, vegetables, meat, poultry, game and fish. They were also intrigued by the local specialities of tripe and drisheen. Among the visitors was the late Jan Weimer from the influential Los Angeles-based *Bon Appetit* magazine, who commented to a local journalist: 'I must admit that I didn't really think of Ireland as an international gourmet centre, but what we have seen at Ballymaloe has changed many of our opinions. We are very impressed with the way the Allen family have been able to use the natural resources'.

From the beginning of the first 12-week course in 1983, we have always taken the students on a tour to help them to appreciate the wealth of produce in Ireland. The object of the exercise is not just a jolly 'skite', although we always have a fun day, but for them to see for themselves the variety of enterprises; the different ways of adding value to a product like milk, e.g. farmhouse cheesemaking, and to understand the effort and skill that goes into producing these delicious ingredients. The 'Shanagarry Express' pulls out of the Ballymaloe Cookery School car park at about 7a.m., complete with bleary-eyed students and a picnic including coffee machines, plus hampers of homemade jam and pickles as presents for the artisans and farmhouse cheesemakers we will visit during the day.

We choose the mix of venues very carefully in order to introduce the students to as many diverse food operations as possible. We always visit a farmers' market, usually at Mahon Point on a Thursday morning – a superb mix of local farmers, fishermen

Above: Foraging on the seashore with Myrtle Allen. Ireland has 1,448 miles of coastline, so we have a wealth of wild produce on offer with rich pickings of seaweed and shellfish including mussels, sea urchins, limpets, razor clams and cockles. When foraging for these wild foods you need to ensure that the water is clean and unpolluted and also that you harvest sustainably, for example seaweed should be snipped and the holdfast left attached to the rock.

and food producers (several of whom are past students making their living from the food skills and techniques they learned at the Cookery School). The produce on offer ranges from desserts and confectionery to jams and pickles, sauces, salads, cake pops, sushi, homemade lemonades and cordials plus gluten-free baked goods. We often include an artisan smoker on the trip; perhaps Bill Casey who smokes fish on our farm, or Frank Hederman from Belvelly near Cobh, who does both cold- and hot-smoked fish, as well as more unusual produce such as smoked garlic, oatmeal and butter. A visit to a farmhouse cheesemaker is a highlight of the day. We have visited Milleens, Gubbeen, Ardrahan, Durrus, Cashel Blue, Coolea, Bay Lough, St. Tola, Desmond and Gabriel, Fermoy, Carrigaline, Inagh, Hegarty's, Ardsallagh (goat's cheese), Toons Bridge (buffalo cheese) and Knockalara (sheep's cheese) – a who's who of the Irish cheesemaking world. This gives the students the opportunity not only to meet the cheesemakers and experience their passion but also to visit the farms and see the process, in some cases from beginning to end. They see the rich pastures that the cows, goats, sheep or buffalo feed on to produce the top-quality milk needed to produce superb cheese, and they begin to understand and appreciate the phenomenal amount of work and tender loving care that goes into making these handmade cheeses. With this understanding, they rarely complain about the price ever again. Instead they are hugely impressed by the dedication and skill of the artisans and the passion they have for their produce.

We may have our picnic there on the farm, sharing it with our hosts and enjoying their cheese with the students' homemade bread. A visit to a café, tea shop and restaurant or country house hotel is also part of the experience. If there's time we visit a craft brewer, the whiskey distillery in Midleton or a pub that does good food. We might visit a garden, an old orchard or an apple farm to see how apple juice and cider are made and explore the ways of adding value to an apple crop, such as jams, jellies and apple cheese. Each experience highlights opportunities in food production.

As well as giving our students an appreciation of and pride in our Irish produce and ingredients, we also acknowledge and stress the importance of preserving and encouraging Irish culinary traditions. In the early 1990s I recognised that, with the passing of one more generation, a whole culinary tradition, with its considerable range of curious regional variations, was in imminent danger of being lost. That was the starting point for my book *Irish Traditional Cooking* and writing it was a labour of salvage as well as one of love.

Following a huge response to my requests for recipes in the regional papers, I set off on a voyage of discovery. In Ballyheigue in Co. Kerry, I spent a memorable day with John Guerin and his mother Bridget, learning how to collect bairneachs (barnacles) off the rocks to make traditional Irish Good Friday soup. In Co. Monaghan, Granny Toye, well into her eighties, described in vivid detail how to make the boxty pancakes of her youth. As my collection of recipes built up, I realised how common the misconception is, even among Irish people, that Ireland has no culinary tradition to speak of. There is much more to it than bacon and cabbage and Irish stew, delicious as they are.

Ireland's farming heritage has given a variety of methods for cooking meat, poultry and eggs. The potato, so central to Irish subsistence (half an acre of cultivated ground could feed a family for a year), is the main ingredient in an array of dishes with infinite regional variations. Oatmeal has always been important too, used in many interesting ways. Most exciting, perhaps, is Ireland's strong tradition of home baking, with its encyclopaedic range of breads and cakes traditionally made with flour from home-grown wheat. Again, regional differences are noteworthy, with the North an especially rich source of recipes. From the dining rooms of grand houses to the kitchens of the poorest cabins, Ireland has had a strong tradition of generous hospitality from Pagan times right up to the present day.

The time is certainly ripe for a revival of interest in traditional Irish cooking – the wholesome, comforting food that nourished our ancestors for generations and is just as delicious today. The next step must be for more young Irish chefs to include it in their menus and to cook these dishes with pride. We can all learn a great deal from a gastronomic tradition that is based around fresh local ingredients, simply and succulently cooked. Sadly, the reality is that many Irish people don't really believe that we have a food culture to be proud of.

2013 is the year of the 'Gathering' here in Ireland, a tourist initiative which encourages all of us to invite as many of our family and friends to return to Ireland and bring their friends to introduce them to what Ireland has to offer, not just warm, friendly, welcoming people and a beautiful ever-changing landscape, but the renaissance in food and the emergence of an artisan food culture. I've been encouraging chefs, restaurateurs, pubs, cafés and caterers to proudly feature at least one Irish traditional recipe on their menu every week. To facilitate this, in 2013 I created a website, www.irishrecipes.ie, of well-tested traditional recipes for people to access easily.

Homemade Mayonnaise

I know it is very tempting to reach for a jar of the well-known brand, but homemade mayonnaise can be made in 5 minutes, even by hand. If you decide to use a food processor, it's even faster and so worth the effort. As ever, the quality of the eggs really matters. Use the best organic eggs you can find and really good-quality sunflower and olive oil and wine vinegar.

Makes 300ml (½ pint)

2 organic egg yolks
¼ teaspoon salt
¼ teaspoon Dijon mustard or pinch of English mustard powder
1 dessertspoon white wine vinegar
225ml (8fl oz) oil (7 parts sunflower to 1 part olive oil or 6 parts groundnut to 2 parts olive oil)

Put the egg yolks into a medium-sized Pyrex bowl with the salt, mustard and white wine vinegar. Pour the oil into a measuring jug. Take a whisk in one hand and the oil in the other and drip the oil into the egg yolks, drop by drop, whisking at the same time. (If using a food processor, you need to use a minimum of four egg yolks otherwise the blades won't be able to catch the egg at first and the mixture may curdle.) Within a minute you will notice that the mixture is beginning to thicken. When this happens you can add the oil a little faster, but don't get too confident or it will suddenly curdle because the egg yolks can only absorb the oil at a certain pace. Taste and add a little more seasoning and vinegar, if necessary.

If the mayonnaise curdles, it will suddenly become quite thin and, if left sitting, the oil will start to float to the top of the sauce. Should this happen you can quite easily rectify the situation by putting another egg yolk or 1–2 tablespoons boiling water into a clean bowl, and then whisking in the curdled mayonnaise, a half teaspoon at a time, until it re-emulsifies.

Any leftover mayonnaise can be stored in a sterilised jam jar in the fridge for a week to ten days.

Variation – Dill Mayonnaise
Add 2–3 tablespoons finely chopped fresh dill to the basic mixture, folding it in at the end. If you add fresh herbs to mayonnaise this shortens its shelf-life, so any left over will keep at its best for only a couple of days.

Ballycotton Prawns Whole in their Shells with Watercress and Dill Mayonnaise

Not cheap, but always a wow. You may be able to buy them already cooked from your fishmonger, however they are very simple to cook at home. Homemade mayonnaise is a must to embellish these beautiful fresh prawns. Make sure you open their heads and scoop out the soft tomalley. Provide a prawn cracker to crack the claws so you can extract every last sweet morsel, then save the shells for a prawn bisque; chefs often make more money from the bisque than they do from the prawns. Prawns are very expensive and, believe me, there is a world of difference between really fresh prawns and prawns that have been 'dipped' in sodium bisulfite or sodium tripolyphosphate to extend their shelf-life. Ask the fishmonger if the prawns have been dipped – if they have, don't waste your money.

First cook the prawns. Bring the water to the boil and add the salt (it may sound a lot, but this is the secret of real flavour when cooking prawns or shrimps). Do not be tempted to cook too many prawns together, otherwise they may overcook before the water even comes back to the boil; cook them in two or three batches.

Put the prawns into the boiling salted water and, as soon as the water returns to a rolling boil, test a prawn to see if it is cooked. It should be firm and white, not opaque or mushy. If cooked, remove the prawns immediately with a slotted spoon. Very large prawns may take 30 seconds–1 minute more. Set aside to cool in a single layer on a tray. Uncurl the tails.

To serve, arrange five or six cooked whole prawns on each plate. Spoon a tablespoon or two of homemade Dill Mayonnaise into a little bowl or oyster shell on the side of the plate. Pop a wedge of lemon on the plate, garnish with some fresh wild watercress, and serve with fresh crusty brown soda bread and Irish butter.

Serves 8

40–48 large, very fresh prawns – preferably Ballycotton langoustines
  in their shells
3.6 litres (6 pints) water
3 generous tablespoons salt

To serve
4–8 tablespoons homemade Dill Mayonnaise (see opposite)
4 lemon wedges
a handful of watercress leaves
crusty brown soda bread and Irish butter

Tripe with Tomatoes

Tripe is the lining of a cow's stomach. The stomach is divided into two parts, and there are three distinct types of tripe: plain tripe, which comes from the first stomach chamber; honeycomb tripe, which comes from the second stomach chamber; and packet tripe, which comes from the far end of the second stomach chamber. Honeycomb tripe is by far the most tender and flavourful, and is my preferred option. Nowadays it's the plain one that's commonly sold and it usually comes ready blanched.

Serves 6

For the tripe
900g (2lb) honeycomb or book tripe
1 tablespoon salt
225g (8oz) carrot, roughly chopped
1 medium onion, quartered
2 bay leaves
2 sprigs of thyme
2 sprigs of flat-leaf parsley
6 black peppercorns
2 tablespoons white wine vinegar

For the sauce
2 tablespoons extra virgin olive oil
5 garlic cloves, peeled and sliced
1 red chilli, deseeded and sliced
2 medium onions (approx. 350g/12oz), sliced
3 celery stalks, cut into 1cm (½in) dice
1 red pepper, cut into 1cm (½in) dice
1 green pepper, cut into 1cm (½in) dice
2 teaspoons sweet paprika
1 bay leaf
1 teaspoon thyme leaves
2 x 400g (14oz) cans of tomatoes, chopped
300ml (10fl oz) chicken stock
sea salt, freshly ground black pepper and sugar

To serve
3–4 tablespoons roughly chopped flat-leaf parsley
potatoes or plain boiled rice

First prepare the tripe. Wash the tripe very thoroughly in several changes of barely warm water. Drain and put in a bowl. Rub the salt into the tripe and set aside for 30 minutes. Drain and rinse well.

Put the tripe into a large saucepan with the carrot, onion, bay leaves, thyme, parsley, peppercorns and white wine vinegar. Cover with cold water. Bring to the boil and simmer for 1½–2 hours or until the tripe is tender. Strain off the cooking liquor, discard, and cut the tripe into slices 1cm (½in) thick and 5cm (2in) long.

Meanwhile, prepare the sauce. Heat the olive oil in a saucepan, add the garlic, chilli, onion and celery and cook over a low heat without colouring for 5 minutes. Then add the red and green pepper and cook for a further 5 minutes. Next add the paprika, bay leaf and thyme, stir and cook for 1 minute. Add the canned tomatoes and cook, uncovered, for 10 minutes. Season with salt, pepper and sugar. Add the sliced tripe and chicken stock and simmer away gently for 10–15 minutes or until the sauce has reduced slightly. To serve, scatter with parsley and accompany with potatoes or plain boiled rice.

Carrageen Moss Pudding with Poached Apricot and Sweet Geranium Compote

Carrageen is a small, scratchy seaweed that grows around the coast on the little rocks from which it takes its name in Gaelic. Traditionally, it was harvested after the Spring Tides every year. The purpley-wine coloured seaweed was then spread out on the grass, to be washed by the rain and bleached in the sun, for about ten days, by which time it would be a very pale, almost translucent colour. It can then be stored for many years and is a powerhouse of iodine, minerals and trace elements. It is packed with natural gelatine and has many commercial uses, but we use it to make this delish Carrageen Moss Pudding to Myrtle Allen's recipe, which I think is the best I've ever come across. The challenge is to use little enough; carrageen is so light, it's difficult to weigh. In Ballymaloe, we serve it with a compote of seasonal fruit. We all love it and wean our babes onto carrageen. It's possibly the most traditional of all the desserts we serve in Ballymaloe.

In the summer term, when we take the students foraging, we show them how to harvest carrageen moss sustainably on Ballyandreen strand, to the west of Ballycotton.

Serves 6

7g (¼oz) cleaned, well-dried carrageen moss (a semi-closed handful)
850ml (1½ pints) full-fat milk
1 split vanilla pod or ½ teaspoon pure vanilla extract
1 organic egg
1 tablespoon caster sugar

For the Poached Apricot and Sweet Geranium Compote
4–6 large sweet-scented geranium leaves (*Pelargonium graveolens*)
225g (8oz) caster sugar
225ml (8fl oz) cold water
450g (1lb) fresh apricots, left whole or cut in half and stoned

To serve
softly whipped cream

To make the pudding, soak the carrageen in a little bowl of tepid water for 10 minutes. It will swell and increase in size. Strain off the water and put the carrageen into a saucepan with the milk. If you are using a vanilla pod rather than extract, add it now. Bring to the boil and simmer very gently, covered, for 20 minutes. At that point, and not before, separate the egg. Put the yolk into a bowl, add the sugar and vanilla extract (if using) and whisk together for a few seconds. Pour the hot milk and carrageen through a strainer onto the egg yolk mixture, whisking all the time.

By now the carrageen remaining in the strainer will be swollen and exuding jelly. You need to press out as much of this as possible through the strainer and whisk the jelly into the egg and milk mixture. Test for a set by placing a teaspoon of the mixture on a cold saucer; it should hold its shape but still be a little wobbly. If it's too stiff, add a little more milk, and if it's too soft, push some more of the carrageen through the sieve. In a separate bowl, whisk the egg white until stiff, and fold or fluff it into the custard; it will rise to make a fluffy top. Divide the mixture between six 175ml (6fl oz) ramekins and set aside to chill in the fridge for 7–8 hours or overnight.

To make the apricot compote, put the sweet geranium leaves into a saucepan with the sugar and water and bring slowly to the boil. Drop in the apricots, cover with a lid and simmer until the apricots are soft, approx. 15–30 minutes depending on ripeness. Set aside to cool, and then transfer the compote to the fridge to chill.

Serve the carrageen moss pudding with the chilled apricot compote and softly whipped cream.

The Fruit Garden

In 1989 my friend, garden designer Jim Reynolds of Butterstream, Trim, Co. Meath, designed a fruit garden for us that was intended to be decorative as well as productive. It is situated in front of the Blue Dining Room at the Cookery School, with steps of Liscannor slate leading down into a gravelled area below the windows, where the students can choose to have lunch in the warmer months beneath the large parasols. The soil is good, having been enriched by farmyard manure, seaweed and compost over the years. Jim designed a formal layout to accommodate a wide variety of fruit so the students could see many different types of fruit blossoming and growing and have the opportunity to pick their own and bring it into the kitchen and eat it. Many who are unfamilar with how fruit grows are intrigued to see how currants hang in clusters and gooseberries hide beneath the leaves and need to be topped and tailed before eating.

Strawberries, loganberries, tayberries, gooseberries, red and yellow raspberries, Worcesterberries, jostaberries, boysenberries, cranberries, blackberries, blueberries, red, black and white currants and crab apples are all planted here. Greengages, plums, peaches, apricots and rhubarb are planted around the perimeter. Pears and heirloom apples, including several old Irish varieties are trained over metal arches. We also grow more unusual varieties, such as a delicious early apple called Irish Peach, which has been grown in Ireland for more than two centuries and is still appreciated and sought out by those who like flavoursome apples. We chose apple varieties no longer easily available in the shops and supermarkets: American Mother, Egremont Russet, Lane's Prince Albert, Pitmaston Pineapple, Arthur Turner, Beauty of Bath and Lady Sudeley. We did this for two reasons: to have more choice than the predictable varieties available in the shops, and to preserve and reacquaint people with these almost forgotten flavours, many of which have a delicious, bittersweet taste.

The black mulberry in the centre, underplanted with autumn crocuses, is just beginning to produce fruit at last. It was planted in 1989 and took over ten years to produce even a small crop.

Green Almonds

Timmy ambles in – I know by his non-committal expression that he has something exciting to announce!

'Have you looked at your almond tree recently?'

I need no more prompting; I race across the dining room out onto the steps overlooking the fruit garden. I don't believe it: my almond tree is covered with soft, furry, green almonds. I'm wild with excitement. Madhur Jaffrey told me how delicious they are eaten at this green stage. I eat one whole. Umm, I'm not sure if that is what she meant. Then I take a knife and cut through the protective outer green husk and taste the moist, white flesh of the green almond inside – delicious. In the Mediterranean countries where they grow, they are eaten, green husk and all, when they are young and tender. The Greeks love them sprinkled with lemon juice and sea salt. The French like to marinade green almonds in verjus. We now have a little almond feast every year. We eat them fresh off the tree in April or early May, sitting under the almond tree with a little paring knife.

Left: We have trained old varieties of apple over the arches in the fruit garden, for example we grow Egremont Russet, Lane's Prince Albert, Arthur Turner, Beauty of Bath, Pitmaston Pineapple and Irish Peach (yes, it is an apple!). This shows the view from the fruit garden, looking up towards the little wood and kitchen garden.

The fruit resemble long, winey blackberries. Two weeping white mulberries frame a garden seat. The almond trees bear abundant furry fruits, which split to release the stones from which the sweet kernels can be extracted. Few students have seen almonds grow, so they are fascinated to see the furry green pods and to know they can be eaten at several stages.

One surprising success has been the Asian pear or nashi; the trees have produced excellent, crisp fruits, which are apple-like with a heavy russet. The elders (*Sambucus nigra*) that grow along the stone wall to the south of the garden include Wildings and the dark purple-leaved cultivar named Guincho Purple. From the end of May for about a month we use an abundance of elder blossoms for cordial, lemonade, fritters and elderflower fizz, and the berries are used for jams and jellies in autumn. Figs grow against the wall of the Cookery School, and there is an olive tree too, although sadly this does not produce enough fruit to make olive oil – still, it earns its place in the fruit garden, as students can see what an olive tree looks like.

The fruit garden is underplanted with spring bulbs, so it is especially joyful in spring when the Lenten roses and bulbs bloom – snowdrops, grape hyacinths and countless crocuses, fritillaries, snowflakes and tiny *Iris reticulata*. Here too, in the shade of the elders, I replanted the Kinoith violets that Lydia Strangman and her brother Wilson, who were the last members of the Strangman family to live in our house at Kinoith (Lydia was also a keen watercolour artist), once picked and sent to London, in conjunction with a number of other farms in East Cork. The violets were tied into little bunches, wrapped in a violet leaf and taken to Cork to be exported to London on the ship, *Innisfallen*. Ladies wore them on their lapels and enjoyed the beautiful scent of the dark purple violets. The violets were bunched in the 'Violet Loft', now a part of the Pink Cottage, which overlooks where Lydia's garden once was. The flowers are sweetly fragrant, and while most abundant in winter and early spring, there are stray flowers in other seasons. Nowadays we use these fragrant flowers at the School and at Ballymaloe House to make pretty crystallised violets to decorate cakes and pastries.

In the mid-1990s we planted white peaches and apricots on the south-facing wall of the dining room. The white peaches, Peregrine, particularly love it there and we usually have an abundant crop to enjoy. We use this glut to make bellinis and both sweet and savoury salads. White peaches are meltingly sweet and juicy but bruise really easily. Ice-cream maker extraordinaire, Kitty Travers of La Grotta Ices, gave us a tip about peeling and dropping them into hot syrup first – this prevents them from discolouring, which they do immediately otherwise. We also show the students how to use the peach leaves in ratafias, panna cottas and crème brûlées, and to make a simple peach leaf tea from fresh or dried leaves, which has many nutritional and therapeutic qualities – it is reputed to be good for cleansing the kidneys, and in the past peach leaves were used to treat worms, bronchitis and whooping cough. Peach is also one of the first fruits to flower in the garden, appearing as early as April; the pale pink blossoms are a joy after the long, sullen winter.

The Beginning of Television

My first foray into television wasn't part of a master plan, it was almost accidental. Keith Floyd, who was extremely well-known on television in the UK, was a great friend of Ireland and had a house in Kinsale in West Cork for many years. Claudia Roden had told him about the School, so when he was visiting in 1986 with a film crew he asked to do a short piece. Our first film crew – we were excited and terrified. He arrived hours late, which made me even more apprehensive. I'd never even seen a television camera up close before. I was nervous and felt really silly in front of my class.

The first take was all arranged – there would be a shot of me teaching the class then suddenly I would catch a glimpse of Floyd reading the *Racing Times* at the back of the class, look shocked and tell him to put the paper down and concentrate. The first take was perfect but Floyd forgot my name. So we had to do it again and again and again. The more takes we did the worse I got, so Floyd had a brilliant idea. Let's stop and have a glass of wine! So we did and everything went swimmingly after that. I don't remember what we cooked – I think it was Irish stew, but I just remember the relief when it was over.

Afterwards Floyd said to Tim, 'You know Darina should do TV, she's a natural'. We all thought that was hilarious, considering I'd found it so nerve-wracking, and at that time I had no plans to do any more television. However, sometime early in 1987, a letter arrived in the post from RTÉ Head of Features, Clare Duignan, asking whether Myrtle and I would be interested in doing a pilot of a cookery series. We decided to have a go and the pilot was shot at the School in August 1987. It took a week to make an hour-long programme. With just one camera, every scene had to be shot twice. There was no playback, unthinkable nowadays when most series are made with four cameras and spontaneous editing. Continuity was a nightmare but it was certainly a good way to 'cut our teeth'. Eventually RTÉ came back to us and said they would like to make a series. They wanted to shoot it in July and August 1988 – a very difficult time for Myrtle, bang in the midst of the tourist season – so she encouraged me to go ahead on my own.

I was dithering: what if it was a disaster, it's so easy to make a fool of oneself in front of the cameras. Eventually, I decided to go for it, preferring to live with the possibility that it wouldn't necessarily be a smash hit, rather than wondering what if I'd had a go!

Colette Farmer, a producer/director who had worked for many years on the *Late, Late Show* with Gay Byrne, which was at that time an unmissable programme for half of Ireland, was assigned to the programme by Clare Duignan. We had a small crew of five, who soon became like family: Roy Bedell was the cameraman, Pat Johns was on sound, Sean Keville was the 'sparks' (electrician) and Patricia Swan was the production assistant for the first series: she was followed by Mary Power and then Kevin Cummins ably took on the role for the following years.

I was adamant that the show should be shot here at the School where I had a well-equipped kitchen and easy access to beautiful, fresh produce. We could also pick up evocative background shots of the farm, gardens and local area. When I agreed to do the series, I explained that I had absolutely no idea how to go about it. Everyone promised to help, but the crew had never done a food programme before either, so we were all learning together. Fortunately I remembered that Claudia Roden and Madhur Jaffrey, who had been guests chef at the School, had done many TV series, so I called them. They were wonderfully generous and put us in touch with their production teams who gave me practical advice, such as rehearsing first and weighing up three sets of ingredients.

For me, the aim of *Simply Delicious* was to take the mystery out of cookery and to incorporate technique into every programme while keeping the food simple and delicious, just as I taught at the School. Colette and I argued constantly about the content of the episodes; I always wanted to squash more into each programme. She wisely knew that less is more and also knew my limitations. My style and the format of the programme were very different from cookery programmes nowadays, which are geared more towards entertainment than tutorial. I was very earnest about the whole exercise and determined that people should really be able to learn from the programmes, which they did.

Initially, it took a day and a half to make a 30 minute programme. Floyd may have thought I was a natural but in reality I found it incredibly stressful, particularly the simple pieces to camera, which I always seemed to have to do over and over again. The series was eventually 'in the can' and disappeared off to RTÉ Donnybrook to be edited. We waited with mixed emotions of excitement and apprehension.

At some stage while we were filming it occurred to me that we would need a cookbook with the series. Colette didn't think it was necessary because the recipes would be published in the RTÉ Guide every week. But I could foresee people either mislaying the

Above: A publicity picture for the first series of Simply Delicious *of me with a selection of dishes from the book, taken outside in the courtyard of the School. The series featured simple recipes such as Kerry Pie, Blackberry and Apple Tart, Bacon Chop and the classic Ballymaloe*

Brown Yeast Bread. The presentation is certainly very of its time and rather different to how we would present dishes today. My trademark glasses are blue instead of red here, possibly in an attempt to co-ordinate with the apron!

guide or not buying it and just phoning me for the recipes instead. I was determined to do a book, but Colette was still hesitant as we would need lots more recipes than were in the series. This was no problem as we already had several thousand recipes in our files. Michael Gill of Gill & Macmillan publishers had approached me a few years earlier to ask if I'd do a book but at that stage I wasn't quite ready. When approached by RTÉ, he jumped at the idea.

I had no idea how to go about writing a book, but Michael assigned me a wonderful editor, Dee Rennison, who explained matter of factly, 'We need 90 recipes and a bit of blurb for each one before the deadline of March'. We chose the content and I tested, tested and re-tested; I was determined that the recipes would work easily for all my new readers. My brother Rory O'Connell and I cooked all the food for the photos – Rory did most of the food styling as well. It was to be a paperback and the cover was grey (what was I thinking?!) with a (very predictable) photo of me in my apron complete with those dreadful huge red trademark glasses.

The first programme was to be shown on Monday 13 March 1989 at 7.30p.m. On the Saturday before, Gay Byrne invited me to be a guest on the *Late, Late Show*. This was a huge deal. Colette had asked him to introduce me and the series to the Irish people. I was never so scared of anything, before or since. This was *live*! We cooked a whole array of food to bring into the studio as an example of what I would be covering in the series. I needn't have worried, Gay was kind and supportive – I was launched. The following day my life changed forever; suddenly I was recognised as I walked along the street; the windows of Easons, Waterstone's and Hodges Figgis were full of my cookbook. I found this surprisingly difficult to cope with and was relieved to be able to disappear back into the relative obscurity of my home in Shanagarry.

Soon after the series was aired, all hell broke loose – the books, which were reasonably priced, started to sell in huge numbers and people queued around the corner when I did book signings in Dublin, Cork, Galway, Waterford and Kilkenny. People rang into RTÉ and radio stations and complained that there were

arguments in their house because *Simply Delicious* was aired at the same time as *Coronation Street*. This was the era when there was definitely only one television in most houses and no playback. RTÉ responded and put on a repeat of each programme. Both RTÉ and Gill & Macmillan were amazed by the reaction to the programme. Journalists kept calling for interviews. People kept telling me how much they were enjoying it; I was obviously very pleased, but had nothing to measure the reaction by and honestly didn't register quite what a phenomenon it seemed to be. Two things gave me an inkling, the first was from Kevin Myers, who wrote ' An Irishman's Diary' in *The Irish Times* and published a piece in his column on 26 April 1989 on how Irish publishing history was being made by a cookbook, of all things. The second hint that it was creating a real stir was sometime in the late autumn – possibly October or November. I had just completed a book signing in Waterstone's in Cork and as we were leaving the Gill & Macmillan representative met a colleague from another company who inquired how things were going, to which the Gill & Macmillan rep replied, 'We're having a fantastic year, this woman's book *Simply Delicious* is selling in telephone numbers!' I thought, 'Wow, that's my book they're talking about'. When we got to the car I asked for the first time how many books I had sold. The answer was over 60,000 copies. At that time successful cookbooks usually sold 3,000–5,000 copies.

Since then there has been the phenomenal rise of the celebrity television chef. Some are more decorative than functional, but others, like Jamie Oliver and Hugh Fearnley-Whittingstall, have a strong social mission and have used their platform to effect political change and raise food issues, such as the dismal quality of school lunches, the plight of intensively-produced poultry and overfishing, for which I admire them greatly. I feel strongly that those of us who are fortunate enough to have the opportunity to be television presenters have a responsibility to educate and contribute to the greater good in some way, rather than merely filling airtime!

Despite the enormous increase in the number of cookery programmes on TV, it is a matter of conjecture and some dispute

An Irishman's Diary

Darina Allen . . . 2 lb of gremlins in her Christmas pudding recipe

POOR Darina Allen. The phone can't go down in Ballymaloe Cookery School in Co Cork without her leaping under a table, sitting on her head, putting her fingers in her ears and screeching: "I'm not in. I'm not in. I'm not in." Because the one thing that a cookery expert hates above all things has happened to her. There is a mistake in her recipe for Christmas pudding in her latest book, and what's worse, it's the recipe for her mother-in-law's Christmas pudding. Oh mercy. Myrtle's rolling pin coming down onto daughter-in-law's cranium.

The error is this. The recipe for the Christmas pudding contains all the normal goodies, but the error is a subtle one. It does not then suggest that you add 13 lb of quick-setting concrete, and bung in a half bucket of rusting nails, or season the mix with a half pint of ox blood and 20 finely ground cloves of garlic. You might, just might, have detected an error there, though I personally doubt it. My own experience of any cookery book suggests that the reader goes into a trance of kamikaze obedience, and would unquestionably chuck a kilo of lightly minced rats' eyelids into a vegetarian hotpot.

Believable Error

But, as I say, Darina's error, the one that has her screeching with horror every time the phone tinkles, is of a more subtle order. In the recipe entitled "Myrtle Allen's Christmas pudding", she has said that you should use 2 lb of bread crumbs. The insidious thing about this error is that it is believable.

The figure should not be 2 lb. It should be seven ounces. But all over the island people have been throwing 2 lb of bread crumbs into the mix. (And all over the island is no exaggeration. Darina is the Harold Robbins of cookery writing, though normally her recipes are not quite as fictional as this Christmas pudding one).

And they have then cooked their Christmas pudding, and some of them have already — oh impetuous souls — decided to eat some of it 'early. And there at the table husband has looked at wife and asked: "What did you say this is

called?" "Myrtle Allen's Christmas pudding," she has replied, with downcast eyes.

And the entire family has nibbled with polite decorum at what they think is Myrtle Allen's Christmas pudding; except, of course, it is not. For it tastes like sliced pan and may justifiably be called mother's pride. And this might even be the case on Christmas Day, in which case people will soundly curse the name of the Allen family, or, if they are suitably drunk, will blame the ozone layer, and lament for the Christmasses of their youth, when there was snow and holly and Christmas pudding that tasted of Christmas pudding rather than the bread sauce that went with the turkey.

A Breaking Heart

The error, you see, is simple and subtle. You should put seven ounces of bread crumbs into your mix, not 2 lb, and that way you'll have the true Myrtle Allen pudding, the one she nourished all 30 (or whatever: it's something like that) of her children on.

And now you know, though that is little consolation for poor Darina. "It breaks your heart," she hissed homicidally, "putting all these recipes together and proof reading, going over the bloody thing endlessly, and then you get an error like this." She stamped a foot and put her heel through the floorboards, and then ground her teeth, loosening half a dozen molars. You know they're angry in Ballymaloe

when the word bloody finds its way into the list of expletives.

"And the infuriating thing is that they are absolutely super recipes. I've had an awful week, and I don't want people not to buy this book because they think it's full of errors."

And it's not. All the other recipes are right, though the recipe for St Stephen's Day pie neglects to point out that the amount of onions you will need is 12 oz, and Mary Joe's cookies should have a half pound, not 1 lb, of chocolate. What's the difference?"

"It's a hell of a lot richer," said Darina, grimly.

Fiendish Recipe

But that's it. The latest copies of the book have errata slips, and one of the features Darina is particularly fond of is the recipes for children. No, this is not a cannibal's cookery book. This is something infinitely more fiendish. It is a plan to introduce children and foodstuffs into the same kitchen simultaneously, and then let them at one another, the winner being first to claim three falls or a submission. Though ideally, an adult should be present, and the idea is for the children to make things like a chocolate Christmas tree, rather than to eat 15 lb of cooking chocolate, and then to proceed to make the only restitution that is in their power.

"I'm so fragile," whispered poor Darina. "You won't over-emphasise that single error, will you?"

Wouldn't dream of it.

Melodic Numbers

Just as Darina is dodging telephones, Miriam Blennerhassett is dodging 'flu bugs, so that she is in good voice for her concert in St Anne's in Dawson Street in Dublin tomorrow at lunchtime. If she gets the cold the Diary has, she'll be known as Mucous Blennerhassett. Miriam has chosen a brilliantly melodic programme for this concert in which she is accompanied by Clive Shannon. Songs by Dowland, Faure, Mahler, Beckett, and virginal, hitherto unheard numbers by Michael McGlynn which Miriam will sing (or snuffle, as the case may be). 1.10 pm, St Anne's, all right?

KEVIN MYERS

---

as to whether people are actually cooking more or simply sitting back on the sofa enjoying the show – indulging in a little 'armchair cooking'. I'm not sure how one can quantify this, certainly there's a lot of produce on supermarket shelves and at farmers' markets, so someone must be doing something with it.

The myriad of cookery programmes on offer has had varying effects on attitudes to food. In my experience series such as *Masterchef* have had two effects, either they intimidate total beginners, who feel that cooking is all too complicated to attempt, or they make others feel that cooking is all about water baths, siphons, foams and gels. The latter often come to the Cookery School keen to learn complex skills and skip the basics; they are convinced that it is totally irrelevant to learn how to make a pâte à choux or silky béchamel. They are desperate to learn how to put skid marks on the plate before they have mastered knife skills, which can be a challenge!

Plum Pudding

Within the first few months of the publication of *Simply Delicious*, Michael Gill, owner of Gill & Macmillan, approached me and asked whether I could very quickly write a Christmas cookbook. I wanted to include recipes for both my mother's and Myrtle's plum puddings. The latter had been passed down the Allen family for several generations and called for a 2lb loaf for the breadcrumbs.

Because of the rush to publish, Gill & Macmillan offered to do the recipe conversions for the book. However, the person who was charged with the task didn't realise that a 2lb loaf didn't mean 2lb of breadcrumbs! (A 2lb loaf would normally produce approx. 7oz of breadcrumbs.) No one spotted the mistake until the book went into the shops, then about a week later the phones started to ring. I still remember the sinking feeling when my PA, Rosalie Dunne, called me to the phone to speak to an irate woman who told me the recipe was wrong; she had got five puddings instead of the three the recipe said and they were all 'very bready'. My heart sank as it gradually dawned on me what had happened. We contacted Gill & Macmillan and explained the problem. They generously suggested that I blame the publishers but I was not prepared to leave it like that. Even in the short time that the School had operated and we'd made one *Simply Delicious* series, I had built up a bond of trust with my readers and they really were using my cookbooks.

Having chatted to Michael Gill, I was determined to go on radio to explain and to try to stop other people from making the same mistake. I contacted Gay Byrne and he had me on his morning radio show where I explained to the Irish people about the mistake in the recipe. It caused a whole spate of hilarious jokes and was even the subject of a cartoon in the *Sun*. They say that there's no such thing as bad publicity and after that interview and the subsequent newspaper coverage, the bookshops reported a surge of people pouring into their shops looking for the 'book with the mistake in it'!

Fig, Bocconcini and Mizuna Salad with Opal Basil

Not everyone can have a fig tree, but it's definitely worth considering. They grow happily in this climate, both outdoors against a warm south-facing wall (contain the roots), or in a tunnel or greenhouse, where the fruit will ripen better. We also use the leaves on the cheeseboard and to wrap fish or to flavour raspberry granita, a trick shown to me by Kitty Travers of La Grotta Ices when she came to teach at the School.

It really isn't worth bothering with figs unless they are in season and freshly picked – otherwise use dried Turkish figs rather than under-ripe imported ones.

Serves 4

12 bocconcini or small balls of fresh mozzarella
1 bunch of mizuna or rocket
1 bunch of Thai basil or opal basil
75ml (3fl oz) extra virgin olive oil
6 fresh figs, preferably Turkey or Black Mission
freshly squeezed lemon juice
Maldon sea salt

Bring a saucepan of water to the boil. Drain the cheese and put the balls in a thick plastic bag.

Mix the mizuna or rocket leaves with the basil in a large salad bowl. Drizzle with some of the olive oil and toss gently to coat. Pile the salad leaves into the centre of four plates. Trim the stem from each fig and gently pull each one in half with your thumbs. Lay the fig halves open-side up on the salad.

Drop the bag of bocconcini or mozzarella into the hot water for 2–3 minutes, then remove the cheese from the bag and scatter over the salad.

Drizzle with a little more olive oil, sprinkle with a few drops of freshly squeezed lemon juice and scatter over a few flakes of Maldon sea salt.

Raspberry and Fig Leaf Granita

This recipe was shown to me by Kitty Travers when she taught an ice cream course in the summer of 2012. She introduced us to some delicious and unusual flavours such as Rhubarb and Angelica Sorbet and Nectarine Leaf Ice Cream. Look out for her cart at Maltby Street Market, London.

Serves 10

60g (2½oz) granulated sugar
250ml (9fl oz) water
3 fig leaves
500g (18oz) fresh raspberries

To serve
Crème Chantilly (see below)

Put the sugar and water into a medium saucepan, stir to dissolve the sugar, then bring up to a simmer.

Rinse the fig leaves under some running water and rip them into a few pieces if they are large. As soon as the sugar syrup reaches a simmer, add the fig leaves to the pan, remove from the heat and cover with clingfilm to infuse for 15 minutes. Strain the leaves, pressing gently on them to extract as much perfumed syrup as is possible.

Add the raspberries to the still warm syrup and blitz with a stick blender. Strain the purée through a sieve to remove the pips.

Pour the mixture into a shallow metal tray, cover with clingfilm, and put flat on a freezer shelf. Stir with a fork after 1 hour, breaking up any large lumps of ice. Keep stirring every 45 minutes thereafter.

The desired end result is a beautiful heap of fine, snowy crystals. This ought to be achieved after 3–4 hours. Serve with homemade Crème Chantilly (see below).

Crème Chantilly

½–1 tablespoon icing sugar
2–3 drops pure vanilla extract
300ml (10fl oz) softly whipped cream

Add the icing sugar and vanilla extract to the cream and fold gently to mix.

Green Gooseberry and Elderflower Trifle

Our repertoire of trifles continues to grow – this green
gooseberry and elderflower one is a fairly recent addition.

Serves 16–20

150ml (5fl oz) elderflower cordial

For the sponge
125g (4½oz) butter, softened, plus extra for greasing
175g (6oz) plain flour, plus extra for dusting
175g (6oz) caster sugar
3 organic eggs
1 teaspoon baking powder
1 tablespoon milk

For the green gooseberry and elderflower compote
3–4 elderflower heads
400g (14oz) caster sugar
600ml (1 pint) cold water
900g (2lb) green gooseberries

For the egg custard
450ml (16fl oz) milk
150ml (5fl oz) cream
1 vanilla pod, split lengthways
3 organic eggs, plus 3 organic egg yolks
4–6 tablespoons caster sugar

To serve
600ml (1 pint) softly whipped cream
gooseberry leaves and sweet geranium flowers or fresh mint leaves
    and elderflowers, to decorate

Preheat the oven to 190°C/375°F/gas 5. Grease two 18cm (7in) cake
tins with melted butter, dust with flour and line the base of each one
with a round of greaseproof paper.

For the sponge, cream the butter, gradually add the sugar and beat
until soft and pale. Add the eggs one at a time, beating well between
each addition. (If the butter and sugar are not creamed properly, and
you add the eggs too fast, the mixture will curdle, resulting in a heavy
texture.) Sift the flour with the baking powder and fold in gradually.
Mix all together lightly and add the milk to moisten.

Divide the mixture evenly between the two tins, hollowing it
slightly in the centre. Bake in the preheated oven for 20–25 minutes
or until cooked – the cakes will shrink away slightly from the sides of
the tin; the centre of the cakes should feel exactly the same texture as
around the edges. A skewer should come out clean when put into the
centre of the cake. Turn out onto a wire rack and set aside to cool.

Meanwhile, make the compote. Tie the elderflower heads in a
little square of muslin and put into a stainless steel or enamelled
saucepan – alternatively, you can just put them in loose. Add the
sugar and water, bring slowly to the boil and continue to boil for 2
minutes. Put in the gooseberries and simmer just until the fruit bursts.
They must actually burst, otherwise the compote of fruit will be too
bitter. Set aside to cool.

To make the egg custard, heat the milk and cream with the vanilla
pod in a heavy-bottomed pan until it reaches the 'shivery' stage.
Meanwhile, whisk the whole eggs and egg yolks with the sugar until
pale and frothy. Pour the hot milk and cream mixture over the egg
mixture, whisking all the time. Return the custard to the pan and stir
over a gentle heat until the custard is thick enough to coat the back
of the wooden spoon. Don't let it boil or it will curdle. Remove the
custard from the heat and continue to stir as it cools. Remove the
vanilla pod. Set aside to cool.

To assemble the trifles, spoon one-sixth of the custard over
the base of two 850ml (1½ pint) glass serving bowls and top with
one-sixth of the gooseberry compote. Split the cakes in half, place
a layer of cake on top of the compote and drizzle one-quarter of
the elderflower cordial over each. Top each with another layer of
custard, some more compote, the last layer of cake and the rest of the
elderflower cordial. Finish with the rest of the gooseberry compote
and a final layer of custard. Cover each bowl with clingfilm and
transfer the trifles to the fridge to settle, preferably overnight or for at
least 2 hours.

To serve, spoon a layer of softly whipped cream over the top each
trifle. Decorate with gooseberry leaves and sweet geranium flowers or
simply fresh mint leaves and elderflowers.

Autumn Peach, Blueberry and Raspberry Crumble Tart

Peach, blueberry and raspberry is a delicious combination of fruit, but this recipe can be used as a base and topping for many other tarts using whatever seasonal fruit is available. We find that people love simple, homely desserts like this and they are also a great attraction on a café menu.

First make the pastry. Sift the flour onto a work surface and rub in the butter. Add the sugar. Make a well in the centre and break in the egg. Use your fingertips to gently bring the mixture together, pulling in more flour from the outside as you work. (If the mixture is very crumbly, you may need to add a few drops of water.) Knead with the heel of your hand, making three turns. You should end up with a silky smooth ball of dough. Wrap in clingfilm and set aside in the fridge for at least 1 hour before using. (If not using the pastry straight away, it will keep for a week in the fridge and it also freezes well.)

Preheat the oven to 180°C/350°F/gas 4. Line a 22cm (9in) tart tin with the pastry and then line with greaseproof paper and fill it to the top with dried beans to hold the paper in place. Bake for 20–25 minutes. Remove from the oven and set aside to cool slightly.

To make the crumble topping, put all the dry ingredients into a bowl and rub in the butter until the mixture resembles coarse flakes.

To make the filling, slice the peaches or nectarines into a bowl and carefully stir in the blueberries and raspberries (if using). Sprinkle in the cornflour and mix well. Taste – if the fruit is unusually tart, you may need to add a little sugar.

To assemble the tart, spoon the fruit into the pastry case and top with an even layer of crumble topping – a generous 1cm (½in) thick.

Bake in the preheated oven for 45 minutes–1 hour or until the topping is crisp and the fruit is tender. The juices should bubble up around the edges.

Serve with softly whipped cream with lots of freshly chopped mint folded in.

Serves approx. 8

For the sweet shortcrust pastry
175g (6oz) plain white flour
75g (3oz) diced butter, softened
40g (1½oz) caster sugar
1 large organic egg, beaten

For the crumble topping
25g (1oz) plain white flour
50g (2oz) soft light brown sugar
75g (3oz) oat flakes, organic if possible
$^1/_8$ teaspoon freshly ground cinnamon
25g (1oz) butter

For the filling
700g (1½lb) peaches or nectarines
225g (8oz) blueberries or 110g (4oz) blueberries and 110g (4oz) raspberries
1 tablespoon cornflour

To serve
softly whipped cream
a small handful of fresh mint leaves, finely chopped

Keeping Cows

In 1990, Tom Ferguson of Gubbeen Cheese in Schull took me to see a beautiful herd of Kerry cows grazing on the hillside overlooking Roaring Water Bay in West Cork. Memories came flooding back of the little black Kerry house cow my family had in Cullohill and the delicious raw milk we had as children. (It was a tradition in Ireland to have a special cow to provide milk for the household and the Kerry breed is known to have particularly delicious and nutritious milk.) Tom has a great fondness for the Kerry and the superior quality of their milk and had serious concerns about their dwindling numbers. I resolved there and then to buy a Kerry to enlarge the gene pool and to have access to raw milk once again, not just for myself, but also for my children and grandchildren.

I bought my first pure-bred Kerry cow, Fortagusta Natasha (Fortagusta was the name of the herd and farm and she was already

named Natasha), in 1990 from an organic farmer in Wexford called Ivan Ward, who didn't quite realise that he was going to have to provide years of 'after sale service' as I slowly learned the ropes. The Kerry is a dual-breed, which thrives even on poor or marginal soil, and is used for both dairy and beef. We rear the male calves for beef – the meat is succulent and flavourful with a rich covering of yellow fat – while we keep the females to provide us with a range of dairy produce. Sadly that first beautiful, elegant cow is no longer alive, but one of her daughters has given birth to seven healthy calves. We now have three Kerry cows and a herd of five Jersey cows, which we milk every day. We opted for Jersey because these lovely cows are gentle and docile and the milk is sweet and delicious, the cream rich and unctuous.

I feel very strongly about the health-giving properties of raw milk from a small, well-managed herd of healthy cows. A growing body of epidemiological research is reinforcing this belief in the health-giving and anti-allergic properties of raw milk, which significantly protects against asthma, eczema and hay fever.

There is a global resurgence of interest in this issue and growing demand for raw milk. In May 2011 the first international Raw Milk Conference was held in Prague on the Risks and Benefits of Raw Milk, and subsequent conferences have been held in 2012 and 2013 in Vancouver. Regulations vary from country to country, but Ireland is particularly famous for the quality of its dairy products.

Every shop and petrol station in Ireland sells pasteurised, homogenised milk, but I feel strongly that people who wish to should be able to choose to buy raw milk. It would seem grossly unfair if Irish people were to be deprived of the opportunity to

Left: One of our herd of five Jersey cows, which provide us with rich milk and cream to make butter, buttermilk, yogurt and a number of cheeses, which then feature in many of the dishes that we make at the School. Right: Eileen O'Donovan bringing her beloved herd of cows in for the morning's milking.

choose. In 2011 the government announced its intention to ban the sale of raw milk to the public in the Republic of Ireland. There was a spirited campaign against an outright ban. We called for a geographical spread of farms around the country to be regulated in order to sell unpasteurised milk to the public who wish to have a choice. We argued that anyone who wants pasteurised homogenised milk can buy it in any shop in Ireland, whereas those who feel strongly about raw milk have a right to choose.

At Ballymaloe we sell the fresh, unpasteurised Jersey milk and cream from a refrigerated unit in our Farm Shop to local people. Some customers drive up to 50 miles to buy it if their children have asthma or eczema and report dramatic improvement in their conditions. Ireland has the fourth highest prevalence of asthma in the world and 18.9 per cent of Irish 13–15 year olds have asthma.

Some customers just want to drink a glass of chilled milk in the shop. Interestingly, there is a small but growing demand for raw milk in the US and many European countries. Several milk bars have opened in New York alone, such as Momofuku and Ronnybrook, where customers can have a glass of pasteurised milk from a variety of breeds.

At the School we offer both pasteurised, organic milk and our own raw milk carefully labelled, so the students can make a choice. Many students are apprehensive at first, having being conditioned to be wary of raw milk. I remind them that milk was first pasteurised in Ireland in 1954 for a very good reason. During the 1950s there

was a serious problem with tuberculosis and brucellosis in cattle. Milk from many farms with varying degrees of hygiene was mixed together, so pasteurisation was desirable. I explain both the risks and benefits of raw milk to our students, give them access to the papers from the Prague Conference on the subject and let them make up their own minds. When they taste the milk they are usually hooked – raw milk from a small herd of healthy cows, which graze on rich and varied pasture, is a nourishing, health-giving food. Even some students who are convinced that they are dairy intolerant discover that they can eat our yogurt and drink our milk.

Learning how to milk a cow is an 'extra-curricular activity' on the 12-week course, but virtually every student grasps the opportunity to learn a skill that few are likely to need unless they want to impress a dairy farmer. We started to offer this activity when we built our new dairy in 2009 and were astonished by the positive response. Students experience first hand just how milk is produced and are totally intrigued by the whole experience. They enjoy connecting to where their food comes from. It gives them yet another insight into how their food is produced and an appreciation of the work of a dairy farmer. They also realise that cows need to be milked twice a day, seven days a week, all year round and that includes weekends, bank holidays and Christmas!

It has to be said this is not an opportunity one gets at many cookery schools, and the students love and really value the experience. After they help to milk the cows they see the milk

Rose Gray and Ruth Rogers

In 1987, I got a postcard from my friend Julia Wight in London saying: 'I've found a wonderful place over in Hammersmith; they're serving beautiful, simple food made with exquisite fresh produce in the mode of Elizabeth David – come quickly'.

When people realised that Rose Gray and Ruth Rogers at the River Café were interested in fresh, unusual, wild produce, they wanted to participate. People started to arrive at their kitchen door with all kinds of offerings. A woman from a local allotment brought them surplus sorrel in the early spring. In April, a friend would pick stinging nettles by the bagful on his farm in Hampshire. Other enthusiasts appeared with seakale from the south coast beaches. Later in the year their builder exchanged the huge puffball mushrooms that grew near his house for bottles of Chianti Classico. I rushed over and we had a memorable meal there – no silly frills or flounces, just really delicious food that sang on every plate.

When I came home, I immediately invited Rose and Ruth to the School as guest chefs and they came in July 1990. We had such fun; they loved the herb and vegetable gardens, the greenhouses and the fresh fish from Ballycotton. They explained how their passion for vegetables and fruit in season has been at the heart of the River Café since they first opened in 1987. Their philosophy echoed our own, hence my eagerness to invite them here. They described how every day outside the kitchen they would pick from their organic garden many varieties of basil, marjoram and mint, and interesting leaves such as purslane, cicoria and treviso to use in their recipes. The recipes they taught at the School were heavily influenced by their love of Italy, their many visits over the years and their growing appreciation of the glorious variety of Italian food. These were not complicated recipes and their message was simple: good cooking is about fresh seasonal ingredients, organic wherever possible, used thoughtfully. It is something the Italians and all good cooks have always known. Rose and Ruth suggested to the students that if you have a garden you should experiment with growing your own. If not, try farmers' markets, pick-your-own farms and organic box schemes. But, above all, develop a relationship with your greengrocer, urging him to supply interesting varieties.

Ruth's husband Richard Rogers, the acclaimed architect of the Pompidou Centre in Paris, Lloyd's of London Headquarters, and Millennium Dome fame, also came and mused over our miscellaneous barn conversions. Later that year I was able to spend a couple of days in the kitchens of the River Café and many of our students, including well-known chefs Stevie Parle, Thomasina Miers, Jordan Bourke and Gillian Hegarty (now joint head chef at Ballymaloe after being a teacher here for many years) have gone on to work there. We have always had an empathy with their philosophy and are deeply grateful to both Rose and Ruth for their inspiration.

Rose Blossom Panna Cotta with Crystallised Rose Petals

Rose blossom water varies incredibly, so you may need to add a little more or less depending on strength. We also make a buttermilk panna cotta from our own buttermilk, which is less rich but equally delicious.

Lightly brush 6–8 x 75–110ml (3–4fl oz) moulds with the non-scented oil, such as sunflower or groundnut.

To make the panna cotta, put the cream into a heavy-bottomed saucepan with the vanilla pod and caster sugar. Set over a low heat and bring to the 'shivery' stage. Meanwhile, 'sponge' the gelatine: put the water in a bowl, sprinkle over the powdered gelatine and set the bowl over a pan of simmering water until the gelatine has dissolved completely and turned transparent. Remove the vanilla pod from the cream. Add a little of the cream to the gelatine, mixing well, and then stir both mixtures together. Add the rose water and rose syrup, stir and pour into the moulds. Set aside to cool, and then cover the panna cottas with clingfilm and transfer them to the fridge to set, preferably overnight.

Meanwhile, make the crystallised rose petals. Break up the egg white slightly in a little bowl with a fork. Using a small paintbrush, paint the egg white very carefully over each petal and into every crevice. Pour the caster sugar over the petals with a teaspoon. Arrange the crystallised petals carefully on baking parchment so that they retain a good shape. Leave to dry overnight in a warm, dry place such as close to an Aga, over a radiator or in an airing cupboard. When properly crystallised, the rose petals will last for months, even years, provided they are kept dry. We store them in a pottery jar or a tin box.

To serve, turn out each rose blossom panna cotta onto a chilled serving plate. Garnish with crystallised rose petals and a few fresh raspberries, if available.

Serves 6–8

non-scented oil such as sunflower or groundnut, for brushing

For the Panna Cotta
600ml (1 pint) double cream
1 vanilla pod, split lengthways
50g (2oz) caster sugar
2 tablespoons water
scant 2 teaspoons powdered gelatine
1 teaspoon rose water
1½ teaspoons rose syrup

For the Crystallised Rose Petals
organic egg white
rose petals (use the petals from fragrant old roses, e.g. Madam Isaac Perriere, Charles de Mille, Celeste, Celcina, William Lobb, Felicity Parmentier or Rosamuny)
caster sugar – this must be completely dry (if necessary, spread it over a baking tray and dry out in a low oven at 150°C/300°F/gas 2 for 30 minutes)

To garnish
fresh raspberries (optional)

Caramel Ice Cream with Salted Peanuts, Caramel Popcorn and Dark Chocolate Sauce

It's a bit of a mission to get all the elements together for this dessert, but the end result is so decadent it is definitely worth the effort. This recipe, made using an Italian egg mousse base, is particularly good for home cooks because there's no need for an ice-cream maker as you just fold the cream into the basic mousse and pop it into the freezer. It's inspired by a dessert I enjoyed at ABC Restaurant in New York.

First make the ice cream. Put the egg yolks into a mixing bowl and whisk until light and fluffy (keep the whites for meringues). Combine the sugar and cold water in a small, heavy-bottomed saucepan. Stir over a gentle heat until the sugar has completely dissolved, and then remove the spoon and boil until the syrup caramelises to a chestnut brown. Quickly pour in the hot water. Do not stir. Boil gently until the caramel thickens to a smooth, thick syrup and reaches the 'thread' stage: 106–113°C (223–236°F). It should look thick and syrupy when a spoon is dipped in. Pour this boiling syrup onto the egg yolks. Add the vanilla extract and whisk until the mixture forms a thick, creamy mousse. Fold the softly whipped cream into the mousse, pour into a bowl, cover and freeze.

Meanwhile, make the caramel popcorn. Combine the sugar and cold water in a small heavy-bottomed saucepan. Stir over a gentle heat until the sugar has completely dissolved, and then remove the spoon and boil until the syrup caramelises to a chestnut brown. Spread out the popcorn on a silicone mat or oiled tin and drizzle the hot caramel over. Set aside to cool and harden.

To make the chocolate sauce, put the cream in a heavy-bottomed, preferably stainless steel saucepan and bring it almost to the boil. Remove from the heat and add the chopped chocolate. With a wooden spoon, stir the chocolate into the cream until it has completely melted. Add a little vanilla extract (or coffee or rum) to taste.

To serve, choose wide, shallow serving bowls. Pour approx. 3 tablespoons of hot chocolate sauce into the base of each bowl. Arrange three balls of Caramel Ice Cream on top, sprinkle a couple of tablespoons of peanuts and some caramel popcorn around the base and some extra popcorn over the top. Shape a little ball of whipped cream and put it in the centre to serve.

Serves 6–8

For the Caramel Ice Cream
2 organic egg yolks
50g (2oz) granulated sugar
125ml (4fl oz) cold water
125ml (4fl oz) hot water
½ teaspoon pure vanilla extract
600ml (1 pint) softly whipped cream

For the Caramel Popcorn
225g (8oz) granulated sugar
150ml (5fl oz) cold water
oil, for greasing (optional)
50g (2oz) popcorn

For the Dark Chocolate Sauce
225ml (8fl oz) double cream
225g (8oz) best-quality dark chocolate
a little pure vanilla extract (or coffee or dark rum)

To serve
110–150g (4–5oz) salted peanuts, lightly crushed
softly whipped cream, lightly sweetened with icing sugar
  and flavoured with a few drops of pure vanilla extract

Homemade ice cream has always been a feature of the dessert trolley at Ballymaloe House.

Foraging

As children growing up in the country village of Cullohill, Co. Laois, in the Irish midlands, we were always foraging, except we didn't call it that. The year was punctuated by foraging expeditions. In early spring we went down the lane to the Chapel Meadows with my second mammy, Mrs Lawlor, to pick wild watercress from the stream. We'd bring it home and have 'salad' for tea. This consisted of hard-boiled eggs, tomatoes, spring onions, watercress and Chef Salad Cream. Later in the season, we picked cowslips, fresh nettle tops, primroses, wild garlic, elderflowers and wood sorrel.

When I came to Ballymaloe in 1968, Myrtle made 'butterfly sandwiches' for the children's tea with the freshly picked watercress. In the autumn there was an abundance of berries, nuts and fruit including damsons, sloes, hazelnuts, elderberries, rose hips and rowanberries. All these became part of the bounty of the year and were incorporated into jams, jellies and miscellaneous dishes, and featured on the menu at Ballymaloe House.

On Fraughan Sunday, around the ancient Celtic festival of Lughnasa, we went on a fraughan-picking expedition up Cullohill Mountain. The tiny tart berries (also known as bilberries) were mashed and eaten with cream, or piled onto a sponge cake. Served

with carrageen moss pudding, they were also part of our wedding feast at Ballymaloe House. So collecting wild foods was an integral part of our lives and something we very much took for granted.

In 1991 I travelled to Vancouver to attend and speak at the IACP (International Association of Culinary Professionals) Conference. The theme that year was 'Pacific Encounters: West meets East'. It was a revelation – I met Ron Zimmerman of The Herbfarm in Washington, and Dr. Sinclair Philip, whose menu at Sooke Harbour House was composed entirely of wild and foraged ingredients, organic local greens, edible flowers and shellfish. I realised then that in the US there was a huge revival of interest in wild food, and that what we'd been doing all those years both at home and at Ballymaloe had a much cooler name – 'foraging'. Not only that, but it was now very trendy as top restaurants were incorporating wild foods into their menus. In the US, restaurants from coast to coast were employing foragers, full or part-time, to gather wild foods to use in their dishes. I suddenly realised that the innate knowledge I had gleaned from my childhood forays was of immense value and should be passed on – so I thought it would be fun to incorporate foraging into the Cookery School schedule.

The Mushroom Hunt, which we ran from October 1993 (originally with Roger and Olivia Goodwillie from Lavistown in Co. Kilkenny), was the first in a whole series of Forgotten Skills courses. Some wild foods are very easy to recognise but with others, like wild mushrooms, one needs to more cautious, as some edible varieties are similar to poisonous species. It is prudent to go on a couple of guided mushroom hunts with skilled and knowledgeable botanists before you go mushroom hunting yourself. If in doubt, act with caution until you've got a trained botanist (or forager) to identify the species for you.

From late summer into autumn, one of our local foragers, Melissa Odendahl, regularly brings baskets of wild mushrooms to the School, starting with chanterelles or girolles (*Cantharellus cibarius*) in August followed by cauliflower mushrooms and porcini (*Sparassis* and *Boletus edulis*) and later yellow legs (*Cantharellus*

tubaeformis). The students really love to learn how to recognise and cook these mushrooms. Wild fungi have disappeared from many intensive farms, but because the farm here at the School is organic we occasionally find field mushrooms on the lawn and on the path up to the Shell House when the weather is warm and moist in early autumn. Mushrooms invariably come up in the same place every year. But they can also be very erratic, depending on the weather. We often have a couple of giant puffballs (*Calvatia gigantea*) on the lawn which we enjoy in breadcrumbs or in a stir-fry – that's if we

Left: A selection of wild mushrooms foraged by our local mushroom expert, Melissa Odendahl. Over the last decade there has been a revival of interest in the wealth of wild mushrooms available. It is best to go on a guided walk with an expert to gain confidence as there are several varieties that look similar, but some can be toxic.
Above: Collecting sea urchins from the rock pools on the island of Inishmaan off the west coast of Ireland.

can get to them before my grandson Jasper decides to kick them into smithereens! A couple of shaggy parasols also pop up every year on the edge of the lane close to the back gate lodge in early October – they too are delicious while still young and are easy for the students to identify.

In September 1996 we ran our first foraging course: A Walk on the Wild Side with Darina Allen. The walk takes place around the farm and gardens and even in the greenhouses where wood sorrel (*Oxalis*) and bittercress (*Cardamine hirsuta*) flourish in the damp atmosphere. I begin the day's foraging literally outside the Cookery School door to emphasise to participants that there are edible wild plants everywhere around us during every month of the year, even in the depths of winter. It's an endless voyage of discovery. Just last year I discovered, in New York of all places, that the peeled stalks of the dreaded Japanese knotweed (*Fallopia japonica*) are delicious to eat. At Noma in Copenhagen I ate Iceland moss

Above: A Walk on the Wild Side with Darina Allen. We now run this one-day course several times a year and the numbers of participants continue to grow.

(*Cetraria islandica*) and several other wild foods, which I had never encountered before. When I returned home I searched around us here and found many, including sea (or shoreline) purslane (*Sesuvium portulacastrum*), beach mustard and marsh samphire, also known as common glasswort (*Salicornia europaea*), some on our own land close to the seashore.

The reaction to our foraging courses is fascinating, people are really excited to discover that so many of the 'weeds' around them are not only edible but delicious. There seems to be a real, almost primeval, excitement as people reconnect with their inner hunter/gatherer. For many it's a life-changing experience, and going for a walk in the country or the park, or by the seashore will never be the same again; where hitherto they saw weeds, now they see dinner – sea spinach soup, forager's salad, crystallised primroses, nettle pasta. From a nutritional point of view there's a very convincing argument for incorporating wild foods into our diet. Unlike intensively-produced and processed foods, they still have their full complement of vitamins, minerals and trace elements, many of which are lacking in our modern diet and which can be accessed free in the wild when we know how to recognise and gather nature's bounty.

Foraging has also become an integral part of our 12-week certificate course. Wild and foraged foods are incorporated into the menus on a weekly basis and the students are encouraged to learn about wild food, greens, plants, flowers, nuts and berries, both on the land and by the seashore. The students have the opportunity to learn where and how to pick wild watercress and to distinguish between this and fool's watercress (*Apium nodiflorum*), which always grow side by side in the river. It's been a long tradition on each 12-week course to take the students down to Shanagarry Strand to show them how to gather periwinkles from the rock pools at low tide. We teach them how to tell the difference between periwinkles and the similar sea snail, which the locals call the 'horse perry'. The latter is easy to recognise due to its mother of pearl interior. Older people caution against eating it even though no one seems to be quite sure why. I have deep respect and pay attention to these 'piseógs' of older people. Sometimes they are just superstitions but it's better to be safe than sorry, so I tend to act on the precautionary principle until proven otherwise.

Slow Food has taken me to many remote places around the globe in search of ancient cultures and indigenous foods. On one memorable occasion I found myself in Sápmi (Samiland) in northern Sweden – the land of the midnight sun. Since time immemorial

an indigenous race called the Sami (the reindeer people), have lived in an area called Sápmi that extends across four countries from the Kola Peninsula in Russia to northern Finland, Norway and Sweden. Like all indigenous tribes they live in harmony with nature, including foraging with the seasons to survive.

Their diet consists of a lot of reindeer and elk meat, fresh, dried, salted and smoked. In summer, they eat more fish and vegetables, in late summer and autumn, a variety of berries, wild mushrooms and fruit. Lingonberries and other wild berries are used for sauces, preserves and desserts. One evening we had cloudberry jam with waffles and cream. Cloudberries look like yellow raspberries and grow in mossy areas and across the tundra. We also ate wild mushrooms in many guises: morels and delicious chanterelles in soup, little quiches and as a sauce with reindeer and arctic char – a pink fish with pale flesh not unlike trout. The wild mushrooms are dried during the season and are much loved.

Sami are expert at preserving their foraged finds – in the past their very survival depended on it. Originally they stored food in underground water holes, but now freezers are more common. In early spring they eat the young shoots of rowan and beech and make a soup from spruce leaves and a syrup from the needles. Angelica grows wild; the young stalks are peeled and eaten raw as a vegetable or candied as a sweetmeat. They also pick buckets of wild sorrel in early summer and cook it in a little water until it wilts. Then it can be stored for months. The Sami women explained to me that the children love to eat bilberry flowers in early June. When I walked up the hill I nibbled some; they tasted of sweet honey. As with many indigenous communities, they know the medicinal value of each plant and food.

Foraged foods are always fresh, always in season and, better still, free, once you have the ability to recognise them. Most years almost all of this free bounty is left to rot because people don't know what to look for. In autumn I encourage people to organise blackberry picking expeditions as, whether you live in the city, town or in the country, you won't have to travel far to find brambles laden with this prolific wild fruit. In recent years it's wonderful to see that foraging has virtually become mainstream. The Nordic food revolution, which started in Copenhagen with chefs like René Redzepi at Noma, has recently reinvigorated the trend and inspired others to celebrate the wild and foraged food of their local area and incorporate it into their menus. I ate a truly memorable meal in Noma in 2012 and was thrilled to see that René had my *Forgotten Skills of Cooking* book in his kitchen library!

Wild Things

Inside the door of the School there's a blackboard where the gardeners write up what vegetables, fruit and herbs from the farm are on the menu that day. Occasionally we have our own pork and beef as well. Even in winter the blackboard is full; in summer and early autumn it overflows onto several boards. Now that foraged foods have become a part of almost every day, we have recently added a 'Wild Things' board to highlight the seasonal wild foods that grow in the fields, hedgerows and woods around us. Today, in February, we have wild watercress, bittercress, pennywort, wild sorrel and Alexanders.

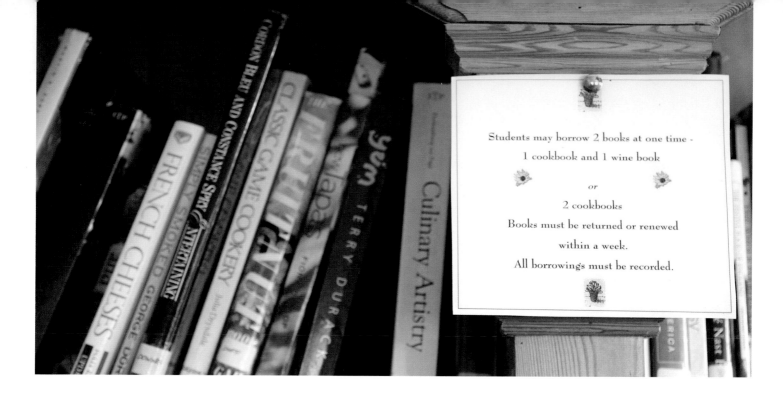

Students may borrow 2 books at one time -
1 cookbook and 1 wine book

or

2 cookbooks

Books must be returned or renewed
within a week.

All borrowings must be recorded.

The Ballymaloe Cookery School Library

The first cookbook library was situated under the roof beside my PA Rosalie's office, in the playroom where the original Cookery School started. There were about 20 books including Jane Grigson's *Good Things*; *The Conran Cookbook* by Terence Conran, Caroline Conran and Simon Hopkinson; Margaret Costa's *Four Seasons Cookery Book*; Katie Stewart's *The Times Cookery Book*; *Mastering the Art of French Cooking* Vol. 1 and 2 by Julia Child, Louisette Bertholle and Simone Beck; Marcella Hazan's *The Classic Italian Cookbook*, Jacques Pépin's *The Art of Cooking*, volumes 1 and 2, and *La Methode*; Harold McGee's *On Food and Cooking* and then of course there was Roger Vergé's *Cuisine of the Sun* and *Cuisine Minceur* by Michel Guérard, the bibles of nouvelle cuisine, which we pored over in the 1970s and early 1980s.

In 1991 an English couple, Stephen Massil and Brenda Goldstein, enrolled on several cookery courses. After they left I had a letter; they had seen our little fledgling library and realised that we could do with a bit of guidance. They offered to catalogue it and put in a system; we gratefully accepted the offer and bartered a few cookery courses. We later discovered that Stephen was the keeper of the library at Sir John Soane's Museum in London.

The library space has increased many times throughout the years and we are once more bursting at the seams. Our latest library is beautiful, it stretches all along one wall of the upstairs office, in what was the apple barn. We started to convert it when we moved

into the new School in 1989. The slightly classical shelves were made in 1990 by our local carpenter, Noel Barry. My collection of cookery books has grown exponentially over the years and is now in excess of 2,000 tomes, with many treasures including *Honey from a Weed* by Patience Gray; Elizabeth David's *French Provincial Cooking* and *An Omelette and a Glass of Wine*; *The Way to Cook* by Julia Child; *Wild Food* and *Mushrooms* by Roger Phillips; Alan Davidson's *North Atlantic Seafood*; *First Catch Your Hare* by Hannah Glasse and *Larousse Gastronomique*.

Whenever I travel to New York I pop into Kitchen Arts & Letters to check out the latest interesting cookbooks and invariably either carry or send a stack of the most exciting and topical volumes home. I always enjoy chatting to the sometimes grumpy owner Nach Waxman, with whom I had a funny first encounter. On my first visit in 1990 I made a pilgrimage to the shop. Having walked for numerous blocks I eventually found it. It was firmly shut, but when I peered through the door I saw a gentleman working inside, so I knocked. He looked up and gestured for me to go away. I tried again and got the same response, but this time he was even more impatient. Eventually, he stormed towards the door and told me in no uncertain terms to go away; he was closed and busily trying to catch up on his work. I explained that I had come all the way from Ireland and asked if I could come in for a few minutes. He looked at me grumpily and said, 'From Ireland, I don't suppose you can tell

me how to get hold of that Ballymaloe girl's book I keep getting asked for?' To which I replied somewhat shyly, 'I am Darina Allen!' 'Well, in that case come in!'

The library is a brilliant resource for the students. Apart from cookbooks, there's a whole section of wine books and another on food issues alongside hundreds of food magazines, including copies of *Gourmet* from the 1980s. Taking pride of place are the cookbooks written by past students, now numbering over 40, which include:

Rachel Allen *Rachel's Favourite Food*; *Rachel's Favourite Food for Friends*; *Rachel's Favourite Food at Home*; *Rachel's Food for Living*; *Bake*; *Home Cooking*; *Entertaining at Home*; *Easy Meals*; *Cake*; *Rachel's Irish Family Food*; *Rachel's Everyday Kitchen*

Hugo Arnold with Leylie Hayes *Avoca Café Cookbook* and *Avoca Café Cookbook 2*

Gillian Berwick *Making Your Own Chocolates*

Jordan and Jessica Bourke *The Guilt-free Gourmet*

Prue Browne *Commonsense Catering*

Jez Felwick *The Bowler's Meatball Cookbook*

Catherine Fulvio *Eat Like an Italian*; *Catherine's Family Kitchen*; *Catherine's Italian Kitchen*; *The Weekend Chef*

Tiffany Goodall *From Pasta to Pancakes: The Ultimate Student Cookbook*; *First Flat Cookbook*

Emma Hannigan has written several novels: – *Designer Genes*; *Miss Conceived*; *The Pink Ladies Club*; *Keeping Mum*; *Driving Home for Christmas*; *Perfect Wives* – and her memoir called *Talk to the Headscarf*.

Lilly Higgins *Make, Bake, Love*; *Lilly's Dream Deli*

Rosemary Kearney with Darina Allen, *Healthy Gluten-free Eating*

Clodagh McKenna *The Irish Farmers' Market Cookbook*; *Fresh from the Sea*; *Homemade*; *Clodagh's Kitchen Diaries*

Thomasina Miers *Cook*; *The Wild Gourmets*; *Mexican Food Made Simple*; *Wahaca – Mexican Food at Home*

Sophie Morris *Sophie Kooks*

Ann Mulligan *The Irish B&B Cookbook*

Stevie Parle *My Kitchen: Real Food from Near and Far*; *Dock Kitchen Cookbook*; *Spice Trip*

James Ramsden *Small Adventures in Cooking*; *Do-Ahead Dinners*

Sam Stern *Cooking up a Storm*; *Real Food Real Fast*; *Get Cooking*; *Sam Stern's Student Cookbook*; *Sam Stern's Eat Vegetarian*; *Virgin to Veteran*

Maureen Tatlow *Back to Basics*

Eleanor Walsh and Michael Durkin *Eden Cookbook*

Barbecue Course

Our first one-day barbecue course ran in 1991 – it was a huge success and so over-subscribed that we decided to run two the following year and have continued to do so every year since. We wanted to encourage people to widen their repertoire and produce something more exciting for what at that time was an occasional al fresco meal. The course explained the importance of good sauces and marinades and the unexpected thrills of the charcoal grill.

Over the years we've come from teaching the absolute basics of how to light a barbecue and cook chicken breasts, sausages and steaks to tackling just about anything on the grill. In 2001 we explored American regional grilling and barbecuing. This is not my particular area of expertise so I invited Elizabeth Karmel, who grew up in North Carolina and was raised on barbecues, to the School. To say that she has a passion for barbecue and grill is an understatement. She plays with fire virtually every day and cooks on a barbecue spring, summer, autumn and winter – everything from hamburgers to suckling pig.

Since our first barbecue course people have become hugely skilled and adventurous. Where Irish barbecues were traditionally carnivorous affairs, with perhaps the odd green salad, now the menu can be far more sophisticated with multi-ethnic flavours and accompaniments. We encourage people to incorporate Mexican, Middle Eastern, Thai and Indonesian flavours into their barbecuing. Those who own a Weber-style barbecue can attempt larger joints of meat: duck, chicken, guinea fowl, even a turkey.

Once one grasps the simple principle and technique of grilling, the possibilities are endless. We love to have a vegetarian barbecue for a change, with delicious grilled vegetables, melted cheese parcels, bean, grain and lentil salads, freshly picked sweetcorn in the husk – not even the carnivores miss the meat.

Wild Garlic Custards

This recipe comes from my brother Rory O'Connell. During the 5–6 weeks when wild garlic is in season, it is woven in and out of the menu at the School every day. There are two types of wild garlic: the wider-leafed *Allium ursinum*, which grows in shady places along the banks of streams and in undisturbed mossy woodland, and *Allium triquetrum*, with long thin leaves, which grows alongside roadsides and country lanes. The latter is also known as the three-cornered leek or snowbell because it resembles white bluebells.

Serves 8

melted butter, for greasing
250ml (9fl oz) double cream
250ml (9fl oz) milk
4 organic egg yolks
100g (3½oz) Parmesan or Coolea cheese, finely grated
pinch of cayenne pepper
3 tablespoons finely chopped wild garlic
sea salt and freshly ground black pepper

To serve
wild garlic flowers, to decorate (optional)
fingers of plain toast or triangles of Melba toast

Preheat the oven to 150°C/300°F/gas 2 and brush the inside of eight deep ovenproof pots or ramekins (approx. 75ml (3fl oz)) – we use deep shot glasses – with melted butter.

In a mixing bowl, whisk the cream and milk with the egg yolks and the finely grated cheese. Season with salt, freshly ground pepper and a pinch of cayenne pepper. Whisk again. Add the wild garlic to the custard at the last minute and immediately pour into the pots or ramekins.

Fill a roasting tin with hot water and put in the pots; the water should come about two-thirds of the way up the sides. Cover the tops with a sheet of greaseproof paper. Depending on the depth of the pots, bake for 30–45 minutes in the preheated oven or until the mixture has just set. A skewer inserted into the centre should come out clean when they are ready.

Serve decorated with some wild garlic flowers, if using, and a few fingers of plain toast or triangles of Melba toast.

Buffalo Mozzarella with Spruce Syrup
and Wild Bitter Greens

This Noma-inspired salad uses spruce syrup, which was a revelation when I tasted it there. It initially took some courage for me to try the spruce tips off the trees around Ballymaloe, but they are delicious and tender and taste very much like spruce smells.

Serves 4

4 handfuls of wild bitter greens, e.g. wood sorrel, watercress, bittercress, dandelion, pennywort, etc.
extra virgin olive oil
2 balls of fresh buffalo mozzarella (we use Toons Bridge)
2 tablespoons Spruce Syrup (see right)
sea salt and freshly ground black pepper

To serve
crusty white bread

Toss the greens in the extra virgin olive oil and season with sea salt and pepper. Strew on a plate, top with torn mozzarella and drizzle over the spruce syrup. Serve with crusty white bread.

Spruce Syrup

We collect the spruce tips in April while they are soft and green. Any leftover syrup can be stored in the fridge for 1–2 months. Serve with cream cheese or soft goat's cheese.

Makes 300ml (10fl oz)

100g (3½oz) fresh spuce tips
150ml (5fl oz) cold water
200g (7oz) granulated sugar
freshly squeezed juice of 1 lemon
pinch of salt

Whizz the spruce tips in a food processor. Transfer to a saucepan with the cold water and sugar. Bring to the boil and simmer for 1 minute. Set aside to cool.

Strain the syrup through a sieve lined with muslin into a clean jug, discarding the solids. Stir in the freshly squeezed lemon juice and season with a pinch of salt. Store in a sealed jar in the fridge until needed.

Dandelion Flower Fritters

~❧~

We use blanched dandelion leaves in salads, however the students also love these flower fritters. We cook elderflowers and cowslips in the same way. I suppose everything tastes good tossed in Madagascar vanilla sugar!

Serves 4–5

24–30 fully open dandelion flowers
sunflower oil, for frying
vanilla sugar, for sprinkling

For the batter
110g (4oz) plain flour
pinch of salt
1 organic egg
150ml (5fl oz) lukewarm water

First make the batter. Sift the flour and salt into a bowl. Make a well in the centre and break in the egg. Using a whisk, bring in the flour gradually from the edges, slowly adding the water at the same time.

Preheat the oil in a deep-fat fryer to 180°C (350°F) or use a shallow pan with at least 2.5cm (1in) of oil.

Shake the flowers just in case there are any insects hidden inside. Holding each flower by its stalk, dip them in the batter (add a little more water or milk if the batter is too thick) and fry in the hot oil a couple at a time until puffed up and crisp – approx. 2 minutes. Drain on kitchen paper. Toss in vanilla sugar and serve straight away.

Blackberry Vodka

~❧~

We use many different fruits to add flavour to alcohol and have fun experimenting with different combinations. Sloes, damsons, orange rind, wild garlic, rhubarb, peaches and apricots are all good options.

Makes 600ml (1 pint)

600g (1¼lb) blackberries
600g (1¼lb) granulated sugar
600ml (1 pint) vodka or gin
3 sweet geranium leaves

Put all the ingredients into a sterilised 1 litre (1¾ pints) Kilner jar and set aside in a cool, dark place to mature for a couple of months, shaking the contents every so often to dissolve the sugar.

Strain after 2–3 months, reserving the booze-sodden blackberries, which can be served with yogurt, panna cotta or in a fruit salad. Return the strained vodka or gin to the bottle and store in a cool, dark place for up to a year, but ideally consume within a couple of months as it gradually loses its freshness and appeal.

Marcella Hazan

" When Darina Allen asked us to come to Ballymaloe, her School in Ireland, we accepted the invitation notwithstanding the discouraging descriptions we had heard of Irish food. To our surprise, the ingredients we found were superb. The seafood – I remember the Dublin Bay prawns (known as scampi in Italy), the turbot, the hake, the monkfish – was equal to the best and freshest we had ever had on the Adriatic. The cheeses, breads and jams were wonderful. To this day, it is Irish butter that I use in my kitchen. We didn't know any of that, however, before going. What we knew is that we loved Darina, and we were grateful that she had forgiven the hard time she had had one day in Bologna when she had been our student.

In Bologna, it had been one of Victor's responsibilities to accompany the class on its field trips and to maintain strict observance of the schedules we had so laboriously worked out. Our longest trip was the one we made to Parma to observe the entire production cycle of Parmigiano Reggiano cheese, an eight-hundred-year-old process. We had arranged with a dairy to hold back, in the morning, a batch of the milk from which they made the cheese, so that the students could watch it being cooked in copper cauldrons of ancient design. They would then have the opportunity to follow the subsequent steps in the cycle, to see the cylindrical mould that shaped the soft mass of the previous day's cheese, a two-day-old cheese being unmoulded, a firm month-old round soaking in its brine bath and a year-old 34kg (75lb) wheel of Parmigiano ageing in the cathedral-like space of the maturation vaults. The class had to be on the bus no later than 8a.m. to leave for the one-hour drive to Parma where the dairy master was waiting. Victor had announced on the previous evening that the bus would pull out at exactly 8a.m., whether or not every student was on it.

No one had ever been late for that appointment – except for Darina. Diligent, dependable, respectful Darina. She had been in the lobby on time, but then she had returned to her room to look for her camera. Victor didn't know. When she returned, the bus had left. Poor Darina. She hired a taxi to take her to the dairy, but when she got there, the demonstration was over and the class was gone. She continued by taxi to all the other stops on the tour, always arriving too late. Fortunately, she did make it in time to the restaurant by the Po River where a midday banquet in grand Parma style awaited the class and applause awaited her.

Darina and her husband, Tim, met us at Cork Airport and drove us first to her mother-in-law's inn at Ballymaloe, where we would be staying. When we had checked in, she asked, 'Would you like to see the School now?' 'Certainly,' I said. She drove us to a large property in the country. 'It was Tim's farm,' she said. The stables had been converted into small but charming rustic rooms for resident students. Chickens scampered over the grounds. A disused truck had been filled with straw and turned into their roost. We passed by row after row of vegetables. 'It's where we grow the produce for our classes,' Darina said. We walked to the large main building. As I remember it, the first floor had the students' spacious kitchen, with six or more four-burner stoves; the teachers' room; a well-equipped pantry; an auditorium with closed-circuit TV monitors for lectures and demonstrations and a beautiful dining veranda with many tables facing a flower garden. The second floor held a splendid library, Darina's office and the administrative offices.

I had never seen a cooking school like it and I was both awed and made uneasy by its scale. I had said that the classes I would teach would permit full participation by the students.

'How many people are you expecting?' I asked Darina.

'Sixty.'

I thought the English language was tripping me up again. I have difficulty discriminating between the sounds of 'sixty' and 'sixteen'. 'Did you say sixteen?' I asked.

'No, sixty, six-zero.'

'How can that be? I have never done a full-participation class larger than twelve. You must do something. Return the deposits. Get the class down to no more than fifteen, *fifteen*.'

Darina smiled. 'There is no way I can do that. Many students are already here. Others are on the way. Some are coming from as far

as Australia and South Africa. And everyone is so excited by your being here. It will be all right, you'll see.'

Victor smiled too. '*Non fasciarti la testa*,' he said, alluding to the family proverb about not bandaging your head before it is broken. 'I'll give you a hand.'

And he did. I see him still, on the day we made risotto. All the stoves were going, and Victor was flying from pot to pot, making sure that everyone was stirring correctly and that when they ladled in the broth, it was neither too much or too little. We came up with a new cooking statistic: sixty pairs of hands can make wonderful risotto.

My course was the last of the school year at Ballymaloe. When all the students had left, Darina invited me to join her and her staff for a farewell dinner at an unusual restaurant. The chef opened only when he had a minimum of twelve guaranteed reservations. When fewer than those had booked, they were not confirmed until enough other bookings came in to complete the necessary number. The restaurant was on Hare Island, a stony lump breaking the surface of the Atlantic Ocean. Transportation to it was in an open dinghy. It could give us a feeling, Darina said, of what living on the wild west coast of Ireland could be like.

The day started out with a grey sky that soon produced that steady, light drizzle that the Irish affectionately call 'soft rain'. It may have been soft, but by the time we reached the shore and the dinghy's landing, it was a very wet and cold rain. Out of the trunks of our cars came blankets and towels, into which we snuggled up to our eyes. I felt like a refugee being driven to the sea. We stepped into the open dinghy, the water on its bottom an inch deep. I could see nothing but water: water above, water below, water ahead. By the time we had been rowed to the shore of what looked as inhabitable as a piece of the moon, I was as wet as I could ever be short of dissolving into a puddle. We made land, but our trek wasn't over. We were on a scraggly path, which we followed until we reached the first white stone house, one of two on Hare Island. There still was water above, but at least we had solid land below. When we eventually came to the house, I went in not knowing what I might find or whether there would be any hope of returning to a less liquid state. It was cheerful inside, warm and cosy. We dropped our soaking blankets and, like puppies released from their bath, shook off as much water as we could. Dry towels appeared, and what was even more effective, whiskey and wine. The dinner – I remember a perfect lamb rack – was comfort and salvation. We ate, we drank, we sang, we were happy. On the way back, the sun came out. **"**

Above (left): Marcella and Victor Hazan shelter from the rain under an umbrella on a visit to Hare (as known as Heir) Island.
Above (right): The intrepid group outside the restaurant on Hare Island. Rachel Allen is on Marcella's right and I can be seen to the right of the group wearing a bright blue jumper and my red glasses.

Marcella Hazan's Penne with Cauliflower, Garlic and Oil

Marcella explains that: 'One of the basic mother sauces for pasta is *aglio e olio*, garlic and oil. From it has spawned a multitudinous breed of sauce where we find most varieties of vegetables. An example is this one, featuring cauliflower. In this family of sauces, additional flavourings such as parsley, hot pepper and anchovies may be used, although not all need to be present. They are almost invariably *sughi in bianco*, "white" sauces – that is, without tomato. They are supposed to be served without grated cheese, and that is how I prefer them. But one may do as one pleases, and choose to have either Pecorino or Parmesan cheese, depending upon whether one wants the sauce more or less sharp.'

Strip the cauliflower of all its leaves, except for a few of the very tender inner ones. Rinse it in cold water, and cut it in half.

Bring 4–5 litres (7–8¾ pints) of water to the boil in a large saucepan, and then add the cauliflower. Cook until tender but compact – approx. 25–30 minutes. Test it with a fork to know when it's done. Drain and set aside.

Put the oil, garlic and chopped anchovies into a medium sauté pan. Turn the heat to medium and sauté until the garlic becomes golden brown. Stir occasionally with a wooden spoon, mashing the anchovies.

Add the boiled cauliflower and break it up quickly with a fork, crumbling it into pieces no bigger than a peanut. Turn it thoroughly in the oil, mashing part of it to a pulp.

Add the chilli flakes and a liberal amount of salt. Increase the heat and cook for a few minutes more, stirring frequently. Then remove from the heat.

Bring 4–5 litres (7–8¾ pints) of water to the boil in a large saucepan and add plenty of salt. As soon as the water returns to the boil, add the pasta. When cooked al dente – tender but firm to the bite – drain the pasta well and transfer it to a warm serving bowl.

Very briefly reheat the cauliflower and pour the contents of the pan over the pasta, tossing thoroughly. Add the chopped parsley, toss again and serve at once.

Serve 4–6

1 head of cauliflower (approx. 700g (1½lb))
8 tablespoons olive oil
2 large garlic cloves, peeled and finely chopped
6 flat anchovy fillets, chopped
¼ teaspoon chilli flakes
450g (1lb) penne or other macaroni
2 tablespoons freshly chopped flat-leaf parsley
salt

Cauliflower is an underrated vegetable that deserves to be more widely used. Not many people think of serving it with pasta, but this dish is an example of Marcella's brilliance in combining simple ingredients.

Bistecca alla Fiorentina – Grilled T-Bone Steak, Florentine style

'One of Italy's two prized breeds of cattle for meat – Chianina beef – is native to Tuscany. Its only rival in the country is Piedmont's Razza Piemontese. The latter is the more tender of the two and as sweet as cream, whereas the Tuscan is firmer and tastier. A Chianina grows rapidly to a great size so it is butchered when the steer is a grown calf, *vitellone* in Italian. To Italians who love beef, a T-bone grilled in the Florentine style is the ultimate steak. It owes some of its appeal, of course, to the distinctive flavour of the meat, but as much again can be attributed to the Florentine way of preparing it, which can be applied successfully to a fine, well-hung steak anywhere.' Marcella Hazan

Serves 2

1 well-hung T-bone beef steak, 4cm (1½in) thick
– ask your butcher for Aberdeen Angus, Hereford, Shorthorn
or one of the traditional crosses
1 garlic clove, peeled and cut in half (optional)
black peppercorns, coarsely ground or crushed with a pestle
and mortar
extra virgin olive oil
Maldon sea salt

Light the barbecue in time so the charcoal will be red and glowing with white ash around the outside. Alternatively, preheat a cast-iron griddle pan to very hot.

Rub both sides of the steak with a cut garlic clove (if using) and some ground or crushed peppercorns. Score the fat side. Drizzle with a few drops of extra virgin olive oil. Grill the steak to the degree desired. In Tuscany it is eaten very rare, approx. 5 minutes on one side and 3 minutes on the other. After turning, sprinkle salt on the grilled side. When the other side is done, turn it over and sprinkle with salt.

When the steak is cooked to your taste, transfer it to a warm platter and serve at once on a bed of rocket leaves accompanied by cannellini beans or rustic roast potatoes. To serve, cut the meat off the bone with a serrated knife and cut across the grain into thick slices.

Zabaglione Semifreddo

I don't love warm Zabaglione, but when it's frozen into a semifreddo it's completely delicious. The praline can be in sheets or more of a crunchy brittle.

Serves 6

sunflower oil, for greasing (optional)
4 organic egg yolks
110g (4oz) caster sugar
60ml (2½fl oz) dark rum
60ml (2½fl oz) sweet sherry – we use Harvey's Bristol Cream
300ml (10fl oz) double cream

For the praline
50g (2oz) unskinned whole almonds
50g (2oz) granulated sugar

First make the praline. Put the almonds together with the sugar into a heavy-bottomed saucepan. Set over a low heat until the sugar melts and turns a rich caramel colour – do not stir. When this stage is reached, and not before, carefully rotate the pan until the nuts are completely covered with the caramel. When the nuts go 'pop', pour the mixture onto a lightly oiled Swiss roll tin or marble slab. Set aside to cool and harden. When the praline is cold, break it into chunky pieces – this can be done by crushing it with a rolling pin or by whizzing for a few seconds in a food processor if you want it a little finer.

Now for the zabaglione. Choose a medium saucepan, half fill with water and bring to the boil. Meanwhile, put the egg yolks into a Pyrex bowl that will fit over the pan. Add the sugar and whisk until the mixture is pale and fluffy. Whisk in the rum and sherry. Sit the bowl over the pan of simmering water and continue to whisk until the mixture has at least doubled in volume. Remove from the heat, sit the bowl in iced water and keep whisking until the mixture is cool.

Whip the cream in a separate bowl and fold it into the cold zabaglione, mixing well. Spoon the mixture into a plastic box or lined loaf tin or divide between six small stemmed glasses. Cover and freeze until firm, approx. 1½ hours. Serve in the glasses or alternatively on pretty, chilled plates, sprinkled with the crunchy praline brittle.

Myrtle Allen

Myrtle Allen's family came from Cork and her father, Henry Hill, was one of a long line of eminent architects. She never cooked as a child and remembers the cook chasing her out of kitchen. She enrolled at The School of Commerce in Cork but failed the cooking exam; she never even went back to get her results, as the liver and bacon she'd made had been spoiled by someone inadvertently turning up the oven and she fled in tears.

She married Ivan Allen in 1943, and they used to joke that they learned lots about each other on their honeymoon. He discovered that she couldn't cook at all, so on their first night at home upon their return, he showed her how to cook scrambled eggs. Ivan was unquestionably a gourmet (rare in those times). He was also a progressive and nationally-known farmer. Being surrounded by wonderful local produce as well as an appreciative husband to enjoy her efforts, encouraged Myrtle to learn more about cooking. She taught herself, sometimes by trial and error, with the help of cookbooks by authors such as Elizabeth David and Philip Harben.

Thanks to Ivan's reputation, they regularly had groups of farmers visit the farm. On one such occasion, Paddy O'Keeffe, of

the *Irish Farmers Journal*, brought a group and Myrtle cooked lunch for them. Paddy asked her if she might consider writing a cookery column for other farmers' wives. Myrtle mulled over the idea and agreed. She carefully researched for her weekly column, cooking many versions of every recipe until she was happy. These columns eventually led to *The Ballymaloe Cookbook*, which was originally published by the *Irish Farmers Journal* in 1977.

When their six children left home for boarding school, Myrtle began to think about starting a small restaurant, encouraged by the reaction of her friends when they came round to dinner. Myrtle and Ivan had bought Ballymaloe House in 1948, so Ivan suggested they set up a restaurant in their home. This was unheard of in Ireland in the early 1960s – there were no country house hotels. They opened in May 1964 and when the children returned home in the school holidays they were excited at the prospect of finding 'real' restaurant food waiting for them, so were surprised and somewhat disappointed to find her serving exactly the same kind of food she'd always served to her family. Some of the dishes, such as a delicious chicken liver pâté, are still made at Ballymaloe House today.

Myrtle was also keen to expand her culinary repertoire and visited Le Cordon Bleu in London for a week to learn how to make meringues, soufflés and parfaits. She later attended L'Ecole des Trois Gourmandes in Paris where she had a lesson with Julia Child and Simone Beck, who taught her how to create chicken terrine and rum baba, and she bought savarin moulds and genoise tins to bring home with her. Myrtle was no ordinary farmer's wife and was very unusual in 1960s Ireland; she had her finger on the pulse of the international scene.

Ballymaloe House is out in the country far from any centres of population. After a couple of years, people started saying they wanted to stay the night. Myrtle and Ivan discovered that if they opened ten bedrooms to the public, they would automatically get a spirit licence. Getting a spirit licence was very expensive and they wanted to sell local spirits such as Irish whiskey and Cork gin. And so Ballymaloe House Hotel was born.

Myrtle and Ivan wanted their visitors to feel as though they were guests of the family. Children were always warmly welcomed: there were special children's teas – always beautiful food that they really loved, but homemade. If Myrtle made chips, she made them from scratch. People came back time and again, and now those who visited as children are bringing their own children back to Ballymaloe. It is not unusual to have visits from families who have been coming here for three generations.

I first met Myrtle when I came to Ballymaloe in 1968. I had heard of the farmer's wife from Co. Cork who cooked delicious food with local ingredients and wanted to learn more, so I wrote to her and asked if I come and work for her. Unlike many of my friends who were trying to find jobs in the industry and were dealt with rather formally, being shown round to the tradesmen's entrance, I received a friendly handwritten letter inviting me to Ballymaloe. Myrtle told me she had children my age, and welcomed me warmly into the kitchens at Ballymaloe House Hotel.

She told me almost the opposite of what I'd learned at hotel school. She taught me to focus on the freshest seasonal ingredients and to cook them simply so they taste delicious and are wholesome and nourishing. Myrtle has a brilliant palate and the confidence to do things simply. Her staff worked with her rather than for her, and she was a strong supporter of small local producers. The farmhouse cheesemakers loved her – she included a cheese course in the price of the menu at Ballymaloe House, and, in line with the rest of the food, all the cheeses were Irish.

When I started the School in 1983, Myrtle taught two days of classes while I taught the remaining three. She was inspiring and patient, always able to get the essence of something across. She felt very strongly that the students needed to learn basic things like how to roast a beautiful free-range chicken, how to make stuffing, how delicious green cabbage could be if it was cooked correctly. She even taught students how to cut a loaf of bread properly – to use the knife in a sawing motion without squashing down the bread. People were used to ready-sliced loaves, and cutting bread properly was a simple skill that was getting lost. Myrtle always encouraged people to season with their fingers rather than with a spoon, as she felt that you were removed from the food with a spoon. This is one of her many wisdoms that I pass on to the students.

As well as starting Euro-toques Ireland, Myrtle taught right into her seventies, and now in her late eighties she still gives inspiring talks and continues to encourage people who share her values, just as she encouraged me.

Above (top): Ballymaloe House.
Above (bottom): Myrtle imparting her jam-making wisdom.
Left: Myrtle and me teaching a cookery class together at the School in the mid-1980s.

Hot Buttered Oysters

These wonderfully curvaceous oyster shells tend to topple over maddeningly on the plate so that the delicious juices escape. In the restaurant at Ballymaloe House we solve this problem by piping a little blob of mashed Duchesse potato on the plate to anchor each shell. We sometimes place some Oyster leaves around the edge of the plate too.

Serves 4

12 Pacific (Gigas) oysters
25g (1oz) butter
½ teaspoon finely chopped flat-leaf parsley

To serve
4 lemon wedges
4 ovals of hot buttered toast (optional)

Open the oysters and detach completely from their shells. Discard the top shell, but keep the deep shell and reserve the liquid. Put the shells into a low oven (110°C/225°F/gas ¼) to heat through. Melt half the butter in a pan until it foams. Toss the oysters in the butter until heated through, approx. 1 minute.

Put a hot oyster into each of the warm shells. Pour the reserved oyster liquid into the pan and bring to the boil, whisking in the remaining butter and the parsley. Spoon the hot juices over the oysters and serve immediately on hot plates accompanied by the lemon wedges.

Alternatively, discard the shells and just serve the oysters on the hot buttered toast. The toast will soak up the juice – simply delicious!

Part of Myrtle's genius is to use ingredients as simply as possible. Customers at Ballymaloe House come repeatedly to eat these delicious oysters when they are in season.

Baked Trout with Spinach Butter Sauce

We can sometimes get lovely fat pink trout, about 2 years old, which have a wonderful taste – much better than the smaller ones. This is a horrendously rich-sounding sauce but it tastes delicious and the flavour is sublime.

Serves 4

2 x 900g (2lb) whole Rainbow trout
25–50g (1–2oz) butter, plus extra for greasing
2 sprigs of fennel
sea salt and freshly ground black pepper

For the Spinach Butter Sauce
75g (3oz) spinach leaves
150ml (5fl oz) double cream
75g (3oz) butter

Preheat the oven to 190°C/375°F/gas 5. Gut the trout and wash well, making sure you remove the line of blood from the inside near the back bone. Dry on kitchen paper and season inside and out with salt and freshly ground pepper. Put a blob of butter and a sprig of fennel into the centre of each trout. Take a large sheet of foil, smear a little butter on the centre, put the trout onto the buttered bit and fold over the edges into a papillote shape. Seal well to ensure that none of the juices can escape. Repeat with the other trout.

Put the two foil parcels on a baking tray, making sure they are not touching, and bake in the preheated oven for approx. 30 minutes.

Meanwhile, make the sauce. Remove the stalks from the spinach, wash and cook in 600ml (1 pint) salted boiling water. Cook for 4–5 minutes or until just soft and tender, then drain. Press out every last drop of water and chop finely. Put the cream into a saucepan and simmer on a gentle heat until reduced to about 3 tablespoons or until it is in danger of burning. Then, over a very low heat, whisk in the butter bit by bit as though you were making a Hollandaise sauce. Stir in the spinach.

When the fish is cooked, open the parcels – there will be lots of delicious juices, so use some of these to thin out the sauce. Put the two parcels onto a hot serving dish and bring to the table. Skin the fish and lift the juicy pink flesh onto hot plates. Spoon the spinach sauce over the fish and serve immediately.

Ballymaloe Chicken Pie

We make this pie from scratch, so it takes a lot of work, but there are few dishes as comforting and satisfying. It is a good recipe to teach the students, as it covers a range of skills.

Preheat the oven to 180°C/350°F/gas 4.

First make the puff pastry. Sift the flour and salt into a bowl and mix to form a dough with 225–300ml (8–10fl oz) of cold water (depending on the flour) and the lemon juice (if using). Cover with greaseproof paper or clingfilm and leave to rest for 30 minutes in the fridge. The roll the dough into a square approx. 1cm (½in) thick. If the butter is very hard, then beat it (still in the wrapper) with a rolling pin until pliable but not sticky. Unwrap the butter and shape into a slab approx. 2cm (¾in) thick. Put in the centre of the dough and fold over the edges of the butter to make a neat parcel.

Dust your work surface with flour, then flatten the dough with a rolling pin, and continue to roll out into a rectangle approx. 45cm (18in) long and 16cm (6½in) wide. Fold into three with the sides as accurately aligned as possible. Seal the edges with a rolling pin. Give the dough a one-quarter turn (90°), it should now be on your work surface as though it was a book with the open ends facing north/south. Roll out again, fold in three and seal the edges with the rolling pin. Cover with clingfilm or greaseproof paper and leave to rest in the fridge for 30 minutes. Repeat the rolling process another two times to give the dough six rolls altogether with a 30-minute rest in the fridge between every two turns. Chill for at least 30 minutes before using.

Put 5cm (2in) water or chicken stock in a heavy casserole and add the vegetables, peppercorns and bouquet garni. Lay the chicken on top and cover with a tight-fitting lid. Bring to the boil and then transfer to the oven for 1–2 hours, depending on the size of the bird. Watch that it does not boil dry.

Meanwhile, fry the whole or sliced flat mushrooms in half the butter in a hot pan, and season with salt and freshly ground pepper. Sweat the onions in the remaining butter in a small, covered casserole until soft. Cut the cooked bacon into cubes.

Once the chicken is cooked, remove it from the casserole onto a large platter and carve the flesh. Degrease the cooking liquor. Arrange the sliced chicken in layers in 1 large or 6–8 individual ovenproof pie dishes, covering each layer with bacon, onions, mushrooms and peas, if using (no need to cook).

To make the sauce, put 600ml (1 pint) of the strained and degreased cooking liquor and the dry white wine into a saucepan and bring to the boil. Whisk in the roux. Cook until thick and smooth. Add the cream and bring to the boil again. Taste and correct the seasoning, then set aside to cool.

Serves 6–8

500g (18oz) puff pastry
water or chicken stock
2 large carrots, cut into chunks
2 large onions, quartered (don't bother peeling)
2 celery stalks, cut into small chunks
6 black peppercorns
bouquet garni and a sprig of tarragon
1 large (2–3kg (5–6lb)) organic chicken or boiling fowl
16 mushrooms (I like to use 'breakfast flats'), sliced if large
25g (1oz) butter
16 button onions, peeled but left whole
450g (1lb) streaky bacon (in the piece), cooked
110g (4oz) peas (frozen are fine), optional
150ml (5fl oz) dry white wine
110g (4oz) roux
250ml (8fl oz) double cream
500g (18oz) puff pastry
eggwash (1 organic egg beaten, plus 1 tablespoon milk), to glaze
sea salt and freshly ground black pepper

For the puff pastry (Makes approx. 1.1kg (2½lb))
450g (1lb) chilled strong flour, plus extra for dusting
pinch of salt
squeeze of lemon juice (optional)
450g (1lb) butter, firm but pliable

To serve
green salad

To assemble the pie(s), pour the cool sauce over the filling and cover with puff pastry. Decorate the top(s) with any leftover puff pastry – have fun, we sometimes make funny faces, write messages such as 'yummy', 'scrummy' or 'yippee', or put a fine pastry cockerel on top if our guests are not too sensitive! Refrigerate until required. (Note: The pie can be prepared ahead up to this point.)

Preheat the oven to 230°C/450°F/gas 8. Just before cooking, brush the top(s) of the pie(s) with eggwash. Bake in the hot oven for 10 minutes, and then reduce the temperature to 200°C/400°F/gas 6 and cook for a further 15–20 minutes or until golden brown (the invidual pies will take approx. 5 minutes less cooking time). Serve with a good green salad.

Ballymaloe Brown Yeast Bread

This bread, a version of the Doris Grant 'no-need-to-knead bread' Loaf, has been made in Ballymaloe for over 60 years. It's eaten freshly baked on the day it's made, but is also delicious three or four days later and toasts brilliantly. It's a particularly good bread recipe to introduce students to yeast breadmaking, as there's no kneading involved and only one rising. You don't need any special equipment or conditions to make this bread. If your kitchen is warm enough for you, the bread will rise!

When making Ballymaloe Brown Yeast Bread, remember that yeast is a living organism. In order to grow, it requires warmth, moisture and nourishment. The yeast feeds on the sugar and produces bubbles of carbon dioxide, which cause the bread to rise. Heat of over 50°C (120°F) will kill yeast. Have the ingredients and equipment at blood heat. White or brown sugar, honey, golden syrup, treacle or molasses may be used. Each will give a slightly different flavour to the bread. At Ballymaloe we use treacle. The dough rises more rapidly with 25g (1oz) yeast than with 20g (¾oz) yeast.

We use a stoneground wholemeal flour. Different flours produce breads of different textures and flavour. The amount of natural moisture in the flour varies depending on atmospheric conditions. The quantity of water should be altered accordingly. The dough should be just too wet to knead – in fact, it does not require kneading. The main ingredients – wholemeal flour, treacle and yeast are highly nutritious.

We usually bake this in a standard loaf tin (as seen on page 27), rather than the shallower loaf tin pictured. You can also make three smaller loaves using 14.5 x 7.5cm (5¾ x 3in) tins. These loaves make an ideal present for anyone living alone as they are the perfect size for one person.

Note: Dried yeast may be used instead of baker's yeast. Follow the same method, but only use half the weight given for fresh yeast. Allow longer to rise. Fast-acting yeast may also be used (follow the instructions on the packet).

Makes 1 loaf

EITHER 450g (1lb) strong stoneground wholemeal flour OR 400g (14oz) strong stoneground wholemeal flour PLUS 50g (2oz) strong white flour OR 400g (14oz) strong stoneground wholemeal flour PLUS 50g (2oz) rye flour
1 teaspoon salt
425ml (15fl oz) water at blood heat
1 scant teaspoon black treacle or molasses
20g–25g (¾–1oz) fresh non-GM yeast
sunflower oil, for greasing
sesame seeds (optional)

Preheat the oven to 230°C/450°F/gas 8. The ingredients should all be at room temperature.

Mix the flour with the salt in a large mixing bowl. Measure out 150ml (5fl oz) of the water in a small bowl or Pyrex jug, stir in the treacle or molasses and crumble in the yeast. Set aside in a warm place for 5 minutes to allow the yeast to start to work. Meanwhile, grease a 13 x 20cm (5 x 8in) bread tin with sunflower oil. Check to see if the yeast is rising: it should have a creamy and slightly frothy appearance on top.

Give the yeast a quick stir and pour it over the flour, along with the remaining 275ml (10fl oz) water. Mix well to form a loose, wet dough; the mixture should be too wet to knead. Put the mixture into the greased tin. Sprinkle the top with sesame seeds, if using. Transfer the tin to a warm place – somewhere close to the cooker or near a radiator perhaps – and cover the top with a tea towel to prevent a skin from forming. Set aside for 10–20 minutes, depending on the temeperature of your kitchen, or until the bread rises just to the top of the tin. The bread will continue to rise in the oven; this is called 'oven spring'. Don't allow the bread to rise beyond the top of the tin before it goes into the oven or it will continue to rise and flow over the top.

Bake the bread in the hot oven for 20 minutes, and then turn the temperature down to 200°C/400°F/gas 6 and bake for a further 40–50 minutes or until it looks nicely browned and sounds hollow when tapped underneath. We usually remove the bread from the tin about 10 minutes before the end of cooking and put it back into the oven to crisp all round, but if you like a softer crust there's no need to do this. Cool on a wire rack.

Versatile Vegetables

My fourth book and TV series, produced in 1994, was called *Simply Delicious Versatile Vegetables*. At that time in Ireland we had a deeply ingrained meat-eating culture; people didn't feel they were adequately fed unless the meal contained meat or fish. However, we also had a very strange attitude to fish. Owing to Irish Catholic customs, Friday was considered by many a 'fast day'; people abstained from eating meat but were allowed to eat fish, if available. Most of the fish was transported inland by bus or by train and so was often at least a week old by the time it reached its final destination. I remember, in my home village of Cullohill, when the fish arrived on the bus from Dublin on a Thursday evening. The choice was limited and generally comprised of whiting, occasionally plaice, and a bright, psychedelic orange smoked haddock. Understandably, eating fish began to be regarded as a penance rather than a pleasure, until thankfully the Vatican lifted this rule in the 1980s, making 'fast day' a voluntary choice rather than an obligation.

Potatoes were of course essential to every meal and in fact, up until recently, it was not uncommon to be served potatoes in three ways in a country hotel, without anyone thinking it at all unusual. However, vegetables in general were looked down on as second class citizens and it was against this background that I made my TV series, with the aim to present them in a new light and move them centre stage. I wanted to encourage people to be more adventurous, to expand their horizons beyond cabbage, carrots and parsnips and the odd swede turnip, and to get them thinking about growing and eating their own. How times have changed! All this is very trendy nowadays, but it certainly wasn't back then as, particularly in rural Ireland, there was the attitude that if you grew vegetables and potatoes 'the neighbours would think that you couldn't afford to buy them'!

At home in Cullohill, my family had always had a kitchen garden and so when Tim and I got married I was longing to start a little vegetable patch of my own. We were young and enthusiatic and so decided to clear a bed at the edge of the orchard close to the wood. We grew an extensive range of vegetables, including many

Left: Courgette blossom, gold rush and coco elle courgettes, sweet Genovese basil, nasturtium flowers and parsley, freshly picked to make a salad.
Above: A selection of sweet home-grown peppers from the greenhouses at Ballymaloe: Atris, Marconi rossa *and* Oro.

varieties of beans, brassicas, root vegetables, beets, leeks and both globe and Jerusalem artichokes, plus more unusual ingredients such as seakale and cardoons. My confidence grew and, after a year or two, I persuaded Tim to let me take over the old haggard where the hay ricks would have been built in earlier years. By then I had travelled quite a bit and was intrigued by the kitchen gardens of the French potagers. I loved the pictures of gardens I'd seen that combined vegetables and flowers and, though a relatively uncommon concept at the time, I decided that the garden ought to be decorative as well as functional.

Frank Walsh, who originally worked with the Strangmans, later with my father-in-law Ivan Allen, and eventually with us at Kinoith for over 60 years, painstakingly laid the paths of old brick in a herringbone pattern for the vegetable garden. Andy Grierson, a school friend of Tim's and a gifted blacksmith, made many of the garden seats and the metal tripods for the sweet peas and runner beans to scramble up.

The vegetable garden is 45.7m (50 yards) long and 20m (22 yards) wide. The main design is a diamond bisected by a cross with boxwood parterres at either end. There's a raised summer beech

house at the west end, which was originally made of trellis but the beech hedge we planted has now grown all over the frame to create a little beech house with a garden seat inside. On the north side there's another trellis-covered seat with a golden hop tumbling over the top and sides. This vegetable garden is our gardener Eileen O'Donovan's pride and joy. The beds are crop-rotated every four years in a complex planting system that ensures no two related vegetables are planted in the same place within a four year cycle. Each plant guzzles a particular set of nutrients from the soil and so keeping them in strict rotation provides you with strong, healthy plants that can resist disease.

The beds are planted to create a pattern of colour, texture and form. Edible flowers, like marigolds, nasturtiums, love-in-a-mist (*Nigella*) and little violas (we call them Johnny-jump-ups) attract beneficial insects into the garden, which help with pollination. Globe artichokes are planted along the south-facing wall and under-planted with catmint (*Nepeta*). This is an old variety of artichoke, which has been passed from one generation of Myrtle's family to another and came from the garden at St Aubyn's in Monkstown to the walled garden at Ballymaloe House, and then onwards to us at Kinoith; it's got a fantastic flavour and a wonderful rich purple colour, although sadly we don't know the name. Four clipped mop head bays punctuate the four large vegetable beds and give height to the scheme.

Even though the vegetable garden is small, less than half an acre, we grow a huge variety of vegetables and herbs. Many, such as globe and jerusalem artichokes, are heirloom varieties and grown primarily for flavour rather than yield. Several types of beans, including French, broad, and scarlet runner; beets; carrots; parsnips; celeriac; a couple of types of chard; courgettes; Florence fennel; leeks and the onion family – shallots, salad onions, red onions – all feature. We also grow a few varieties of salad potatoes; Pink Fir Apple and Ratte are my favourites. There's a great variety of pumpkins and squash as well as aubergines. We've been delighted with the success of scorzonera and salsify, certainly not easy to find in the shops. We don't grow brassicas or spinach here because the pigeons kept devouring them despite our watchful wicker scarecrows, and it was too labour intensive and ugly to keep netting them. We also grow a selection of flowers: marigolds, Echinacea, sunflowers, *Nigella*, poppy, catmint, cornflowers – some for cutting, like sweet peas, others for adding to salads, such as the nasturtiums and violas, and others for companion planting, like *Tagetes*. The soil in the vegetable garden is friable and fertile, the result of years

Left: This variety of artichoke has been passed down the generations of Myrtle's family. Sadly we have never been able to identify it by name.
Above (left): The herringbone paths in the vegetable garden were painstakingly laid over a period of several months by Frank Walsh, who worked with the Allen family for over 60 years and lived in the courtyard at Kinoith. The Ballymaloe Cookery School gardens are open to the public from Easter to the end of October so visitors can enjoy wandering through the gardens, maze, greenhouse and do a self-guided farm walk. We also offer a guided tour for pre-booked groups.
Above (right): Globe artichoke growing in the vegetable and herb gardens. This variety has less flavour than its rich purple counterpart, so we often let them go to flower in early August when they look particularly stunning.

of enriching the soil with well-rotted farmyard manure, compost and seaweed.

However, even though the variety is large, we are restricted for space in the kitchen garden and the quantities of each crop are small. Therefore, in 2007, Tim started to prepare a patch in the field close to the greenhouses to plant long drills of both annual and perennial vegetables. There's an asparagus plot and several drills of seakale, a big patch of Jerusalem artichokes and rhubarb plus a couple of rows of strawberries. Leeks, swede turnips, carrots, Brussels sprouts, kohlrabi and others take their turns at either side of the grass path leading from the wildflower meadow to the greenhouses.

We are acutely aware that the maxim 'all good food comes from the good earth' sounds a bit hippyish, but then I am, after all, an aged hippy, and we are passionate about caring for and feeding

the soil that feeds us. Unless we have rich fertile soil we won't have good food or clean water. To quote Lady Eve Balfour, founder member of the Soil Association: 'Agriculture must be looked upon as one of the health services, in fact the primary health service.'

This is a fundamental truth that we try to pass on to the 12-week students who pick the vegetables and see them grow. Throughout the seasons, but particularly in summer, the gardeners arrange a plate of freshly picked raw vegetables – crunchy radishes, pea pods, broad beans, florets of Romanesco, beans, baby carrots – on the hall table, with a sign saying 'Help Yourself to Food from the Farm', for the students and visitors to munch on ; for most people the taste of freshly picked organic vegetables is a total revelation. In autumn, Eileen O'Donovan, our gardener for the past 25 years, piles the squash and pumpkins along the window ledges so the students can learn to identify the different varieties. I love it when I see them all piled up and feel very blessed to live in the middle of a farm.

The huge Irish wooden salad bowl in the Blue Dining Room is legendary; it was hand-turned from Irish beech by Keith Mosse, the most extraordinary and talented woodturner that Ireland has ever produced. Every day, the students fill it with lettuces, salad leaves, both wild and foraged greens and edible flowers from the garden and greenhouses. At lunchtime it's tossed with a variety of freshly made dressings, but sometimes just with beautiful cold-pressed extra virgin olive oil and a fine wine vinegar. The students love the salad and many tell me they pine for it when they leave.

We use the School as an indoor classroom and the farm, gardens, greenhouses and seashore as an outdoor classroom. All around the School on the windowsills, in the hall, conservatories and garden there are edible plants, several varieties of rose geranium, lemongrass and chilli plants, stevia (a powerful sweetener), wasabi, and various citrus including kumquats, lemons and satsumas.

We've taught a Vegetarian Course at Ballymaloe, virtually every year for the past 30 years. In 1996 we started to classify all the recipes at the Cookery School with symbols, including V for vegetarian and VV for vegan. In 1998 we added a vegetarian option to our daily menus and, in 2011, a Salad of the Day made from the seasonal vegetables, fresh herbs and salad leaves, often paired with pulses and grains. In a further effort to highlight the bounty of the seasons, we have a blackboard just inside the door of the Cookery School where we chalk up the produce from the farm and gardens every day. This emphasises the 'farm to table' experience and gives the gardeners a feeling of pride when they see their work being celebrated and acknowledged.

I love the vegetable dishes that I have tasted in Italy, Morocco and India and I long for the day when Ireland values vegetables and pulses in the same way. In Thailand and Vietnam, the food uses lots of fresh herbs and vegetables and only a little meat. I don't necessarily want to encourage people to become vegetarian but rather to inspire them to eat less but better-quality meat and to enjoy and value vegetables more – after all, they are unquestionably the most important food group.

Research study after research study reminds us what we already know: that our global consumption of meat is unsustainable and so I'm hopeful that change is afoot. Meat or fish used to be the star on restaurant plates, with a mere nod to vegetables as a pretty garnish, but this is not so much the case any more. In 2011, Hugh Fearnley-Whittingstall produced a TV series and bestselling book called *River Cottage Veg Every Day!*, encouraging people to see veg as healthy, cost-effective and, above all, delicious. In the US, Dan Barber at Blue Hills at Stone Barns has raised the farm-to-table dining experience to a new high, serving what's best from the farm and gardens on the menu every day, exactly as Myrtle Allen has been doing since she opened a restaurant at Ballymaloe House in 1963.

Veganism is also gaining popularity with many high profile fans, including Brad Pitt, Demi Moore and Venus and Serena Williams embracing a plant-based diet, initially for health concerns, but also for environmental and ethical reasons. Vegans do not eat dairy, eggs, honey or anything that originates from animals. Some feel that it is part of a more humane and caring lifestyle, particularly if they have concerns about how poultry and animals are handled in mass-production facilities. Vegan diets are low in cholesterol and saturated fats, so it makes it easier for those who may be at risk of heart disease and circulatory problems to follow a recommended diet.

Bill Clinton, who visited Ballymaloe House in 2012 for the Ireland Fund Dinner, had a legendary appetite for fast food – burgers, steak, fried chicken – but now finds himself the poster boy for veganism after shedding 20 pounds. Vegan cookbooks are now outselling vegetarian cookbooks, and one of my favourite food trucks, Cinnamon Snail in Manhattan, serves vegan food. So watch this space – I reckon it's a global trend.

Left: Sharlene Smit, an intern from Durban, South Africa, with a big bowl of freshly picked salad for lunch at the Garden Café.
Right: My daughter Lydia writing the Food from the Farm board, which we update daily to highlight the wealth of fresh produce from the surrounding farm and gardens. In the summer and early autumn we often run out of space to list all the available ingredients on the board.

Brussels Sprouts with Avocado and Pecans

Brussels sprouts have a bad reputation in general but roast Brussels sprouts are very trendy in the US right now – they are certainly an acquired taste, which I have grown to love, although there is a fine line between charred and burnt! However, they're also delicious raw, grated into salads, or the fresh outer leaves used to make soup. This recipe uses the outer leaves to make a wonderful salad (it is difficult to give an exact quantity). Roast Pumpkin seeds or hazelnuts would also be good here.

Serves 8

approx. 900g (2lb) Brussels sprouts
1–2 blood oranges (depending on size), peeled
2 avocados, sliced
25–50g (1–2oz) pecans, toasted
a large handful of small flat-leaf parsley sprigs

For the dressing
finely grated zest of 1 lemon
2 tablespoons freshly squeezed lemon juice
6 tablespoons extra virgin olive oil
1 teaspoon honey
½ teaspoon Dijon mustard
sea salt and freshly ground black pepper

In a small jar or bowl, whisk all the ingredients for the salad dressing together.

Peel the outer leaves of the Brussels sprouts (keep the centres for another dish) and put into a bowl. Segment the blood oranges and also add them to the bowl. Drizzle half the dressing over the salad, tossing gently.

Turn the salad out onto a wide platter and arrange the avocados haphazardly on top. Sprinkle with the toasted pecans and plenty of flat-leaf parsley sprigs, and drizzle over the rest of the dressing.

Vegetable and Red Lentil Broth

This makes a nice big pot of soup.

Serves 12

1 tablespoon extra virgin olive oil
450g (1lb) onions, sliced
3 garlic cloves, peeled and finely chopped
900g (2lb) carrots, diced into 1cm (½in) cubes
1 head of celery (approx. 450g/1lb), diced into 1cm (½in) cubes
2 tablespoons sweet chilli sauce
1 tablespoon Worcestershire sauce
2.4 litres (4 pints) well-flavoured vegetable or chicken stock
450g (1lb) red lentils
sea salt and freshly ground black pepper

Heat the extra virgin olive oil in a large saucepan. Add the onion, garlic, carrot and celery and sweat for 10 minutes over a low heat.

Add the sweet chilli sauce and the Worcestershire sauce and mix well. Cook for another 5 minutes, and then add the vegetable or chicken stock. Bring to the boil and simmer for 10 minutes.

Add the lentils and continue to cook for a further 20 minutes or until the vegetables are soft and the lentils have lost their bite. Taste and season. Serve in wide soup bowls.

Pumpkin, Goat's Cheese and Kale Tart

My mother always grew curly kale as a winter vegetable in the kitchen garden behind our house in Cullohill. She would wait for a couple of nights of frost before picking it, as she quite rightly felt that the frost sweetened the taste, turning the starches into sugars as it does for many winter vegetables. She served kale, as many people did at that time, in only a couple of ways – in colcannon or as a green vegetable. We now use it at the School in a huge variety of recipes and dishes from salads, quiches and savoury tarts to crisps and healthy, energy-boosting drinks.

Serves 8

For the shortcrust pastry
175g (6oz) white flour, spelt or wholemeal flour
pinch of salt
75g (3oz) cold butter
beaten organic egg with a little water, to bind
beaten organic egg white, to glaze

For the filling
450g (1lb) pumpkin or butternut squash
1 tablespoon extra virgin olive oil, plus extra for drizzling
2 teaspoons fresh thyme leaves
110g (4oz) kale, raw and stripped off the stalk
    or 50–110g (2–4oz) coarsely chopped rocket
75g (3oz) spring onions, chopped
2 organic eggs
3 organic egg yolks
200ml (7fl oz) double cream
25g (1oz) Parmesan cheese, grated
50g (2oz) Gruyère cheese, grated
150g (5oz) Ardsallagh goat's cheese (or another soft goat's
    cheese of your choice)
sea salt and freshly ground black pepper

To serve
green salad

Preheat the oven to 200°C/400°F/gas 6. First make the pastry. Sift the flour and salt into a large bowl. Cut the butter into cubes, toss in the flour and then rub in with your fingertips. Keep everything as cool as possible; if the fat is allowed to melt, the finished pastry may be tough. When the mixture looks like coarse breadcrumbs, stop.

Using a fork to stir, add just enough beaten egg to bring the pastry together. Shape the dough into a ball with your hands – this way, you can judge more accurately if you need a few more drops of egg wash. While rather damp pastry is easier to handle and roll out, the resulting crust can be tough and may well shrink out of shape as the water evaporates in the oven. As a general rule, the drier and more difficult the pastry is to handle, the crisper and shorter the crust.

Flatten the pastry into a round, wrap in clingfilm and set aside to rest in the fridge for at least 15 minutes. This will make the pastry less elastic and therefore easier to roll.

Meanwhile, peel the pumpkin or squash and cut into 2.5cm (1in) chunks. Arrange on a roasting tin and drizzle with extra virgin olive oil. Season with salt and sprinkle over half the thyme leaves. Roast in the preheated oven for approx. 30 minutes or until tender. Set aside to cool.

Bring a large pot of water to the boil, add the kale (if using) and blanch for 2 minutes; drain and refresh under cold running water. If you are using the rocket, there is no need to blanch it.

Line a 23cm (9in) tart tin with the pastry and bake blind for about 25 minutes. The base should be almost fully cooked after this time. Remove the parchment paper and beans, brush the base with a little beaten egg white and return to the oven for a further 3–4 minutes. This will seal the base and prevent the 'soggy bottom' effect.

Reduce the oven temperature to 180°C/350°F/gas 4. Heat 1 tablespoon oil in a sauté pan, add the spring onion, cover with a lid and sweat gently over a low heat for approx. 6 minutes or until almost soft.

Meanwhile, whisk the eggs and egg yolks in a medium bowl. Add the cream, Parmesan, Gruyère, remaining thyme leaves, cooled spring onion and kale or rocket. Mix well and season to taste: heat a frying pan, cook a teaspoon of the mixture over a gentle heat for 2–3 minutes until it coagulates, and then taste. Correct the seasoning if necessary.

Add the chunks of cooled roasted pumpkin to the filling and crumble in the goat's cheese. Pour the mixture into the pastry case and bake in the oven for 30–40 minutes or until the centre has just set. Serve warm with a freshly tossed green salad.

Parsnip and Maple Syrup Cake

Here at the School we subscribe to a variety of food magazines from all over the world. We all love to flick through them – they spark off ideas and occasionally we find a little gem like this recipe for a delicious winter cake, which was inspired by one from *BBC Good Food Magazine*.

Preheat the oven to 180°C/350°F/gas 4. Grease two 20cm (8in) deep cake tins with a little butter and line the bases with parchment paper.

Melt the butter, sugar and maple syrup in a pan over a gentle heat. Set aside to cool slightly, and then whisk in the eggs. Sift the flour, baking powder and mixed spice into a large mixing bowl. Stir in the butter and sugar mixture and mix carefully. Next add the grated parsnip, apple, pecans or hazelnuts, orange zest and juice and combine thoroughly.

Divide the mixture between the two tins and bake in the preheated oven for 35–40 minutes or until the cakes are just starting to shrink from the sides of the tins. Cool on a wire rack.

Just before serving, beat the mascarpone and maple syrup together. Spread over the base of one cake and top with the other. Dust with icing sugar just before serving.

Serves 8

175g (6oz) butter, plus extra for greasing
175g (6oz) demerara sugar
100ml (3½ fl oz) maple syrup
3 large organic eggs
250g (9oz) self-raising flour
2 teaspoons baking powder
2 teaspoons mixed spice
250g (9oz) parsnips, peeled and grated
1 medium eating apple, peeled, cored and grated
50g (2oz) pecans or hazelnuts, roughly chopped
zest and juice of 1 small orange
icing sugar, for dusting

For the filling
250g (9oz) mascarpone
3–4 tablespoons maple syrup

I often wonder which thrifty housewife started using courgettes, beetroot, celeriac and other root vegetables in cakes, but it is a more unusual way of cooking vegetables and a useful way to use up a glut, while adding nourishment to something sweet.

Keeping Pigs

In the mid-eighties, when we could no longer buy the sweet, juicy pork I remembered as a child, I decided to get our own pigs. I met a smallholder in West Cork while I was filming one of my *Simply Delicious* series and I bought two weanlings from him. They settled in happily but I needed an unrelated boar. Then, as luck would have it, I was walking in the Knockmealdown Mountains in Co. Tipperary with a few locals and we chatted on and off, as one does on a long walk. I told them about my pigs and one man told me that he also kept a few but was having difficulty selling them in the mart as they were black and tan Tamworths and so considered 'queer looking'. I couldn't believe my ears. He had a black Berkshire boar for sale and this was exactly what I needed. We made a deal, shaking hands as we crossed a stream on stepping stones, and that spot has been known as the Ford of the Black Pig ever since.

We have kept traditional breeds – Saddlebacks, Red Duroc and Gloucester Old Spot for many years and the pork that they produce is completely delicious, sweet and succulent. Our happy, lazy pigs are born in the fields and live freely all their lives – rooting in the ground and eating organic meal and surplus greens from the gardens and greenhouses. After about 5–6 months they make a short trip to Frank Murphy, our local butcher in Midleton, where they are humanely slaughtered. Frank prepares and splits the carcass and saves everything, from nose to tail, at our request. Many of the students on the 12-week course are delighted to have the opportunity to learn how to butcher (break up) a pig. Being free-range, the pigs have had quite a bit of exercise and developed a fair amount of muscle so we hang them in a cold-room for a week to ten days.

We use every single scrap of the animals: the blood is made into puddings, the head into brawn or head cheese, in which the ears are sometimes included, or they're prepared as crispy pigs' ears. We make lots of sausages, salami, chorizo, and a variety of cured meats,

from bacon and hams to dry-cured jamon – a never-ending journey that continues to thrill both us and many of the students.

In 2006, we introduced a course called How to Cure a Pig in a Day and use every single scrap, as part of our Forgotten Skills series and we've noticed how the interest in keeping a few pigs at home has grown phenomenally since then. In general, people are incredibly keen to relearn the skills needed to rear and grow one's own food – in the US there's a considerable homestead revival and in the UK, allotments are over-subscribed in virtually every city and town. Thankfully there is at least one upside to the downturn in the economy, encouraging us to discover a degree of self-sufficiency and recognise its importance.

In 2008, one of our past students, Ted Berner, started Wild Side Catering and became one of the very first people to bring back the traditional method of roasting pigs and other meat on a spit. It proved a great hit and he is in huge demand at weddings, parties, and music festivals all around the country.

Since 2005, visitors to the School and gardens, which have been open to the public since the late 1980s, can enjoy a self-guided farm walk. We've provided explanatory signs in strategic places around the farm and gardens to provide information about the animals and plants, breeds and varieties. There is also a treasure hunt sheet for children to look out for around the farm.

Left: A Gloucester Old Spot sow with her litter of piglets, which are called 'bonhams' in Ireland, snuffling around the muddy fields. Above: A newborn piglet on the farm at Ballymaloe. We have two litters every year, ranging in size from 10–15 piglets.

Above: Our current sow, a cross between the Gloucester Old Spot and Saddleback breeds. During the outbreak of Foot and Mouth Disease in 2001, when there was a ban on the movement of animals, our Saddleback boar died. We were looking for another boar to replace him, but were advised to try a cross of Gloucester Old Spot and Saddleback, which was believed to produce even better quality meat with a little less fat, so we thought we would try it out and we've been enjoying the results ever since.

Cooking with the Clergy

When I was a child, every parish in Ireland had a priest and every priest had a live-in housekeeper, a woman of 'good repute', usually a spinster or widow, who cooked and cleaned and washed and kept house. By the early 1990s, education, women's liberation and increased opportunities meant that fewer women were prepared to do the housekeeping, so the supply dwindled and many clergy found that when their old housekeeper retired it was impossible to find a replacement. Most priests could scarcely boil water or make toast, so they were unable to fend for themselves and were virtually helpless. After two separate people mentioned that their 'brother the priest' was desperate to learn a little bit of simple cooking and that I'd be doing a great service if I put on a course specifically for priests, I did.

In July 1996 we scheduled a two and a half day hands-on course called A Cookery Course for Clergy and we had eager students enrolling from all over the country. The course itself caused quite a stir and we were inundated with press, including the *Daily Express* and *Irish Catholic*. There were articles in *Esquire* and the *Guardian*, while several TV channels, including the BBC, wanted to film it. However, I was very protective of the privacy of my class and it was a really special few days for all of us as we taught the priests the basics and helped them to hone their culinary skills.

The first day consisted of two long demonstrations, covering everything from breakfast to dinner, from pinhead oatmeal porridge and scrambled eggs to grilled chicken breast with rocket and tomato salad; simple nutritious wholemeal bread; purée of onion soup; lamb stew with bacon, onions and garden herbs; mushrooms à la crème, which they could eat on toast or slather over a steak, and crêpes with orange butter. On the morning of the second day we gave the clergy the chance to practise what we had preached to them, and then followed this up with further demonstrations. On day three, the fathers honed their new skills. It was all very intensive, with an emphasis on the practical application of the lessons. The underlying idea was to teach some basic dishes and then to show how they may be given infinite variety by changing certain ingredients – how the grilled chicken breast can lose its rocket and tomato salad in favour of mushrooms à la crème, which in turn could be used as a pasta sauce. Father Michael said he had learned a lot from the course – 'I didn't know you could cook vegetables in three minutes. I'd say there'll be fewer tins in the garbage can beside the cooker'. Others, like Father Patrick, were

happy that they now felt able to cook for friends who would come round after Mass on a Sunday.

By the end of the course everybody knew a mornay from a roux and how to make meals using each. They could use a chopper, skin a fish and even defrost homemade stock in plastic cartons by putting it in the dishwasher. Some left compiling and comparing lists of cooking equipment they wanted to buy on the way home, while one loaded a starter pack for a fresh herb garden into the boot of his Volkswagen Golf.

● **Food & Drink:** Matthew Fort

Canon fodder

Where does a poor clergyman turn when he loses his trusty cook? Boiling those eggs can be such a problem. Thankfully, help is at hand

Left: The front of the Cookery School – this welcoming seat and some of our fancy fowl, including a Frizzle Bantam pecking around in the gravel are often the first sights to greet students on arrival.
Above: Matthew Fort's article in the Guardian *about the Cooking with the Clergy course – one of the many pieces of press coverage that the class received.*

The Shell House

Perhaps it was because I was born about as far away from the coast as it's possible to be in Ireland that I have always had a fascination for seashells. As children, an expedition to the beach in Tramore, Co. Waterford was the highlight of our summer and I always brought home a little collection of shells in my sand bucket. I'd lay them out on the veranda outside our kitchen and long for the sea.

When I moved to Cork in 1968, within sight and sound of the sea, I continued to collect shells on the nearby beaches and dreamed of making a shell grotto, reminiscent of those I'd seen in *Country Living* magazine. As luck would have it, when I was flicking through a copy of *House & Garden* magazine in early summer 1994 I came across an enchanting article about Blott Kerr-Wilson, a shell artist from Wales who was so crazy about shells that she used them to cover the bathroom in the council house in Peckham in London where she lived at the time. She had won a 'design a room' competition in *The World of Interiors* magazine so her phone number was at the end of the article. I telephoned and left a message on her phone asking if she ever came to Ireland and explaining that I'd been collecting shells for years and would love to chat to her about a shell house. I then thought better of my rambling message and finished by saying that if a man answered when she returned the call to put the phone down!

Blott was obviously intrigued by my long, convoluted message and fortunately I picked up the phone when she returned the call. I asked if she ever came to Ireland. She said she didn't have any plans to but was between jobs and would be delighted to if there were a reason to. I suggested that she try to find a cheap flight and she rang back within hours to say she could come the following week; brilliant, I thought, must tell Tim. However, somehow the right moment didn't present itself and the morning of Blott's arrival, I had to teach so I never had the change to explain to Tim before he left for the airport. On the way back to Ballymaloe, Blott blurted out all my grandiose plans, much to Tim's astonishment, and yet in such a charming way that Tim was delighted with the idea by the time they returned to the School!

Tim and I had decided to build an octagonal folly at the end of the herbaceous borders. Designed by our friend, the renowned gardener Jim Reynolds, it was to incorporate the gothic windows I'd bought from Edward Byrne's architectural salvage yard in Co. Carlow and also the thousands of shells I had collected, many from local strands, others brought home from holidays abroad or sent by friends who knew I loved them. David Hugh-Jones of Rossmore Oysters provided mussel, whelk and oyster shells. Still more mussel and scallop shells were collected by the chefs at Ballymaloe House and Aherne's Townhouse Seafood Restaurant in Youghal, who kindly saved them after their guests had enjoyed the contents. Blott also sourced lots of exotic shells from Marine Arts in Penzance in Cornwall. On 1 June 1995, our builder, Will Kenneally, constructed scaffolding inside the octagonal folly and, like Michaelangelo in the Sistine Chapel, Blott started her work, beginning in the apex of the roof.

I tried to communicate to Blott what I had in mind but neither of us can draw and so Blott decided she should just get started and I could decide if I liked it. If I didn't, we had four hours to change our minds before the tile cement set. However, once Blott started to work, I realised she was so much more creative than I could ever be. The result was completely magical and every panel and window reveal is different. The work took five months and 20,000 shells to complete. Benjamin Krebs, then Blott's boyfriend, now her husband, also helped out and graded and sorted all the pebbles for the floor under a leaky plastic cover – she was surprised he stuck around it was such a horrid job! Perdi Fenn then joined Blott to pebble the floor for a few weeks before the end. A stream of water circulates from a little pool in the centre and around the outside of the floor on a continual basis.

The initials of my four children – I for Isaac, T for Toby, L for Lydia and E for Emily – are incorporated into the shell or pebble pattern, as well as 1995, the year of mine and Tim's 25th wedding anniversary.

The Shell House was officially opened on 27 October 1995, the date of our 25th wedding anniversary, and is considered to be a monument to Tim's patience with all my crazy ideas. However, he also loves the Shell House and reckons it is one of the most exciting things that we've created at Kinoith. In 2006 Blott returned to make and install a 'shelldolier' as a celebration for our daughter Lydia's wedding in the garden.

The Shell House was my way of recycling shells and to this day I can't bear to waste shells; after we eat our 'Plate of Irish Shellfish' lunch, I encourage the students to keep the shells and use them to decorate picture frames or mirrors or to plan their own shell grotto.

Above: A view to the octagonal Shell House from the herbaceous border, which leads up to it. The roof slates are rounded to resemble fish scales. We also fly a coloured pennant (flag) from the top for all celebrations and events.

Right: A window in the Shell House.

Far right: A detail of the Shell House with whelks, cockles, periwinkles, oyster and abalone shells.

Strawberry, Raspberry, Blackberry or Apple Muesli

This fruit muesli is served for breakfast right through the year at Ballymaloe and is a dish we've made from the beginning of the School; the fruit varies with the season. It is a recipe that we teach at the start of the 12-week course to encourage students to eat breakfast and we felt it was useful for the clergy to learn too. It can be made in a matter of minutes and is high GI (glycaemic index), which means that it releases energy slowly to help keep you going throughout the day.

Serves 4

3 heaped tablespoons rolled oatmeal (Quaker Oats)
6 tablespoons water
110g (4oz) fresh strawberries, raspberries, blackberries or grated dessert apple (preferably Worcester Pearmain or Cox's Orange Pippin)
approx. 1 teaspoon honey

Soak the oatmeal in the water for 10–15 minutes. Meanwhile, mash the strawberries roughly with a fork. Stir the fruit into the oatmeal and sweeten to taste with honey – a scant teaspoon is usually enough, but it depends on how sweet the fruit is.

Serve with cream and soft brown sugar.

When buying pork it is important to look for organically reared heritage breeds, such as Saddleback, Gloucester Old Spot, Tamworth, Black Berkshire, Mangalese, Red Duroc...

Pork Belly with Green and Black Olive Tapenade

This recipe is inspired by a dish I ate at Amisfield Winery near Queenstown on the South Island of New Zealand. They sourced high-quality pork from a heritage breed for this dish and, as ever, the resulting texture and flavour was much superior to that of intensively-produced pork. There is usually a higher proportion of fat on these old breeds, as they needed it to protect them outside in winter, which results in juicier and more succulent meat.

Serves 6–8

1 x 2.2kg (5lb) pork belly with skin
rocket leaves
Maldon sea salt and freshly ground black pepper

For the tapenade
75g (3oz) stoned green olives
75g (3oz) stoned black olives
2 large garlic cloves, peeled and finely chopped
2 anchovies (preferably Ortiz), mashed
4 tablespoons extra virgin olive oil, plus extra to serve

Score the pork skin at 5mm (¼in) intervals. Sprinkle both the rind and the flesh side with salt and set aside for 2–3 hours. Wash and dry well.

Preheat the oven to 180°C/350°F/gas 4. Put the pork, skin-side up on a chopping board and season again with salt and black pepper. Pour 1cm (½in) water into a roasting tin, put the pork on a wire rack inside the tin and roast for 25–28 minutes per 450g (1lb). Baste with the rendered pork fat every now and then.

Meanwhile, make the tapenade. Roughly chop the olives and combine them with the finely chopped garlic, mashed anchovies and extra virgin olive oil. Mix and taste.

To serve, cut the pork into 5cm (2in) squares – allow three pieces per person. Drizzle a little of the chunky tapenade over and around the pork and serve with a sprinkle of flakes of sea salt and a drizzle of extra virgin olive oil.

Mummy's Sweet White Scones

These scones are my mother's recipe, which I introduced to a wider audience in my first *Simply Delicious* TV series. I thought this would be a useful recipe to teach the clergy in the special course I ran for them, as it is a simple and quick, but also makes a large amount, so they could freeze any leftovers and reheat them quickly in the oven for any visiting parishioners.

When Mummy made these for us as children, they were always tender and delicious – but adding a few sultanas was as adventurous as it got. Nowadays we teach numerous twists on the original (see right).

Makes 18–20 scones

900g (2lb) plain white flour
pinch of salt
50g (2oz) caster sugar
3 heaped teaspoons baking powder
175g (6oz) butter
3 organic eggs
approx. 450ml (15fl oz) milk

To glaze
eggwash, made by whisking 1 organic egg with a pinch of salt
granulated sugar, for the topping

Preheat the oven to 240°C/475°F/gas 9. Sift all the dry ingredients into a large, wide bowl. Cut the butter into cubes, toss in the flour and rub in with your fingertips until the mixture resembles really coarse breadcrumbs – surprisingly this results in lighter scones. Make a well in the centre. Whisk the eggs with the milk in a jug. Add to the dry ingredients and mix to a soft dough. Turn out onto a floured board. Don't knead but shape just enough to make a round. Roll out to approx. 2.5cm (1in) thick and cut or stamp into scones. Stamp out the scones with as little waste as possible; the first scones will be lighter than the second rolling. If you cut them into squares or triangles with a knife or pastry cutter, as Mummy did, there is no need to re-roll.

Transfer the scones to a baking tray – there is no need to grease it. Brush the tops with the eggwash and dip each one in granulated sugar. Bake in the hot oven for 10–12 minutes until golden brown on top. Transfer to a wire rack to cool.

Serve split in half with homemade jam and a blob of whipped cream, or just butter and jam.

Variations

Sultana Scones
Add 110g (4oz) plump sultanas to the basic mixture after the butter has been rubbed in.

Lexia Raisin and Rosemary Scones
Add 110g (4oz) Lexia raisins and 1 tablespoon of chopped rosemary to the basic mixture after the butter has been rubbed in.

Cherry Scones
Add 110g (4oz) quartered glacé or dried cherries to the basic mixture after the butter has been rubbed in.

Crystallised Ginger Scones
Add 110g (4oz) chopped crystallised ginger (or drained and chopped stem ginger) to the basic mixture after the butter has been rubbed in.

Candied Citrus Peel Scones
Add 110g (4oz) candied orange and lemon peel to the basic mixture after the butter has been rubbed in. Coat the citrus peel really well in the flour before adding the liquid to stop it sticking together.

Sugar and Spice Scones
Add 4 teaspoons of ground cinnamon to the basic mixture with the flour. Instead of dipping the glazed scones in granulated sugar, use 1 teaspoon of ground cinnamon mixed with 50g (2oz) sugar.

Poppy Seed Scones
Add 4 tablespoons of poppy seeds with the dry ingredients. Serve with freshly crushed strawberries and cream.

Chocolate Chip Scones
Chop 110g (4oz) best-quality chocolate and add to the basic mixture after the butter has been rubbed in.

Strawberry, Raspberry or Blueberry Scones
Add 110g (4oz) chopped fresh strawberries (or whole raspberries or blueberries) to the basic mixture after the butter has been rubbed in. Increase the sugar by 25g (1oz).

White Chocolate and Raspberry Scones
Add 75g (3oz) fresh raspberries and 75g (3oz) chopped white chocolate to the basic mixture after the sugar has been rubbed in.

Slow Food

On 7 September 1996 I accepted the SEI (Società Edictrice Nationale) prize for food and wine culture from the Premio Langhe Ceretto in Italy, for my book *Irish Traditional Cooking*, and gave a spirited speech about the effect of EU regulations on our food culture. Ireland became a member of the EU in 1973 and by 1996 we were really beginning to experience the effects of the changing food hygiene regulations – suddenly there were new and more stringent regulations in many areas of food production. The cost of complying with these, e.g. upgrading butcher's shops and abattoirs, was much more than the producers could afford. This was endangering, and in some cases eliminating, food businesses, such as family butchers, bakeries, cheesemakers and home bakers. There were many local home bakers who had cooked a few scones, a couple of loaves of soda bread and maybe an apple tart for the local shops, who found the environmental health officers knocking on their doors asking if they had a licence to do so. Of course they didn't, it had never been required before. Most took fright and stopped. The effect was to eliminate an integral part of our food culture, preventing local people from taking pride and satisfaction in their produce, plus the extra 'pin money' they earned from their baking that in virtually every case went back into the local economy, or perhaps bought a new pair of shoes or music lessons for a child.

In my speech, I warned the Italians, who still have such a diverse food culture, to be on their guard lest they allow the tidal wave of new food regulations to eliminate their artisan producers. Italy has only been a united country since 1861, prior to which it was made up of a patchwork of principalities, each with their unique traditions and jealously guarded recipes, so they have hugely important regional specialties that it is vitally important to safeguard.

After my speech – delivered through an interpreter – received a standing ovation, a gentleman literally ran up to me from the audience and asked, 'Have you ever heard of Slow Food?' I hadn't and he said, 'You have just been giving a speech that encapsulates the philosophy of Slow Food – you must start Slow Food Ireland'. He was one of the founders of Slow Food International. This organisation, which was officially launched in 1986, could be described as the Greenpeace of gastronomy – the antidote to the fast food culture that threatens to engulf us. Slow Food defends biodiversity, encourages and supports artisan food production and safeguards foods and food cultures in danger of extinction. The movement started as a result of Carlo Petrini's outrage when he encountered the smell of mass-produced French fries wafting from the first McDonald's in Piazza di Spagna in Rome. What started as a single group of disenchanted Italians who were passionate about saving endangered foods, farmhouse cheeses, salamis and old seed varieties has developed into a vibrant international movement.

After my return to Ireland, Slow Food Italy wrote asking me to set up Slow Food Ireland, but Tim was adamant that I was already over-committed and must not take on another project. So Giana Ferguson of Gubbeen Cheese launched Slow Food Ireland in the summer of 1998 at a wonderful gathering in Gubbeen, which included the former Irish Taoiseach Garret FitzGerald and legendary artisans such as Bill Hogan, maker of the wonderful Gabriel farmhouse cheese, Sally Barnes who smokes fish, Adele O'Connor from her bakery in Schull and Toby Simmonds of The Real Olive Company. Renato Sardo from the Slow Food office in Italy came over to meet us all and to explain what was involved in setting up a Slow Food Convivium, which is a local chapter or branch of the organisation. Local convivia work autonomously to defend their cultural heritage and support a more sustainable food future. There are more than 1,500 convivia worldwide and they are the backbone of Slow Food.

The Slow Food philosophy of 'good, clean and fair' has been a major influence in my life and an affirmation of the value of the innate philosophy of Ballymaloe. The vision of 'a world in which all people can access and enjoy food that is good for them, good for those who grow it and good for the planet', is one that I can readily identify with.

I eventually set up the East Cork Slow Food Convivium at the Ballymaloe Cookery School in 1999 and we have had regular Slow Food events ever since, some based at the school, others on local farms or in local restaurants where the menu celebrates the local food of the area. We now have over 100 members in East Cork. In 2005, we launched the East Cork Slow Food Educational Project with four local schools – the list has now expanded to nine. The children visit Ballymaloe several times a year and are split into two groups. The first group heads out on to the farm and learns about livestock and growing, while the second group has a cooking lesson and prepares a delicious lunch for everyone to share.

On Palm Sunday, 16 April 2000, the West Cork Convivium held its second Slow Food Celebration of Taste at the West Cork Natural Cheese Farm. The weather forecast was appalling, yet

Above: The launch of Slow Food Ireland, Gubbeen House, Schull, in August 1998. Pictured are, left to right: Annie Barry, chef at Ballydehob; Sally Barnes, of Woodcock Smokehouse, Skibbereen; Bill Hogan, of West Cork Natural Cheese in Schull; Giana Ferguson, of Gubbeen Farm; Myrtle Allen; former Irish Taoiseach (Prime Minister) Garret FitzGerald; and me.

about 100 like-minded people made their way up the winding lane to Bill Hogan's farm where the legendary Gabriel and Desmond farmhouse cheeses are made. The sun shone all afternoon on the merry band of food producers and bon viveurs. The gathering was like a who's who of the artisanal food scene. The party took place indoors, outdoors, upstairs and downstairs. Bill just threw his gates and doors open and delightedly welcomed the eager foodies. Out in the yard, Fingal Ferguson, son of cheesemakers Tom and Giana, who make the much-loved Gubbeen cheese, had set up a beautiful stall and was busy frying slices of his delicious home-cured smoked bacon. Like many of the artisans, he has gone from strength to strength in the intervening period.

During Carlo Petrini's week-long visit to Ireland in 2004 he met with Minister for Agriculture and Food, Joe Walsh, Bord Bia, UCC, food historians, farmers and fishermen, artisan food producers, chefs, fish smokers, butchers, teachers and Slow Food members. His primary purpose in coming to Ireland on this occasion was to announce details of the University of Gastronomic Sciences in Pollenzo and Colorno in Italy. This project, the first in the world, was to help to create a new type of professional: an expert who is able to lead and elevate the quality of production, to teach others how to taste, to guide the market and to communicate about and promote foods and beverages. The stated aim was that: 'The University will provide those with an interest in understanding food with a humanistic, sensory approach, knowledge of traditional and industrial processes, and an appreciation of cooking and gastronomic tourism. In a world where "specialities" and "typical local products" are increasingly important and are raising the standards of the market, gastronomes will be able to communicate a wealth of knowledge, in advising new businesses, designing distribution outlets and advising the restaurant trade. Though undervalued in the past, this profession is destined to become a true interpreter of food culture.' At a dinner at Ballymaloe House, Rory O'Connell's menu reflected an abundance of wonderful Irish produce and the local foods of the area. Among the many delicious dishes served were Carpaccio of Beef with Horseradish Mayonnaise, Ballymaloe Potted Crab, Nora Aherne's Traditional Duck with Sage and Onion Stuffing, all finished off with Carrageen Moss Pudding with new season's Rhubarb Compote.

Many students become Slow Food members after we explain the philosophy and they often attend a couple of events while they are here. I would hope that they continue their membership when they leave the school, possibly join a convivium somewhere else, or go

out there and make a difference.

In 2012 Slow Food offered a special Slow Food youth membership for students under 35, which boosted the numbers. Membership is growing worldwide, with now over 100,000 members in 150 countries around the globe. The events are always good fun and have a strong educational element – it could be a tasting of local honey combined with a talk on how to keep hens; a visit to a local butcher's shop or abattoir combined with a talk on how to recognise and cook lesser known cuts of meat; or a discussion about the risks and benefits of raw milk with chief scientists from Moorepark Dairy Research Station.

A terrifying number of varieties of vegetables and plants have already been lost or are in danger of extinction. Old varieties of fruit and vegetables, traditional and rare breeds of animal, not considered to be of commercial value, are also under threat. According to Edward Wilson's estimate in *The Diversity of Life* (1992), in one century over 250,000 varieties of plant have become extinct – and they will continue to vanish at the rate of three species every hour, or 27,000 a year. Also, according to Food and Agriculture Organization of the United Nations (FAO) estimates, 75 per cent of agricultural crop varieties have disappeared and three-quarters of the world's food comes from only 12 plant and five animal species. In the US, for instance, 7,000 apple varieties and 2,500 pear varieties were once grown, but today just two pear varieties account for 96 per cent of the entire market. Another example is potatoes: it is estimated that at one time over 5,000 varieties existed around the world, while today just four varieties are primarily grown for commercial purposes.

This loss has direct consequences on the food we eat. Out of around 30,000 edible natural species, just 30 crops provide for 95 per cent of the entire world's nutritional requirements. Of these thirty, wheat, rice and corn provide more than 60 per cent of the calories consumed worldwide (FAO, 1999). Domestic animal species are in a similar situation. According to the latest report on the status of animal genetic resources in the food and agricultural sector – published by FAO in 2007 – 20 per cent of the races surveyed in the 169 countries involved in the study are at risk of extinction. About 60 per cent of these are mammals; the remaining 40 per cent are poultry.

Slow Food has done much to highlight the problem of conservation and the importance of action on a national and international scale through its various projects, Presidia, Arc of Taste, Slow Food Awards, Salone del Gusto and Terra Madre. At

Left (top): Bill Casey, our neighbour from the village, cures and smokes salmon in the smokehouse on our farm in Shanagarry and explains the process to the 12-week students. He has been smoking for 20 years and occasionally smokes wild salmon from the Blackwater river especially for us to use at Ballymaloe House and the School.
Left (middle): A glimpse into the dairy and packing area at Gubbeen Farm outside Schull in West Cork, where two generations of the Ferguson family are involved in artisan production. Perhaps most famed for their washed rind cheeses, their son Fingal is also acclaimed for his range of charcuterie and cured meats and daughter Clovisse has created a wonderful organic garden, where she grows a wide range of vegetables and salad leaves to supply local restaurants and farmers' markets. This kind of enterprise is an example of the type of artisan producers that Slow Food encourages and supports.
Left (bottom): Clovisse Ferguson.
Above (top): Fingal Ferguson, one of the new generation of young artisan producers who have blazed a trail, inspired others and won multiple awards. As well as producing his own charcuterie, Fingal also makes beautiful, collectible kitchen knives in his workshop on the farm.
Above (bottom): Giana Ferguson in her dairy at Gubbeen.

*Above (top): Igor harvesting red and white onions on the farm
to dry for use over the winter.*
*Above (middle): James Cullinane and Chris O'Brien hanging bunches
of onions from the rafters of the greenhouses – the perfect airy and dry
environment for curing. You can also see our crop of garlic drying on
lower wires. The garlic cloves are sown around the shortest day of the
year and harvested around the longest day.*
Above (bottom): A bunch of garlic ready to hang in the greenhouses.

Salone del Gusto in Turin, the biggest artisan food fair in the world, hundreds of producers sell their products to a public increasingly craving forgotten flavours. Terra Madre, meaning Mother Earth is an international meeting of food communities held bi-annually in Turin. Slow Food brings 5,000 farmers and food producers from all over the world together there so that they can meet and share concerns and solutions for a sustainable future and thereby build a global network of food 'communities'. Held over four days in the enormous Palazza del Lavoro, the participants represent about 1,000 food communities from 150 countries. Terra Madre provides a meeting place and a forum for people from around the world – for farmers, artisans, food producers, seed-savers, fishermen, distributors, cooks, cheesemakers, fish smokers, cured meat producers, bakers and merchants to come together to exchange ideas, share diverse experiences and to try to find solutions to similar problems.

Some shared aims include protecting the rights of the small farmer and promoting sustainable agriculture as well as uniting against the growing domination of the multinationals and large corporations. Participants often come with an amazing story to tell, some clutching precious seeds, others with grains, all with a deep knowledge of their own food culture. Many dress in their colourful traditional clothes and distinctive headdress – from Indian feathers to cowboy hats, sombreros and headscarves. Masai peasants meet Afghan raisin farmers, American maple syrup producers meet yak herders and cheesemakers from Kyrgyzstan and wild Irish salmon smokers meet Ghanaian fishermen. Speakers stress the need for biodiversity, speak out against transgenic crops, illustrate how globalisation is causing the erosion of rural communities and how the indiscriminate use of pesticides and antibiotics is destroying the land and how the World Trade Organization (WTO) organisation accords affect farmers and food producers. Slow Food, since its inception in 1986, has already battled and successfully saved a growing number of foods and drinks threatened with extinction. It defends our right as consumers to free choice. Prince Charles, an organic farmer himself, addressed the closing session of Terra Madre in 2004. In his speech to the conference, the Prince highlighted the huge social and environmental costs of cheap 'fast food'. His Royal Highness said: 'Any analysis of the real costs would have to look at such things as the rise in food-borne illnesses, the advent of new pathogens such as E.Coli 0157, antibiotic resistance from the overuse of drugs in animal feed, extensive water pollution from intensive agricultural systems, and many other factors. These costs

are not reflected in the price of fast food, but that doesn't mean that our society isn't paying them.'

I have attended every Salone del Gusto and Terra Madre and come back on a high, totally inspired. We bring a delegation of 70–80 people from Ireland and Bord Bia, our National Food Board, and always have a stand at Salone del Gusto to promote and highlight the Irish food products that we are so proud of. Slow Food has granted a *presidia* (a protection) around our Irish raw milk cheeses, so they always have a stand at Terra Madre as well. The Irish Farmhouse Cheesemakers Association (CÁIS), man the stall themselves and charm the Italians and the delegates from all over the world.

During this challenging economic time in Ireland Slow Food membership is falling, but even though membership is considered by many to be a barometer of success, I am not so depressed. I understand that for many nowadays, it's about survival and even though they may not be able to renew their membership, many are still living their lives by the principles of Slow Food – good, clean and fair. This philosophy underpins everything we do at Ballymaloe and the students who spend 12 weeks with us seem to feel deeply committed to spreading the Slow Food philosophy.

Above (top): Watering the many plants in the Ballymaloe greenhouses.
Above (bottom): At the start of every 12-week course I emphasise to the students the importance of good, clean, fertile soil.

A Plate of Irish Charcuterie and Cured Meats

❦

One of my favourite easy entertaining tricks is to serve a selection of Irish artisan charcuterie from inspired producers like Fingal Ferguson and Frank Krawczyk from Schull, West Cork, and James McGeough from Oughterard, Co. Galway. More recently, Martin and Noreen Conroy's son Matthew, from Woodside Farm, is making outstanding salami, chorizo and air-dried meats from their own Saddleback pigs, having spent a considerable period of time apprenticed to Massimo Spigaroli in the Emilia-Romagna region of Italy. The quality of these cured meats is so wonderful that I'm always bursting with pride as I serve them.

a selection of cured meats, such as air-dried smoked Connemara lamb, smoked venison, prosciutto, Gubeen salami, chorizo and chistora, Pat Mulcahy's Ballinwillin House wild boar and venison salami, Derreenatra salami, West Cork Kassler, pork rillettes, brawn, etc.
a selection of crusty country breads, such as sourdough, yeast and soda bread
tiny gherkins or cornichons
fresh radishes, trimmed but with some green leaf attached
good green salad of garden lettuce and salad leaves

Arrange the meats and potted meat on a large platter, open a good bottle of red and tuck in! Accompany with bread, gherkins, radishes and salad.

Smoked Wild Irish Salmon with Horseradish Cream, Arjard and Pickled Red Onions

Wild Irish salmon is a now a rare treat, as for the last couple of years we have managed to get a small number from fishermen on the Blackwater river. We treasure each one and eat some fresh, cure and smoke some ourselves or give them to Bill Casey, our local smoker, to smoke for us. We hot- and cold-smoke the salmon and teach the students both methods of preserving. For this recipe we use cold-smoked salmon, but flakes of the hot-smoked variety would also be delicious.

Serves 4

175–225g (6–8oz) cold-smoked wild Irish salmon,
cut into 1cm (½in) cubes

For the Pickled Red Onions
225ml (8fl oz) white wine vinegar
110g (4oz) granulated sugar
pinch of salt
3 whole cloves
1 cinnamon stick, broken
1 dried red chilli
450g (1lb) red onions, peeled and thinly sliced on a mandolin

For the Arjard (cucumber salad)
2 shallots, peeled and thinly sliced lengthways
1 red chilli, deseeded and sliced into rings
1 green chilli, deseeded and sliced into rings
4 tablespoons sugar
6 tablespoons water
6 tablespoons malt vinegar
½ teaspoon salt
1 cucumber, quartered lengthways and thinly sliced

To serve
chervil sprigs and wild garlic or chive blossom in season
freshly ground black pepper

To make the pickled onions, put the vinegar, sugar, salt and spices in a heavy-bottomed pan and bring to the boil. Put in one-third of the sliced onions and simmer for 2–3 minutes or until they turn pink and wilt. Lift out the cooked onions with a slotted spoon and transfer them to a 350g (13oz) sterilised jam jar with a non-reactive lid. Repeat with the rest of the onions, cooking them in two batches. Top up the jar with the hot vinegar, put on the lid and set aside to cool overnight. Once cold, store in the fridge.

To make the Arjard, put all the ingredients except the cucumber in a heavy-bottomed saucepan. Bring to the boil and simmer for 3–5 minutes. Set aside to cool. Once cold, pour the marinade over the slices of cucumber and set aside to marinate in the fridge for at least 30 minutes.

To serve, arrange the cubes of salmon on a plate, add some Arjard and some pickled red onion and scatter over a few sprigs of chervil, wild garlic or chive flowers. Finish with some freshly ground black pepper over the top.

Ardsallagh Goat's Cheese and Thyme Leaf Soufflé

We have several farmhouse goat's-cheesemakers in Ireland. We use Ardsallagh goat's cheese, St Tola from Inagh in Co. Clare is also heaven, as is Gortnamona from Cooleeney farm in Co. Tipperary and Corleggy from Co. Cavan.

We bake this soufflé until golden and puffy in a shallow oval dish instead of the traditional soufflé bowl. It makes a perfect lunch or supper dish. Little individual bowls are also perfect as a starter. Reduce the cooking time accordingly.

Preheat the oven to 230°C/450°F/gas 8. Brush the bottom and sides of a 30cm (12in) shallow oval dish (not a soufflé dish) or six individual wide, rimmed soup bowls with melted butter.

Put the cream and milk into a saucepan, add the carrot, onion, peppercorns and fresh herbs. Bring slowly to the boil, and then set aside to infuse for 10 minutes. Strain, discarding the flavourings (we rinse them off and throw them into the stockpot if there is one on the go).

Melt the butter, add the flour and cook for a minute or two. Whisk in the strained cream and milk, bring to the boil and whisk until the sauce thickens. Cool slightly. Add the egg yolks, goat's cheese, Gruyère and most of the Coolea or Parmesan (reserving some for the topping). Season with salt, cayenne, freshly ground pepper and nutmeg. Taste and correct the seasoning.

Whisk the egg whites stiffly and fold them gently into the mixture to make a loose consistency. Spoon into the prepared dish, scatter the thyme leaves over the top and sprinkle with the reserved Coolea or Parmesan.

Bake in the preheated oven for 12–15 minutes (or 9–11 minutes for the individual soufflés) or until the sides and top are nicely puffed up and golden – the centre should still be creamy. Garnish with thyme flowers. Serve immediately with a good green salad.

Serves 6

75g (3oz) butter, plus extra for greasing
300ml (½ pint) double cream
300ml (½ pint) milk
a few slices of carrot
1 small onion, quartered
4–5 black peppercorns
a sprig of thyme, a few flat-leaf parsley stalks and a little scrap of bay
40g (1½oz) plain flour
5 organic eggs, separated
110g (4oz) goat's cheese (we use Ardsallagh), crumbled
75g (3oz) Gruyère cheese, finely grated
50g (2oz) mature Coolea or Parmesan cheese, finely grated
good pinch of salt, cayenne, freshly ground black pepper and nutmeg
2 teaspoons fresh thyme leaves

To serve
lots of thyme flowers, if available
green salad

The Maze

Ever since I visited Hampton Court in the 1970s, I was intrigued by labyrinths and mazes and wondered how I could possibly justify planting a maze at Ballymaloe. 1991 was 'The Year of the Maze', so I had a flash of inspiration: I'd give Tim a present of a maze for his 50th birthday – a stroke of genius! As luck would have it, Peter Lamb, a scholarly friend of ours had designed a beautiful Celtic maze, inspired by an illustration from the *Book of Kells*, but didn't have a site so was delighted to share it if there was a possibility of the drawing becoming a reality. Friends who had planted a new maze at Dunbrody in Co. Wexford invited me along to see the site and explained that a maze must have a proper puzzle. A good drawing doesn't necessarily work, people can get hopelessly lost and might never be found again. They introduced me to Lesley Beck, a UK maze designer, who explained that a maze must have a main entrance and a short exit. She worked her magic on Peter's plan and instructed Will Kenneally, our builder, who is happy to tackle anything, on how to mark out the complicated pattern.

We chose a site where the old orchard had been and decided to edge the paths with timber. Kinoith gardens already had several handsome beech hedges so we choose yew, traditionally used in mazes, calculated the number (several thousand) and ordered them from Bill Montgomery in Northern Ireland. We brought electricity and water into the centre of the maze so we could have a fountain, which never materialised, but for years we had fun with a pedal which, when curious visitors pressed it, shot a jet of water 9m (30ft) into the air and drenched them. Initially the plants were only about 46cm (18in) tall. We had hoped they would romp away when they settled in but instead many looked sickly and eventually died. We replanted, but they too died. Everyone was baffled and various theories were put forward: residues of weed killer in the soil, compaction... we still don't know the reason, but I suspect that it was water-logging as that field had a particularly thin topsoil and heavy clay sub-soil. Eventually, in 2003, we decided to try beech and hornbeam as the latter just loves it in Shanagarry and now, 20 years later, we have a fantastic Celtic maze.

From time to time Tim and I would talk about creating a folly in the centre of the maze to tantalise and encourage people. The Petal Folly is the fantasy of architect and friend Jeremy Williams, made from fibreglass in a workshop in Dublin in 2011 and installed in the garden in 2012. We had many chats about the colour; Jeremy favoured wild fuchsia, purple and cherry red, which we thought would be wonderful when the leaves were green in summer, but we weren't so sure they would work with the rusty autumn colours. After much deliberation Jeremy suggested an Irish muralist called Michael Dillon and the result was perfect. The exterior, which is clearly visible over the maze, resembles an Indian tent while the interior is rich red and gold, embellished with exotic birds and flowers. On more than one occasion we've had to rescue people who have got hopelessly lost, including a batch of exuberant students on a moonlit night in mid-summer 2012. The occasional empty wine bottle tells tales of partying too!

Above: The Petal Folly, in the centre of the Celtic maze.

The Memory Arboretum

When news reached us in 1997 of the tragic death of one of our past students, Karen Harte (12-week course, January 1985), who drowned in an accident in the Caribbean, we were all deeply shocked and saddened. Tim and I decided to start a memory garden, close to the avenue, so we planted an apple tree in Karen's memory and have continued to add to it ever since.

We also planted an apple tree for Robert Lett, a copper beech for Thomas Fitzgerald, Lord Earl of Offaly, and a liquid ambar tree for Anna Fitzgerald, who was lost in the tsunami in Thailand in 2004. A crab apple was planted for Philippa Corbin, a sweet chestnut for Geoffrey Harrison and a Japanese walnut for Martin Maher. There are now seven trees with a plaque under each to commemorate the past student and a garden so that visitors can rest and reflect. There are other trees planted in the garden and two rosemary bushes in tubs – rosemary for remembrance. Parents and family of the students occasionally come to visit the memory arboretum and are very moved to see the tree planted in remembrance of their loved one.

Watercress, Sorrel and Wild Leek Broth

My brother Rory O'Connell, author of *Master It* and co-founder of the Ballymaloe Cookery School, introduced us to these light broths. We ring the changes throughout the year, depending on what delicate greens are in season.

Melt the butter in a large, heavy-bottomed saucepan and allow to foam. Add the potatoes, onions, leek and garlic. Coat in the butter and season with salt and pepper. Cover the pan with a butter wrapper or greaseproof paper and a tight-fitting lid. Cook over a very low heat to allow the vegetables to sweat gently until barely tender – approx. 10 minutes. Don't overcook; the diced potato must not collapse.

    Add the stock and bring to a simmer, stirring gently. Cook for 10 minutes; the broth should be barely bubbling. If it cooks too fast at this stage, the delicate flavour of the chicken stock will be lost. Do not replace the lid on the saucepan. Taste and correct the seasoning. (This is the soup base; if necessary, you can set it aside at this stage to finish later.)

    To finish the soup, bring the base back to a simmer. Add the wild garlic leaves, watercress and sorrel and allow them to wilt – this will only take a couple of minutes. Taste and correct the seasoning. Finally, sprinkle the wild garlic flowers over the top and serve immediately.

Serves 4–6

50g (2oz) butter
175g (6oz) potatoes, peeled and cut into neat 1cm (½in) dice
110g (4oz) onions, finely chopped
50g (2oz) wild leek (*Allium babingtonii*), thinly sliced
2 garlic cloves, peeled and finely chopped
1.2 litres (2 pints) chicken stock
150g (5oz) wild garlic leaves, finely chopped
40g (1½oz) watercress, finely chopped
50g (2oz) sorrel, finely chopped
sea salt and freshly ground black pepper

To serve
wild garlic flowers (from either *Allium ursinum* or *Allium triquetrum*, as illustrated opposite), if available

Cabbage, kale, chard and spring onions also work well in this soup if wild garlic and leek are not in season.

Boiled Leg of Mutton with Wild Garlic Sauce

It is very difficult to get hold of mutton nowadays unless you ask a farmer to rear it specially for you. George Gossip, a game teacher at the School, organised for a farmer he knew in Co. Galway to keep four sheep for us for over two years, when they become classified as mutton. They had a rich gamey flavour and we hope to have more again this year. Kay Harte occasionally serves corned mutton at her Farm Gate restaurant in the English Market in Cork city.

Trim the knuckle from the shanks and end. Remove the aitch bones as you would roast lamb. Put the leg of mutton into a deep saucepan. Cover with the cold water, add the salt and bring slowly to the boil. Simmer for 5 minutes and then skim thoroughly. Tuck the vegetables around the edge and add the thyme. Continue to simmer, covered, for 1½– 2 hours depending on the size – as a rough guide, allow 15 minutes per 450g (1lb) plus an extra 15 minutes. Once the meat is cooked, you should be able to pierce it easily with a skewer.

To make the Wild Garlic Sauce, pour the milk into a pan and bring to 'shivering' point. Melt the butter in a heavy-bottomed pan, stir in the flour and cook, stirring, for 1 minute. Remove the pan from the heat and whisk in the hot milk. Return to the heat and stir continuously with a wooden spoon until the sauce thickens. Simmer for 2–3 minutes to cook out the flour and season with salt and pepper. Finally, stir in the chopped capers and wild garlic. Taste and correct the seasoning.

To serve, transfer the lamb to a hot serving dish and surround it with the vegetables. Serve the Wild Garlic sauce separately, sprinkled with some wild garlic flowers if you have some.

Variation – Corned Mutton with Caper and Wild Garlic Sauce
Corned mutton cooked in the same way is, if anything, even more delicious. Brine the leg of lamb for 2–3 days, depending on your taste. Cook in unsalted water.

Serves approx. 8–10

1 leg of lamb, weighing approx. 3kg (6lb 8oz)
4.8 litres (8 pints) water
1 tablespoon salt
4 carrots, peeled and halved (or quartered if large)
2 white turnips, peeled and halved or quartered
3–4 celery stalks, cut into 2–3 pieces
a sprig of thyme

For the Wild Garlic Sauce
600ml (1 pint) whole milk
25g (1oz) butter
1 tablespoon plain white flour
2 tablespoons chopped capers
3 tablespoons freshly chopped wild garlic
salt and freshly ground black pepper

To serve
wild garlic flowers (optional)

Honey Mousse with Lavender Jelly

J.R. Ryall, the pastry chef at Ballymaloe House, loves to make this dessert in June using the lavender from the walled garden at Ballymaloe, just before the flowers open. Using only the best quality local honey will make this feather-light mousse truly unforgettable.

Serves 6

350ml (12fl oz) whipping cream
1 teaspoon gelatine
1½ tablespoons cold water
75g (3oz) best-quality local honey
1 tablespoon Grand Marnier, to taste
1 organic egg

For the Lavender Jelly
110g (4oz) granulated sugar
225ml (8fl oz) water
12 fresh lavender heads
1½ teaspoons gelatine
2½ tablespoons cold water

First make the honey mousse. Whip the cream to soft peaks and set aside in the fridge. Sprinkle the gelatine over the cold water in a small heatproof bowl and allow to 'sponge'. Once fully rehydrated, melt the gelatine by placing the bowl over a saucepan of hot but not boiling water. Add the honey and Grand Marnier and stir until the mixture is an even consistency. Set aside to return to room temperature.

Next, using an electric mixer, whisk the egg to a pale mousse, then gently fold into the whipped cream. Fold the cream mixture into the honey and gelatine in three stages. Pour the mousse into a 1.2 litre (2 pint) serving dish and chill in the fridge until set.

To make the Lavender Jelly, put the sugar and 225ml (8fl oz) water in a heavy-bottomed saucepan and bring slowly to the boil. Once the syrup has boiled, remove the saucepan from the heat and drop in six lavender heads. Set aside to cool to room temperature.

Meanwhile, sprinkle the gelatine over the 2½ tablespoons of cold water in a small heatproof bowl and allow to 'sponge'. Once fully rehydrated, melt the gelatine by placing the bowl over hot but not boiling water.

Strain the cooled syrup through a sieve, add to the melted gelatine and mix well. Arrange six lavender heads on top of the set honey mousse and carefully spoon over enough liquid jelly to cover the lavender. Chill until the jelly is set – approx. 1 hour – then serve.

The Wood-burning Oven

Above: Philip Dennhardt making Saturday Pizzas in the Garden Café at Ballymaloe.
Right: Pizzas cooking in the wood-burning oven.

My first encounter with a wood-burning oven was in Italy in the 1980s and later at Alice Waters' Chez Panisse restaurant in Berkeley, California, where the most irresistible food was emerging from it. I had loved the flavour of the food since tasting Wolfgang Puck's bubbly thin crust pizza in Los Angeles a few years previously and so when we opened the Garden Café at the School in the summer of 1998, I decided I wanted a wood-fired oven of my own. So I went to California on a research trip.

My journey took me to Mendocino County where, behind the community centre in a small town called Elk, we found a clay adobe oven large enough to roast a pig. I soon discovered that the man behind many of the great ovens that I saw was an oven-builder from New Zealand, called Alan Scott who had since returned home to his native country. When I arrived at Chez Panisse, Alice told me all about the vagaries of their wood-burning oven as there had been some teething problems, and suggested I forget about trying to have one built, romantic as that was; better to go to the Italians, who have been making wood-burning ovens for centuries, and buy a kit. She found me the name of a brilliantly efficient Italian company called Refrattari Reggello and, much to my amazement, I had the oven within six weeks. The company gave brilliant instructions for installation in English and I also took my builder over to see the River Café's oven in Hammersmith to observe it in operation. Ruth Rogers and the late Rose Gray have said it is instrumental in their cooking and they use it every day – it was therefore a good place to visit to see how this type of oven could work.

Cooking in a wood-burning oven is quite a different skill to using a standard oven. There's no temperature gauge for a start so one needs to be much more observant and learn to judge the heat of the oven by the intensity of the fire and the colour of the ash. The oven needs to be heated gradually at first as, if the oven is cold, a sudden large fire can crack the base and so permanently damage the oven. The management of the timber is a whole skill in itself, as is knowing which timbers to use, as some generate much more heat than others. It is important not to use any wood that might

have traces of preservatives or residues of paint – these can give off toxic fumes, which of course taint the food. Dry timber gives off more heat than damp timber, which smoulders and so is inefficient. If the oven is not hot enough, pizzas take longer to cook and won't have the crisp base and bubbly edges that we all love so much.

In 1998 we found a young chef, Stevie O'Brien Gleeson, who had been working with a wood oven in Tosca, a pizzeria in Suffolk Street in Dublin. Stevie spent the summer season with us in the Garden Café and taught us how to work with fire. People came from far and wide for the pizza – the café was open seven days a week and the students loved it too. That year, Stevie concentrated on pizza, but the following year my son Isaac became more adventurous – he made a delicious roast tomato soup and we also used the oven to roast fish, meat and vegetables.

In May 2008, ten years after its installation, our son-in-law, Philip Dennhardt, decided to do a 'pop-up' pizzeria for just four hours from 12.30–4p.m. every Saturday in the Garden Café (the school is usually closed on a Saturday so the dining room is open to the public). The pizaa toppings reflect the ingredients in season on the farm and in the gardens and make use of local farmhouse cheeses and occasionally shrimps, squid or fresh crab from the nearby fishing village of Ballycotton. There is always a Pizza Margherita, a Pepperoni and a Marinara and just two others, a vegetarian and a non-vegetarian option. It has proved so popular that Saturday Pizzas are now institution – there's cool music and a fun atmosphere plus the 12-week students get the opportunity to learn how it all works on a rota basis and to cook with fire – the half-day pizza, calzone, panzarotti, piadina and sfinciuni demonstration is an integral part of the course.

Wood-burning ovens are now quite widespread – popular in many restaurants and not just pizzerias. You'll often see mobile ones at farmers' markets and festivals and many people build small versions in their garden. Philip Dennhardt gives a Pizza Workshop using the wood-burning oven at the Ballymaloe Cookery School several times a year and Simon Mould, who now runs the 'Volcano Pizza' stand at Midleton Farmers' Market, is an old student of his. The regulators, who were wary of this trend at the outset, presumably regarding concerns about health and safety, have become more accepting of it and realise that cooking in wood-burning ovens is a time-honoured tradition, which adds immeasurably to the flavour of the food.

Pizza with Roast Peppers, Olives and Gremolata

At Saturday Pizzas the toppings change every week depending on the season. We love to make this one with home-grown peppers in summer but the misshapen Spanish and Italian ones are also fleshy and flavourful. We use Kalamata, Niçoise or green Picholine olives.

First make the dough. Put the water into the bowl of a food processor. Add the mother to the water, if using. Crumble the yeast into the flour and add to the water along with the salt. Mix for 5 minutes at a medium speed. Pinch the dough between your thumb and index finger – it should feel stretchy already. Leave the dough to rest for 5 minutes, then mix for a further 20 minutes. The dough should be smooth and stick to the side of the mixing bowl. (If you don't have a dough hook on your food processor, you can knead it by hand.)

Transfer the dough to an airtight container, which is four times bigger than the size of the dough, to allow for expansion. Transfer the container to the fridge for at least 6 hours, preferably overnight.

Remove the dough from the fridge and sprinkle a work surface with a little flour. Transfer the dough onto the work surface, then weigh and divide into eight 150g (5oz) pieces using a small knife. Knead the dough into round balls roughly the size of tennis balls. Put the dough balls onto a tray, sprinkle with flour and transfer to the fridge to rest for 6 hours. Remove the dough from the fridge 1 hour before you cook the pizza.

Preheat the oven 200°C/400°F/gas 6. To make the tomato sauce, arrange the tomatoes, cut-side up, on a roasting tray in a single layer. Scatter over the garlic cloves and season with salt, pepper and sugar. Drizzle the balsamic vinegar and olive oil over the tomatoes. Roast in the preheated oven for 15–20 minutes until the tomatoes are completely soft and the garlic is squishy.

Meanwhile, put the peppers for the pizza on a separate baking tray, drizzle them with olive oil and roast in the oven for 30–35 minutes until starting to blacken. Remove from the oven, peel, deseed and cut into strips. Set aside.

Grate the mozzarella into a small bowl and drizzle with a little extra virgin olive oil. Set aside.

To finish the tomato sauce, remove the tomatoes and garlic from the oven and push them through a sieve, discarding all the skins and seeds. Taste and correct the seasoning.

Increase the oven temperature to 240°C/475°F/gas 9. Roll out the pizza dough into a 25cm (10in) circle. Sprinkle a little semolina all over the surface of a pizza paddle and put the pizza base on top.

Spread 4 tablespoons of the tomato sauce over the base of the pizza

Makes 1

150g (5oz) pizza dough
½ red pepper
½ yellow pepper
extra virgin olive oil, for drizzling
110g (4oz) mozzarella
semolina, for dusting
75g (3oz) black olives (you can remove the stones if you prefer)
sea salt and freshly ground black pepper

For the pizza dough (Makes 8 x 150g (5oz) dough)
550ml (19fl oz) cold tap water
50g (2oz) mother – leftover dough from the previous batch (optional)
20g (¾oz) fresh yeast
900g (2lb) strong Italian flour, such as Tipo 00 or strong baker's flour, plus extra for dusting
20g (¾oz) dairy salt

For Isaac's Roasted Tomato Pizza Sauce
450g (1lb) very ripe tomatoes, halved
6 garlic cloves, unpeeled
1 tablespoon balsamic vinegar
2 tablespoons olive oil
sugar

For the Gremolata
2½ tablespoons freshly chopped flat-leaf parsley
1 teaspoon grated or finely chopped lemon zest
2 garlic cloves, peeled and finely chopped

(any leftover sauce can be stored in a sealed container in the fridge). Arrange the roast pepper slices and olives over the tomato sauce. Season with a little sea salt and some freshly ground black pepper. Sprinkle the mozzarella over the top of the pizza.

Bake in a wood-burning oven or a fully preheated oven for 10–12 minutes or until the pizza base is crisp and the top is bubbly and golden.

Meanwhile, make the Gremolata by combining all of the ingredients in a bowl. To serve, sprinkle the gremolata over the top of the pizza.

Broad Bean, Blue Cheese, Parsley and Lemon Pizza

When the first of the broad beans and fennel are in season, Philip Dennhardt makes this pizza. Crozier Blue is a gentle blue cheese made by Henry Clifton Brown in County Tipperary from his herd of milking sheep. This fennel sauce is also delicious as a base for a seaweed pizza, or any pizza with fresh greens, like kale, spinach or broccoli. It also freezes perfectly so make the full amount and use as required.

First make the pizza dough according to the instructions on page 168.

Meanwhile, make the fennel sauce. Heat the oil in a pan, add the onions and garlic and sweat until soft but not coloured. Add the fennel slices and water, season with salt and pepper, and simmer for approx. 25 minutes or until soft. Blend until smooth. Taste and correct the seasoning, if necessary.

Preheat the oven to 240°C/475°F/gas 9. Blanch the broad beans in boiling water for 2 minutes. Drain, refresh under cold running water and set aside.

Roll out the pizza dough to form a 25cm (10in) circle. Sprinkle a little semolina all over the surface of a pizza paddle and put the pizza base on top. Drizzle the olive oil over the base of the pizza and sprinkle with a pinch of sea salt. Spread approx. 150ml (¼ pint) of the fennel sauce over the pizza base (any leftover sauce can be frozen until required). Scatter the broad beans and blue cheese on top and sprinkle with the mozzarella.

Bake in a wood-burning oven or a fully preheated oven for 10–12 minutes, or until the base is crisp and the top is bubbly and golden. Sprinkle the chopped parsley over the pizza and serve immediately, accompanied with the lemon wedges.

Makes 1

150g (5oz) pizza dough
20 broad beans
1 teaspoon extra virgin olive oil
pinch of Maldon sea salt
8 cubes of blue cheese, approx. 1cm (½in)
a large handful of grated mozzarella

For the pizza dough (Makes 8 x 150g (5oz) dough)
550ml (19fl oz) cold tap water
50g (2oz) mother – leftover dough from the previous batch (optional)
20g (¾oz) fresh yeast
900g (2lb) strong Italian flour, such as Tipo 00 or strong baker's flour, plus extra for dusting
20g (¾oz) dairy salt

For the fennel sauce
1 tablespoon extra virgin olive oil
2 onions, thinly sliced
3 garlic cloves, peeled and crushed
5 bulbs of fennel, thinly sliced
600ml (1 pint) water
sea salt and freshly ground black pepper

To serve
1 teaspoon finely chopped fresh flat-leaf parsley
lemon wedges

Ballymaloe White Sourdough Bread

Once you have established or acquired a starter, making sourdough bread is a three-day process, and one which, once you get started, will soon become a routine part of your day. Every loaf will be slightly different depending on the activity of the wild yeast starter.

This is the only recipe in the book without imperial measurements because bakers operate using the metric system – you'll find it very convenient too.

STAGE 1 Ballymaloe Sourdough Starter – Levain
Some starter recipes suggest mixing the full amount of flour with water and leaving it for six days. However, we have found that we get a much more active starter when we feed it (i.e. add more water and flour) every day. You will need to allow at least six days for your sourdough starter to fully develop; in fact sometimes, when your starter is new, it is recommended to throw out approx. 300g and feed it again with 150g of water and 150g of strong baker's flour, and leave it for another 24 hours. This helps to make a stronger active yeast, however if you don't want to waste your starter, go ahead and make some loaves. They will be rather flat in the beginning, but do persevere.

You will need:
2-litre airtight jar, such as a Kilner jar
300g pure spring water
300g strong white flour (preferably organic)

Day 1: Choose a large airtight jar that will hold at least 2 litres – a Kilner jar is fine. Put 50g of barely tepid (not hot) pure spring water and 50g of strong white flour into the jar. Mix well, close the jar and set aside at room temperature for 24 hours.
Day 2: You should begin to see some bubbles at this stage. Add 50g of water and 50g of flour. Mix well, close the jar and set aside for a further 24 hours at room temperature.
Day 3: Add 50g of water and 50g of flour. Mix well, close the jar and set aside for a further 24 hours at room temperature.
Day 4: Add 50g of water and 50g of flour. Mix well, close the jar and set aside for a further 24 hours at room temperature.
Day 5: Add 50g of water and 50g of flour. Mix well, close the jar and set aside for a further 24 hours at room temperature.
Day 6: Add 50g of water and 50g of flour. Mix well, close the jar and set aside for a further 24 hours at room temperature.

Your sourdough starter is now ready for use. You should have at least 600g of lively, bubbly starter, enough to make the following sourdough recipe.

Note: It's good to use your starter immediately. However, it can be stored in an airtight jar in the fridge. (It will need to be fed to reactivate it before use.) The more you use your starter the stronger it will get – in fact, the first few loaves may be disappointing, but do persevere; the thrill of taking a beautiful loaf of sourdough out of the oven is worth the effort.

Once you've established the sourdough starter, making a loaf of sourdough bread from start to finish will take anywhere from 24 to 36 hours, depending on how lively the starter is.

Starter Tips
• Your starter should smell distinctly beery, slightly yeasty and fermented, and it should be really bubbly. It may develop a layer of grey liquid on top, but that's fine – just give it a stir.
• Your starter must not be allowed to get too warm.
• Starters grow best at comfortable room temperature.

STAGE 2 – Making the Sponge

You will need:
230g sourdough starter (see left)
240g barely tepid water
240g strong white flour (preferably organic)

Day 1: Put 230g of sourdough starter into a bowl. Add 120g of barely tepid water and 120g of strong white flour. Beat well, cover with clingfilm and set aside at room temperature overnight.
Day 2: Next morning, add 120g of barely tepid water and 120g of strong white flour. Beat well, cover with clingfilm and set aside at room temperature for 6–7 hours.
By now the 'sponge' should be active and bubbling. To check it is ready, carry out the Float Test: fill a measuring jug with cold water, add 1 teaspoon of starter and see if it floats. If it sinks, set it aside to ferment for a little longer.

STAGE 3 – Making the Bread

You will need
340g 'sponge' (see left)
200g pure water at blood heat
20g rye flour
300g strong white flour (preferably organic), plus extra for dusting
10g salt (2 per cent)

You will need a 22cm bread basket (Banneton), lined with
 a well-floured napkin

Put 340g of the 'sponge' into the bowl of a food mixer and put the
remainder back into the starter jar – you have now fed your starter,
ready for the next loaf of sourdough. Add the water to the 'sponge'.
Beat well with a wooden spoon. Add the rye flour, white flour and
the salt.

 Transfer the bowl to the mixer. Insert the dough hook and mix for
a few minutes until the dough comes together. Then rest the dough
for 25–40 minutes – this will make it easier to knead.

 The dough will seem far too wet, but continue to mix it with the
dough hook until the texture of the dough is smooth and it comes
away from the sides of the bowl – approx. 8 minutes. Increase the
speed for a further 5–8 minutes or until you can lift the dough hook
clean out of the bowl. If the dough hook cuts through the dough, put
it back in and mix for a little longer, approx. 3–4 minutes.

 Remove the dough from the mixer and transfer to a clean work
surface (no flour needed). Allow the dough to rest for 1 hour, folding
it like a square parcel (to trap air) every 20 minutes. At first you will
notice the dough spreading, but as you fold it, it will slowly start to
rise, holding its shape.

 It is important to rest the dough after each folding. After the last
folding, dust the work surface with flour. Shape the dough into a
round ball and put it in the floured and lined bread basket. Slide the
filled basket into a large plastic bag and refrigerate overnight.

 The following morning, remove the basket from the fridge and
take it out of the plastic bag. Set aside and allow to rest at room
temperature for 1–2 hours or until doubled in size.

 Preheat the oven to 240°C/475°F/gas 9 and dust a baking tray
with flour.

 Turn the bread out gently onto the floured baking tray and slash
the top with a sharp knife or razor blade. Slide the tray into the oven,
spray the inside of the oven with a water mister – the moisture will
help develop a nice crust – and close the oven door. Mist the bread
at regular intervals and bake for 35–40 minutes or until the bread is
crusty and it sounds hollow when tapped underneath.

 Remove from the oven and set aside to cool on a wire rack.

Going Organic

At Ballymaloe House and the Cookery School, we have always been passionate about sourcing beautiful fresh produce; it's the essence of what we do and we've always understood that unless we put substantial effort into finding the freshest seasonal produce from artisan producers, local farmers and fishermen, we simply can't get the 'wow factor'. Experience has taught me that, the simpler the food, the more vital it becomes to have pristine fresh ingredients, pure and natural, and this is one of the most important things I emphasise to students. The reality is that, unless you start off with beautiful raw ingredients, you need to be a wizard to transform them into something truly delicious and often, that's where all the cheffy bells and whistles, fluffs and foams are needed to compensate for the fact that the flavour isn't there in the first place.

When we opened the School in 1983, the surrounding 100-acre farm was not organic. In the 1970s, the land was farmed conventionally by my brother-in-law, Rory Allen, in a rotation of potatoes, sugar beet and barley. However, as the years passed, I became aware of a growing body of research that warned of the dangers of pesticide and herbicide residues in our food and I grew increasingly uneasy.

One food crisis followed after another: in 1987 the story of BSE (Bovine spongiform encephalopathy) broke about a mysterious and incurable brain disease killing dairy cows that had taken hold in Britain the previous year. Worse still, the meat had entered the food chain and crossed over to humans, and so Variant Creutzfeldt-Jakob disease (vCJD) became an ugly reality. Furthermore, this was just a mere taste of the macabre revelations to come. In 2001 there was the outbreak of Foot and Mouth Disease, both in UK and Ireland, with the consequent slaughtering of huge numbers of cattle. In December 2008, there was the Dioxin scandal when it was found that some of the national pork production was contaminated with dioxins, highly toxic compounds that are the by-product of various industrial processes. On and on it goes, with the most recent being the horsemeat scandal, when horsemeat of doubtful origins was found in beef burgers in many countries across Europe.

Above: Tim inspecting the flat pod French bean crop growing in the greenhouse. We've been growing these for several years and, in general, find them far superior to the round variety.
Right: A fine crop of beautiful tomatoes grown on seaweed- and compost-fed soil.

Above: A wheelbarrow full of sweet Genovese basil destined for the compost heap. We pick off the flowers to encourage the plants to sprout and become bushy rather than going to seed.
Right: A crop of peas growing in the greenhouse. We use them at every stage – the pea shoots, flowers and tendrils, or wizard's whiskers, the mange tout pods and eventually the peas themselves. Tim is vigilant that we don't pick off too many pea flowers as this can endanger the eventual pea crop, which after all, is the object of the exercise!
Far right: An apple ripening on one of our many apple trees.

All these examples are the consequence of pushing animals and plants beyond their natural limit to produce the maximum amount of food at minimum cost in order to fulfil our endless quest for cheap food.

In the early 1980s, a brilliant grower called Jill Gairdner worked with us on the farm and in the greenhouses. She told us about an inspirational organic farmer called Rod Alston in Co. Leitrim, who had gradually turned a patch of wet bog land into fertile soil, which produced a wide variety of organic vegetables, herbs, salad leaves and fruit. When I was filming *Simply Delicious Versatile Vegetables*, I took a television crew there and was mightily impressed by what had been achieved. In 1994, Rod contacted me about his vision to establish an organic centre and research station in Ireland and asked if I would be patron. I agreed and The Organic Centre was established in 1995 on 19 acres of land near Rossinver and has, despite the challenges, gradually established itself and offers a wide range of excellent courses on organic horticulture, green building, seed sowing, planting potatoes, growing in polytunnels and even working with horses. Rod detached himself from the centre in 2000, but he was one of the founding fathers of the organic food movement in Ireland and my involvement in the centre increased my interest in organic produce.

My own 'eureka moment' came one day in 1996, in the middle of a cookery class when I was telling the students yet again about the importance of beautiful, nourishing produce. Out of the corner of my eye, I saw a tractor with a boom spraying goodness knows what onto the field behind the Cookery School. I couldn't bear it; I felt like a total a hypocrite and so resolved at that moment to do whatever it took to go organic. That evening I said to Tim that I knew it was a 'big ask' but we had to farm the land ourselves again. It was a huge request, as previously we had nearly lost the roof over our heads through farming, and Tim was rightly scared that the farm would be a big black hole to absorb the Cookery School's hard-earned profits. However, we struck a deal. I agreed to his condition, that the farm had to at least break even, and he agreed to mine, that I would join the Rural Environmental Protection Scheme (REPS), which gave an increased payment to organic farms during the transition period. A reasonable request you might think, but we have never been fans of the grant system, preferring instead to borrow minimally, work like mad and pay it back. However, Tim agreed that this might tide us over the conversion period.

We applied to the Organic Trust, they inspected the farm and explained the criteria. After we registered we entered a two-year

conversion period, during which the use of any chemicals or sprays was forbidden, but after this time we were awarded full Organic Trust certification. It was a steep learning curve. At that time, the perception of organic farming was far from positive. People imagined weed-infested fields, cosmetically challenged produce, low yields and sick animals that couldn't be treated with antibiotics. Our hugely skilled farm staff, none of whom had any training in organic growing, were quite resistant to the idea at first, convinced I would still want beautiful produce. However, with the acre of greenhouses that we have at Ballymaloe (a relic of our commercial horticulture enterprise), which we use to grow as many as 50 crops a year, albeit in small quantities, we realised that no one in the British Isles was attempting to grow this kind of variety organically and quickly our farm and garden team rose to the challenge.

Good advice was very hard to come by and we were told it would take 20 years to rebuild the fertility of the land. However, fortunately, I had heard about the Soil Association; a membership charity based in the UK, which campaigns for healthy, humane and sustainable food and farming use. We joined in 1998 and attended our first Soil Association conference in Circencester in 1999, which proved another turning point. The Soil Association is a brilliant networking organisation with a palpable generosity of spirit. We heard some truly brilliant and visionary speakers: Patrick Holden, Helen Browning, Professor Jules Pretty, Professor Nic Lampkin, Jonathon Porritt and Richard Young, met so many kindred spirits and received generous advice and support. The conference was totally inspirational and we all returned on a high.

In 2000 we began to see the fruits of our labours when the quality of the crops and the health of the animals stunned all the intial sceptics. The local vet once quipped that 'he would be broke

if he was depending on us' because he was called so seldom. It was such a joy to have our own organic produce, not only for the family and Ballymaloe House, but also for the students who now come from all over the world to participate in a truly organic farm to fork experience.

The organic farm has continued to develop over the years. We have a few pigs – traditional breeds, including Saddlebacks, Red Duroc and Gloucester Old Spot. We also have three, soon to be five, Jersey cows, which we milk every day and, including these, we currently have 20 beef animals – cows and their offspring. A growing body of research reinforces the argument about the benefits of raw milk from a small organic, grass-fed herd and we offer this to the students, many of whom are tasting it for the first time. (It goes without saying that the herd must be healthy and disease-free.)

In 2007, we converted the farm building below the school into a milking parlour and installed the smallest milking system in Ireland. When *Ear to the Ground* came to film, the presenter Daragh McCullough was greatly amused by this and said that it was the only one in Ireland that had a cluster for every cow. In our system, the cows are milked once a day, in the morning. The calf stays with the cow during the day, but we separate them at night, so there's lots of milk for the morning's milking. This system works really well and there's ample milk for us and the calf.

When we increased our herd from two to three Jersey cows, we occasionally had surplus milk. We couldn't bear to waste a drop so Tim and Eileen O'Donovan (our gardener and herself a farmer's daughter), experimented with making yogurt using only live yogurt as a starter and our own rich Jersey milk. The resulting yogurt is utterly beautiful, thick and unctuous, with a layer of Jersey cream on top – no milk powder or aspartamane, no flavouring or colouring – just beautiful milk and live culture. It's a revelation to the students who love to make it, and many past students have now gone on to make their own homemade yogurt and turn it into a small business.

In 2009, Tim bought a 50-litre stainless steel vat from a German company called Asta and started to experiment with cheesemaking; he quickly became completely fascinated. The students were also intrigued and now every batch of 12-week students has the option to learn how to milk a cow, separate the organic milk from the cream and learn how to make many dairy products, including cheese. As each student's cheese matures, they look after them lovingly and as they leave they pack them into their suitcases to share with their family and friends all over the world.

Left (above): We grow a couple of varieties of grapes in the greenhouses: Muscat d'Alexandrie and Black Hamburg. We have also been trialling some varieties of wine grapes for Colm McCan, consultant sommelier at Ballymaloe House, but have so far the results have not been promising and it doesn't look like we are going to be producing Grand Cru wines any time soon.

Left (below): A courgette blossom ready for stuffing or to add to a salad or fritters.

Above (left): Eileen O'Donovan, a woman of many talents – gardener extraordinaire, who also milks the cows and makes butter, cheese and yogurt from their rich milk.

Above (right): Susan Turner, consultant Head Gardener at the School. She also teaches organic gardening to the 12-week students who have a particular interest in the subject, as well as a whole series of day courses on gardening, compost-making, seed-saving and garden design for the general public.

The pigs and cows are also part of the self-guided Educational Farm walk, which my son Toby and his wife Penny initiated in 2009, due to popular demand. The trail takes visitors through the farm and gardens and into the greenhouses and provides interesting information about all their diverse features and activities – the various animals, plant varieties, breeds of poultry, composting, milking parlour, dairy, photovoltaic system and student vegetable beds. We also sometimes lead guided tours of the farm and garden for special interest and team-building groups.

Attitudes to organic food are changing, albeit slowly, particularly during these challenging economic times. Interestingly 80 per cent of sales of baby food in the UK are organic and several of the biggest baby food manufacturers are reported to be considering

discontinuation of conventional baby food. The hope is that this bulge of concern about how food is produced will continue to gather momentum through the generations. All supermarkets now sell a range, sometimes limited, of organic produce, but local farmers' markets sell an extensive range of local and imported organic produce, which was unheard of 15 years ago.

According to Patrick Holden, formerly of the Soil Association and now of the Sustainable Food Trust, the Departments of Health and Agriculture and the farming organisations are ignoring at their peril the detrimental consequences of intensively-produced food – a public health time bomb which needs to be addressed. Even though I didn't get politically involved in the organic movement in Ireland, preferring to lead by example, 14 years later the range of organic produce we grow is arguably the most diverse in the country, in excess of 80 crops. We employ 50–56 people on our 100-acre organic farm throughout the year, depending on the season, which may just be a record in the 'developed world'!

Since 2001, two French horticultural colleges have been sending interns to work in the organic gardens and greenhouses. We were amazed when their lecturers told us that they don't know of anywhere in the whole of Europe where there is such bio-diversity and a wide range of experience for their students, with the extra bonus of good food. Even though the greenhouses are not heated, we grow year round and have planted peaches, nectarines, apricots, figs, kiwis, grapes, loquats and citrus fruit around the perimeter and over the central path. This year's big excitement is our pomegranate tree, which has produced fruit for the very first time. Students and visitors to the garden are intrigued to see these fruits flourishing happily in Shanagarry.

Since about 2008 we have put a farm stand outside the Ballymaloe Cookery School Shop, so local people and visitors can buy fresh organic produce from the farm and gardens, and pick up free recipes and cooking suggestions. We also sell our handmade organic Jersey butter, yogurt and raw milk. The shop, managed by Toby and Penny, also sells a range of craft, kitchen and household items, as well as jam and preserves.

Above (top): My sister Elizabeth O'Connell, who worked in the gardens for many years.
Above (bottom): Haulie Walsh, our farm manager, who has been working with us since his teens.
Right: A crop of peppers flourishing in the greenhouse.

Patrick Holden

❝ It would be hard to overstate the significance of the contribution that Darina Allen and her extended family at the Ballymaloe Cookery School have made towards the development of a new food culture fit for the 21st century.

In my book, Darina is nothing short of an Irish national treasure. Over the last 30 years she and her husband Tim have created at Ballymaloe what I believe should be seen as one of the templates upon which our future food systems are designed. Ballymaloe is a truly inspirational example of a project that combines training and education in culinary skills, local production and sourcing and the integration of the cultural and social dimension, and it is upon this fusion that I believe the long-term success of all truly sustainable food production systems will depend.

I first met Darina around 20 years ago, in the late 1990s, at a time when the Soil Association ran an annual conference on sustainable and organic food production at the Royal College of Agriculture, Cirencester. It was typical of Darina, who was already a well-known food celebrity in Irish circles, with her own hugely

popular television show, that she came year after year as a delegate and participant, thus greatly contributing to the extraordinary conviviality and energy that characterised the Cirencester conferences at that time.

After capitulating to her irresistible offer of a visit to Ballymaloe, I was immediately intoxicated and inspired by the atmosphere of the Cookery School, the openness and generosity of Darina and Tim and the unique and unforgettable Irish hospitality, which has become a hallmark of all the ventures of the Allen family and the Ballymaloe community.

As Darina showed us around the Cookery School, I could only marvel at the story of its genesis, as she related how, when she and Tim took on the 100-acre family farm, situated close to the already famous Ballymaloe House hotel, they not only had the vision to imagine the piggery converted into a cookery school, but also the courage to press ahead and convert the building, despite the polite refusal of the local bank manager to give them a loan!

Since those early beginnings, they have developed the Cookery

School to the point where it now has an international reputation and is widely regarded as the best institution of its kind in the world. It is a remarkable testament to Darina's extraordinary qualities – her tenacity, warmth and enthusiasm, but above all her talent for communicating what she has learned and understood to others.

I can only deeply admire Darina's lifelong dedication to what could perhaps be described as the fusion of science, art and alchemy, required for the successful preparation and transformation of high-quality ingredients into delicious, nourishing food, eaten in the company of friends and loved ones. For me, this must surely be the ultimate physical and cultural expression of quality of life in all civilised societies.

I've always known that high-quality raw ingredients grown sustainably should form an essential element of food culture, but without people like Darina, the sustainable food movement always risked failing to break into the mainstream and remaining confined to a ghetto of well-meaning but worthy practitioners.

By way of a 'case study', my daughter Alice was lucky enough to have more than a taste of the Ballymaloe experience after Darina, at virtually no notice, generously allowed her to join one of her legendary 12-week courses. The experience was to prove a turning point in Alice's career development, not only providing her with the foundation of culinary skills, which have been of inestimable value to her ever since, but of equal significance, through some sort of osmosis, she returned intoxicated with the spirit of Irish magic that pervades Ballymaloe. This has shaped not only her subsequent thinking, but also her career pathway as a grower and champion of the emergent food culture. This has been especially gratifying for me, since it is becoming clear that her generation is now taking over the baton from their ageing parents!

One of the key reasons that this has happened is because in addition to being a cookery school, Ballymaloe has also become a centre for culture and the arts, a magnet for young people who would otherwise have probably migrated to Dublin or equivalent cities, but for whom the combination of the atmosphere and social attractions of a community built on sustainable food foundations with added career opportunities in education and culture, in the end proves to be a more a seductive option.

The entire Ballymaloe project has become one of the beacons of inspiration, which will hopefully inform the evolution of a new 21st-century food culture, and should be regarded as a place of pilgrimage for all those who decide to travel along this path. ”

Left and Above: Beautiful organic produce from the farm and greenhouses at Ballymaloe.

Garden Peas with Fresh Mint

~~~

We eat most of our pea crop raw and fresh off the plant. Durng the pea season, we serve them to our guests in the drawing room at Ballymaloe House so they can nibble the freshly picked peas directly from the pods, either with their drinks or as a first course.

Serves 8
150ml (5fl oz) water
1 teaspoon salt
1 teaspoon sugar
a sprig of mint
450g (1lb) garden peas, freshly shelled
approx. 25g (1oz) salted butter
1–2 teaspoons freshly chopped mint

Bring the water to the boil in a medium saucepan. Add the salt, sugar, mint and peas and bring back to the boil over a high heat, simmering until the peas are cooked, approx. 4–5 minutes. Strain, reserving the water for soup or gravy.

To serve, tip the peas into a serving bowl, add a knob of butter and sprinkle over some freshly chopped mint and a little extra seasoning if necessary. Serve immediately.

Variation
Frozen peas can be extraordinarily good; the cheaper brands tend to lack flavour so buy the best you can afford. A mixture of fresh peas and broad beans, tossed in a little good butter and some freshly chopped mint, is also splendid.

Peas in the Pod

freshly picked peas

Pick the peas and pop them into a deep bowl for each person. Serve as a first course – everyone will love them, both the peas and the experience.

Sweetcorn with Butter and Sea Salt

~~~

Unless you actually grow your own, or are fortunate to have a close neighbour who grows sweetcorn, you'll never be able to taste it at its most exquisite. For perfection it should be cooked within minutes of being picked.

Serves 4
4 ears of sweetcorn, ideally just picked
75–110g (3–4oz) salted butter
sea salt

Bring a large saucepan of water to a fast rolling boil and add lots of salt (3 teaspoons of salt for every 1.2 litres (2 pints) of water). Peel the husks and silks off the sweetcorn and trim the ends. Put the sweetcorn into the boiling water, bring back to the boil and cook for 3 minutes, then drain. Serve immediately with butter and sea salt.

Beetroot Purée with Toasted Cumin Seeds and Buffalo Curd on Poppadoms

A delicious combination inspired by a canapé I tasted at The Dutch House in Galle, Sri Lanka, made by Eloise Schwerdt.

Trim the beets, leaving the whole root and 5cm (2in) of leaf stalks on top. Hold them under a running tap and wash off the mud with the palms of your hands so that you don't damage the skin (otherwise the beetroot will bleed during cooking). Put in a saucepan, cover with cold water and add a little salt and sugar. Cover and bring to the boil, then simmer for 1–2 hours depending on the size of beetroot. You can tell beetroot are cooked if they dent when pressed with a finger. If in doubt, test with a skewer or the tip of a knife.

Drain, peel off the skins and chop coarsely. Put the beetroot flesh into a blender with half of the buffalo curd (or goat's cheese) and a drizzle of olive oil. Blitz to a smooth purée and season to taste with salt, pepper and a drop of balsamic vinegar (if using). Taste and add a squeeze of lime juice if necessary.

Preheat the sunflower oil to 180°C (350°F) in a deep-fat fryer or use a shallow pan with at least 2.5cm (1in) of oil. Cut each poppadom into eight triangles and deep-fry in the hot oil until crisp.

To serve, put a blob of beetroot purée on each poppadom triangle, crumble over a little of the remaining buffalo curd (or goat's cheese) and top with a little pinch of toasted cumin seeds and a fresh coriander leaf.

Makes 30–32

225g (8oz) beetroot
150g (5oz) Buffalo curd or soft goat's cheese
extra virgin olive oil
balsamic vinegar (optional)
1 lime (optional)
sunflower oil, for deep-frying
4 poppadoms
sea salt and freshly ground black pepper

To serve
1 tablespoon toasted cumin seeds, lightly crushed
fresh coriander leaves

Asparagus with Romesco and Crème Fraîche

The asparagus season was in full swing during the Ballymaloe Literary Festival of Food and Wine in May 2013, so Skye Gyngell chose to cook this recipe to celebrate.

Preheat the oven to 180°C/350°F/gas 4.

Put the nuts on a baking tray and roast on the middle shelf of the oven for 3 minutes to colour them slightly. Remove from the oven then roughly pound to a paste using a pestle and mortar.

Blitz the bread in a food processor until you have crumbs, scatter them on a baking tray and bake until golden – approx. 6–8 minutes.

Put the tomatoes on a baking tray and drizzle with a dash of olive oil. Add the whole chilli and roast with the tomatoes for 10 minutes. Remove from the oven and add to the hazelnuts in the pestle and mortar. Pound to a coarse paste. Add the garlic, sherry vinegar and paprika and mix together. Add the toasted breadcrumbs and pour in the remaining olive oil and season to taste. Stir well to combine.

Boil a large saucepan of water and season liberally with salt. While the water is coming to the boil, prepare the asparagus by snapping off their woody ends. Plunge the asparagus into the water and cook until just tender when pierced with a knife. The cooking time will largely depend on the size and thickness of the spears, but as a general rule of thumb, it should take approx. 1 minute. Drain and dress with the extra virgin olive oil, lemon juice and a little sea salt and pepper.

Divide the asparagus between four plates, or one large plate if you prefer. Split the crème fraîche between the plates and sprinkle the Romesco sauce over the top. Serve immediately.

Serves 4

20 asparagus spears
good pinch of sea salt
1 tablespoon extra virgin olive oil
a few drops of lemon juice
sea salt and freshly ground black pepper

For the Romesco
12 blanched almonds
12 hazelnuts
2 ripe tomatoes, peeled
100ml (3½fl oz) extra virgin olive oil, plus extra for drizzling
1 whole red chilli (the ancho variety if you can get hold of one)
2 garlic cloves, crushed to a paste
1 tablespoon good-quality sherry vinegar
1 teaspoon sweet-smoked paprika (I prefer Spanish to Hungarian)
1 thick slice of chewy, peasant-style bread, such as ciabatta

To serve
2 tablespoons crème fraîche

Top (left): My daughter Lydia manning the Ballymaloe Cookery School stand at Midleton Farmers' Market.

Top (right): Myrtle Allen giving a speech at the opening of Midleton Farmers' Market.

Middle (left): We like to make handwritten and illustrated labels for the produce we sell at the stall.

Middle (right): Local artisan fish smoker Frank Hederman's smoked mackerel from his Belvelly smokehouse, near Cobh.

Bottom (left): Mozzarella and a selection of olives at Toby Simmonds' olive stall.

Bottom (right): The range of produce on offer at the Ballymaloe Cookery School stand includes everything from meringues, cakes and granola to homemade jams.

Farmers' Markets

In 1995 I went to San Francisco to visit my friend Mary Risley who owns the Tante Marie Cooking School. I arrived late in the evening pretty exhausted but Mary announced that we must be up early next day to go to see the new farmers' market in a parking lot on the Embarcadero near Green Street. I'd seen tons of great markets in France, Italy and Spain – Boulevard Raspail in Paris, the Rialto Market in Venice and La Boqueria in Barcelona – and wasn't a bit keen to be dragged out of bed at dawn to see a collection of stalls, but Mary is even bossier than me, so I was hiked out of bed at 7.30a.m.

This was like no market I'd ever seen before; stallholders were a mixed bunch of urban farmers and professionals who had chucked in their careers in favour of a more agreeable self-sufficient lifestyle in Mendocino or Marin county. Stalls were piled high with their home-grown organic vegetables, orchard and stone fruit and berries, dried peaches, artisan breads, free-range chickens and eggs, garden flowers, homemade cookies and cakes and one stall sold nothing but bunches of beautiful sweet peas in recycled silver tin cans. Several local restaurants and cafés had decamped to the market because that's where all the action was on a Saturday morning; it was absolutely the coolest place to see and be seen.

Suddenly I had a light bulb moment: during the mid-1990s the supermarkets in Ireland had gone over to a central distribution system, which meant that their shops were discouraged and in some cases actually penalised if they bought more than a couple of per cent of their stock locally. This had a devastating effect on local producers who were too small to be in the system and who relied on local shops for their livelihood. So on one side there were local people who were desperate to buy local food and on the other producers who were desperate to sell, but there was no way they could meet unless customers went directly to the farms, which simply wasn't feasible for the majority of the population. It was suddenly blindingly obvious: local markets were the answer. If we could re-establish the markets then local farmers could sell their produce directly to local people. Bingo!

'Country Markets' were established by the Irish Countrywomen's Association in 1946 for the sale of home-produced food and handcrafts. When first set up it gave women working in the home an opportunity to sell their produce: jams, cakes, bread, hand-knitting, flowers and plants. The markets are still held weekly indoors in many country towns and are well worth visiting, but we thought we could take this idea further with a proper farmers' market selling produce on a larger scale.

My mother-in-law Myrtle Allen loved the idea, so in June 1996 we started the first new-age farmers' market in Ireland on the Coal Quay in Cork city, where there has been a market for over 400 years under the auspices of the Cork Free Choice Consumer Group of which Myrtle was president. The Cork Free Choice Consumer Group was formed in 1989 by the customers of two highly skilled French cheesemakers, Martin Guillemot and Anne-Marie Jaumaud, living in West Cork, whose business was threatened by a raft of new food hygiene regulations. They were unable to save the cheesemakers but continued to find, support and promote producers of high-quality food in Cork city and county, especially small specialists and traditional producers, and to put them in touch with interested consumers. They still meet monthly in the Crawford Art Gallery and have a speaker on a food-related topic. Sometimes small food producers come along and give a presentation and tasting, on other occasions it might be a talk on GM, water quality, where to find a decent chicken or good heritage pork, additives in food, how to cook inexpensive cuts of meat, a healthy diet, fun food for children or making the most of your polytunnel growing winter vegetables.

My *Simply Delicious* series was on television at the time so it was a source of great amusement to all and sundry when I turned up with my stall, two iron trestle tables with a couple of teak boards on top and a blue gingham cloth. I wish I could remember what I brought with me. It was a May weekend, so only the first of the early vegetables were ready to harvest, a few lettuces, bunches of our neighbour Patty Walsh's rhubarb, homemade muesli and

Above: A customer buying delicious fresh produce at the Ballymaloe Cookery School market stall. Every weekend, unless I am away, I am on the stall at Midleton Farmers' Market with my shawl. I love the camaraderie between the stallholders and the banter with the customers is, as Frank Hederman once said, 'like pure therapy'.

granola, some jam, a few chutneys, local honey and some home baking. We printed little flyers and left them in local restaurants and gradually people heard about the market.

The difficulties encountered by small producers of good products was investigated at meetings. A delegation went to Dublin to ask the health and safety officials to reconsider the ban on the sale of goods from home kitchens. A committee was set up to study the risks, and later the Artisan Food Forum was set up in January 2004 to liaise with the Food Safety Authority about the challenges faced by the artisan sector. Much progress has been made.

The Midleton Farmers' Market was launched in 2000 on Saturday 10 June – Whit weekend – with twelve stalls. After initial discussions about the location with the local community it was set up behind the Court House with the full support of the Chamber of Commerce and the Urban Council. From an initial twelve stalls the market has blossomed and gone from strength to strength. Among the original stall holders were Frank Hederman with his smoked fish, Ardsallagh Goat's Cheese, Kate O'Donovan with her salad dressings, Willie Scannell selling floury Ballycotton potatoes, Ted Murphy with vegetable and flowering plants and hanging baskets, Dan Aherne with beef from his farm, which was in the process of converting to organic production at that time, Toby Simmonds' olive stall, Caroline Robinson, who grows the most beautiful chemical-free vegetables on her farm near Bandon in West Cork, Jill Bell, now from Well and Good Health Food Shop in Midleton, and several different bread and cake stalls. Mrs Burns, who has been a vegetable trader for over 40 years, was also one of the founder members, selling a variety of local vegetables, bundles of fresh carrots and turnips, all in season. Before long there was a waiting list for spaces for stalls.

Ballymaloe Organic Farm and Gardens also had a stall from the beginning. The stall sells home-grown organic vegetables, lots of free-range eggs, brown bread, jams and chutneys and over the years has branched out into offering little bunches of sweet peas, Nora Aherne's ducks, fresh herbs, salad dressings, elderflower cordial and occasionally organic free-range pork from our own Saddleback pigs. Nowadays, Julija Makejeva cooks all week for the Midleton Farmers' Market and Farm Shop beside the Cookery School.

Some of the students at the Cookery School are interested in the farmers' market as a career option, so they love to come to the Midleton Farmers' Market weekly on a rota basis to learn how to set up and operate a farmers' market. They also love to help Julija and Igor who man the stall. We do a detailed evening lecture on

every 12-week course for students who are particularly interested in trading in or setting up a farmers' market.

Clodagh McKenna was one of my first students to get involved; she sold homemade chicken liver pâté from the corner of the Ballymaloe Cookery School stall until she got a stall of her own where she sold delicious homemade fresh pasta, parsley pesto, tomato fondue, toffee apples, brown soda bread and seasonal soups and dressings. (Later she went on to write a book and do a TV series on farmers' markets, which has led to a very successful career in food.)

Many stallholders who started selling in a small way at farmers' markets, testing their products and getting the reaction of the public, have gone on to establish successful food businesses, including Deirdre Hilliard of Just Foods. Deirdre started in 2004 with a stall selling her homemade soups using organic and, where possible, local ingredients. She now has a commercial kitchen in Cobh and supplies supermarkets and restaurants. Paddy O'Connell made granola and accessed the market in the same way with the help of his mother Una, who initially toasted tray after tray of grains in their home kitchen. His granola is now very successful nationally. His friend Ross Staunton also started in the farmers' market in Dublin, then spent some time in Australia and on his return opened a gourmet food store and café called The Foodgame in Stoneybatter, Dublin, selling lots of Irish artisan produce.

Farmers' markets are set up with the express intention of providing an outlet for farmers and small food producers to sell local seasonal produce to the consumers who are desperately seeking this kind of food. Farmers' markets are quite different to some of the established markets. Apart from a few rare exceptions like Skibbereen in West Cork, they do not sell clothes, CDs, tools or bric-a-brac but simply sell local food to local people; the producers themselves or an appropriate representative must man the stall. The markets enable farmers and food producers to sell their goods locally, which benefits them and the local community. They keep the money circulating within the local area and attract people to adjacent retail businesses. Farmers' markets also help the environment by encouraging sustainable agriculture and small scale, less intensive production. They reduce the effects of long-distance transport of food and the need for excess packaging. The variety of produce they offer is amazing and, of course, most abundant during the growing season. For example, as you enter the Midleton Farmers' Market area, you might see Kate O'Donovan, who sells her delicious homemade marinades, dressings and dips

Above (top): A busy stand at Midleton Farmers' Market.
(bottom): Students enjoying their time working on the Ballymaloe Cookery School stand. They come weekly on a rota basis to learn how to set up and operate a successful farmers' market. Students also have the opportunity to attend a detailed lecture on the subject as part of the 12-week course.

or Mrs Burns with her selection of local vegetables. Artisan baker Declan Ryan sells his Arbutus, soda, yeast and sourdough breads. Local farmer Dan Aherne and his wife Anne invested in a refrigerated truck and now sell their organic beef. He responded to the numerous requests for free-range organic chickens and now can scarcely fulfill the demand. Oren Little of the Little Apple Co. drives down from Kilkenny every Saturday to sell cooking and eating apples and delicious apple juice, as well as daffodils in spring.

As you enter Midleton Farmers' Market, which moved to a new site in the Circus Field in 2009, you see Willie Scannell selling his Ballycotton potatoes. He, like so many others, was a victim of the supermarkets' central distribution policy, but now that the Midleton Farmers' Market allows him the opportunity to sell his potatoes directly to the consumer his future is secure, and he's branched out into selling a selection of vegetables including lettuces, cabbages, white turnips, radishes and onions.

There are now 26 stalls selling a wide variety of produce from freshly caught fish, which the O'Driscoll brothers from West Cork will fillet as you wait, to O'Connell's handmade chocolates, Woodfield free-range pork and charcuterie, gluten-free produce, Ballyhora wild and cultivated mushrooms, Green Saffron spices, crêpes and lots of organic produce.

From the beginning, the market has been enthusiastically supported, not only by the local community, but also by the local shops that report an increase in business on market day. From a base of one farmers' market in 1996, there are now in excess of 160 around Ireland – some are small, others, such as Mahon Point, Midleton and Douglas, are large and vibrant. It has helped change the way many people shop and provides another option for those who want to engage with the people who produce their food.

From these humble beginnings, farmers' markets have spread all over Ireland and continue to gather momentum. Despite the challenging economic climate of recent years, farmers' markets have held their own, and have meant the difference between survival or not for many farmers, fishermen and food producers.

Of all the projects I've been involved with over the years, I think it's true to say that the re-establishment of the farmers' market is what I am most proud of – several people are on record that they feel they would not be still farming were it not for the fact that they get the full fair price for their product directly into their hands at the farmers' market – how wonderful is that?

Left: The range of delicious, fresh, organic produce on offer at the Ballymaloe Cookery School stand.
Right (top): Organic peppers grown at Ballymaloe.
Right (bottom): Willie Scannell, one of the founder members of the Midleton Farmers' Market, whose floury Ballycotton potatoes draw customers from far and wide.

Heirloom Tomato Salad with Wasabi Mascarpone

We've been growing heirloom tomatoes ever since I first tasted them in San Francisco in 1999. I arrived home with packets of heirloom seeds and our gardener, Susan Turner, also sourced a great selection from the Heritage Seed Library in London. One year we grew over 50 varieties; the flavour, texture and appearance are completely different, some are tiny, others huge, but all are delicious. This salad is inspired by one eaten at Yotam Ottolenghi's NOPI restaurant.

Serves 4

500g (18oz) heirloom tomatoes such as Persimmon, Tibet Apple, red and yellow Oxheart, Lily of the Valley, Black Prince, Gobstopper
3 tablespoons extra virgin olive oil
1 tablespoon Chardonnay vinegar
pinch of sugar (optional)
a handful of micro greens and purple basil leaves

For the Wasabi Mascarpone Dressing
125ml (4fl oz) mascarpone
2–3 tablespoons milk
2–3 teaspoons wasabi
1 tablespoon pine nuts, lightly toasted
1 teaspoon finely chopped tarragon
2 teaspoons finely sliced spring onion
sea salt and freshly ground black pepper

To serve
crusty bread

First make the dressing. Loosen the mascarpone with a little milk. Stir in the wasabi, pine nuts, chopped tarragon and spring onion. Season with sea salt and freshly ground black pepper and set aside to mature for 15–30 minutes.

Slice the heirloom tomatoes in half or into quarters, depending on size, and put them in a bowl. Season with sea salt and freshly ground black pepper. Whisk the oil and vinegar together and drizzle over the tomatoes. Taste, adding a pinch of sugar if necessary. Put a generous tablespoon of wasabi mascarpone in the centre of a white plate or in a small bowl. Pile the heirloom tomatoes onto the plate and scatter over the micro greens and basil leaves. Serve immediately with lots of crusty bread.

Roast Jerusalem Artichoke Slices

What would we do without kale and Jerusalem artichokes in the winter? For us they are must-have winter vegetables, so versatile and madly nutritious. Jerusalem artichokes have the highest inulin content of any vegetable (a prebiotic that helps to develop and preserve a healthy gut flora).

Try to grow them yourself – if you plant one you'll have at least a dozen or more next year as they spread like mad. They have tall green foliage and yellow flowers in early autumn. When they are freshly dug you scarcely need to peel them – a definite advantage. They also make tasty gratins, soups, purées and are delicious raw. You'll need to pop them into acidulated water if you are not using or cooking immediately, because they discolour quickly as they oxidise.

Serves 4–6

450g (1lb) Jerusalem artichokes, well scrubbed
2 tablespoons extra virgin olive oil
a few rosemary or thyme sprigs (optional)
sea salt and freshly ground black pepper

Preheat the oven to 200°C/400°F/gas 6 and line a roasting tray with greaseproof paper.

Slice the artichokes into rounds, 7mm (⅓in) thick. Toss them in extra virgin olive oil and season well with salt. Arrange in a single layer on the prepared roasting tray. Roast in the hot oven for 10 minutes until golden on one side, then flip them over and cook them on the other side until golden. Test with the tip of a knife – they should be tender. Sprinkle with thyme or rosemary (if using), season with black pepper and serve.

Sweet Chilli Sauce

The students adore this Sweet Chilli Sauce. We also make and sell this both at Midleton Farmers' Market and in the Farm Shop beside the School; people love it. We often joke that we need to set up a helpline because it's so popular. Serve with everything!

Makes 12–13 x 275ml (9fl oz) bottles

60 red chillies (we use medium hot Serrano chillies or Dutch chillies)
30 garlic cloves, peeled
3.6 litres (6 pints) white wine vinegar
1.8kg (4lb) granulated sugar
7½ tablespoons salt

Whizz the chillies and garlic in a food processor. Put the vinegar and sugar into a heavy-bottomed saucepan and stir over a medium heat to dissolve the sugar. Add the puréed chilli and garlic mixture to the pan, along with the salt. Bring to the boil, then simmer over a medium heat until the sauce has reduced by half – at least 1 hour. Pour into 12–13 x 275ml (9fl oz) sterilised bottles, put on the lids and set aside to cool. Store in a cool, dark place for up to 12 months.

Madhur Jaffrey

Above (top) and (bottom): Madhur Jaffrey and me in the original Cookery School in 1988.

When the Ballymaloe Cookery School was launched I realised that I had the opportunity to invite my food heroes from all over the world to teach at the School. The fact that they were not only happy, but also excited, to come to Ireland to teach at a little cooking school in the middle of a farm was the most thrilling revelation to me.

Madhur Jaffrey was high on my list of culinary icons. Her Indian cookery series was on television – I couldn't wait to buy the book and was enchanted, though somewhat intimidated, by some of the recipes, long lists of exotic-sounding ingredients and spices. I yearned to learn more. I can't quite remember how I managed to find Madhur's contact details, possibly through Zanne Stewart, then food editor of *Gourmet* magazine. It was one of the first transatlantic phone calls I ever made, and I was over-awed by the reality of being able to talk to someone on the other side of the world, so I really had to psych myself up. I distinctly remember listening to the ring tone and wondering whether Madhur would pick up. She did and I then had to summon up all my courage to ask whether she would come and teach at a little cooking school in Ireland. She graciously said yes to my invitation. I now know that she had read about the Ballymaloe Cookery School in *Gourmet* magazine's cover story in March 1986 and was intrigued. I was totally thrilled and remember coming off the phone, punching the air and rushing off to tell Timmy, my PA Rosalie, and my parents-in-law the good news.

Madhur arrived, dressed in one of her many exquisite saris, with her lovely husband Sanford in July 1986. Even then Madhur had a global following. The course was totally over-subscribed and people flew in from London to attend. Madhur cooked delicious food with a little apron over her saris.

Madhur sent the menu and list of recipes well ahead of time. The challenge for us in July 1986 was to source all of the ingredients. Many were completely unfamiliar, not only to me, but to many of my suppliers. Even some names were different, so Sanford sweetly offered to go to Cork with Tim to choose the correct dals. I knew

about orange lentils (from lentil soup at boarding school) but what on earth was chana dal, rajma dal, urad dal, toor dal (also known as split or yellow pigeon peas) and moong dal…? Then there was amchoor (mango powder made from dried unripe green mangoes), asafoetida, tamarind, gram flour, ajwain (or ajowan) seeds, kalonji, oriental sesame oil, poha, mooli radish and lima beans.

Fresh ginger and spices were easy enough to source from the English Market in Cork, where Mr Bell's stall was a rich source of ethnic ingredients, but some like fenugreek and black cardamom I had never used before. Chillies were also a minefield. We managed to find some dried ones similar to those Madhur needed.

Even rice created a challenge; Tim was intrigued as Sanford showed him how to judge really fine basmati rice by its smell and appearance. The rice shouldn't be dusty in texture or have lots of broken grains. He urged us to buy loose rice rather than pre-packaged so one could examine it for quality. Fresh coriander also had to be imported from London and so sadly was not at its best when it arrived.

So much has changed, all these ingredients are now readily and widely available. Coriander is a must-have herb and we grow it year-round, in the greenhouses in winter and outdoors in the herb garden in summer. We've also learned to use everything from the leaves to the stalks, roots, flowers and seeds in the dishes we cook and teach the students.

On Madhur's last visit she was particularly impressed by the quality of the spices that our past student Arun Kapil, of Green Saffron, imports directly from his relatives' spice gardens in India. Madhur whetted our appetite for India to such an extent that we now make annual visits and each year come back with more recipes, food memories and images to share with our students at the School.

Madhur's classes are not just cookery classes but a lesson in the history, culture and customs of her beloved India. She taught a further four classes at the School in July 1988, July 1991, July 1996 and July 2001 and returned in 2013 for the inaugural Ballymaloe Literary Festival of Food and Wine, giving both a cookery demonstration as well as a talk on her latest book, *Curry Nation*.

Right (top): Me, Dervilla Flynn, Suzanne Walsh, Madhur, Breda Murphy, Claire Cullinane and Rachel Allen.
Right (middle): Me and Madhur enjoying afternoon tea in the conservatory.
Right (bottom): Madhur Jaffrey giving a cookery demonstration at the Ballymaloe Literary Festival of Food and Wine, May 2013.

Prawn Curry

The spicing in Sri Lankan curries is subtle but pretty perky. They are usually served as part of a selection of curries, such as Cashew Nut Curry, Pineapple Curry and Garlic Curry, with lot of raitas and side dishes – truly a feast. (Pictured bottom right on page 203.)

Serves 8

1kg (2¼lb) king prawns in their shells
2 tablespoons vegetable oil
a sprig of fresh curry leaves
25–50g (1–2oz) red onions, finely chopped
4–6 garlic cloves, peeled and finely chopped
3–4 green chillies, finely sliced
1 cinnamon stick
2 teaspoons chilli powder
pinch of ground turmeric
½ teaspoon ground fenugreek
1¼ teaspoons salt
110ml (4fl oz) coconut milk

Peel, devein and wash the prawns, reserving the heads and shells. Set aside.

Put the prawn heads and shells in a food processor with a splash of water and grind to a smooth paste. Set aside.

Heat the oil in a medium saucepan and, once it is very hot, add the curry leaves. Add the onion, garlic, chilli, spices, salt and prawns and stir well over a high heat for approx. 5 minutes. Scoop in the ground extract of prawns, pour in the coconut milk and simmer gently for 7–10 minutes.

Serve as part of a selection of curries or with rice, a green salad and fruit raita.

Pumpkin Curry

Fresh curry leaves are more readily available nowadays and you can usually buy them from Asian suppliers. They may also have pandanus leaves, which make a terrific ice cream and custard also. (Pictured top right on page 203.)

Serves 8

1kg (2¼lb) pumpkin, peeled and cut into 2.5cm (1in) chunks
4 green chillies, finely sliced
25g (1oz) Bombay onions, finely sliced
2 garlic cloves, peeled and finely chopped
a sprig of fresh curry leaves
1 teaspoon salt
1 teaspoon ground fenugreek
1 teaspoon mustard powder
pinch of ground turmeric
110ml (4fl oz) coconut milk

Put all the ingredients in a medium saucepan and bring to the boil. Simmer until the pumpkin is cooked – approx. 10–20 minutes depending on the type of pumpkin.

Serve with a selection of curries or on its own accompanied with rice.

Cashew Nut Curry

The Dutch House in Galle is one of my favourite places on earth to stay. This delicious Sri Lankan curry recipe, plus the others on the previous page, were given to me by Chef Shanti at The Sun House and Dutch House in Galle.

Put the cashew nuts in a saucepan, cover them with boiling water and set aside to soak for at least 3–4 hours, preferably overnight. Drain under cold running water. Return the cashew nuts to the pan, cover with fresh water and cook until tender but not soft – approx. 10 minutes. Drain well.

Preheat the oil in a medium saucepan, add the curry leaves, onions and garlic and fry over a medium heat until the onions are golden – approx. 3 minutes. Add the cashew nuts along with the powdered spices and salt and cook for 5–10 minutes, stirring occasionally.

Pour in the coconut milk, bring to the boil and simmer for 8 minutes. Scatter over the fresh coriander and serve with poppadoms or boiled rice.

Serves 8

500g (18oz) dried unsalted cashew nuts
vegetable oil, for frying
a sprig of curry leaves
2 onions, finely chopped
5 garlic cloves, peeled and finely chopped
1 teaspoon ground fenugreek
3–4 teaspoons chilli powder
1 teaspoon ground cinnamon
2 teaspoons curry powder
¼ teaspoon ground turmeric
1¼ teaspoons salt
110ml (4fl oz) coconut milk

To serve
fresh coriander leaves
poppadoms or boiled rice

Food Allergies

Like many people of my generation I never even realised that food allergies or intolerances existed until the mid-1980s. In fact, I vividly remember the moment at dinner in a very famous restaurant called Spago in Los Angeles while I was over for an IACP Conference in 1986. The waiter seemed to be taking ages to take the order around the table and I overheard several of the American guests saying things like 'I can't do pork', 'I don't eat dairy', 'I'm allergic to chicken', 'No gluten please – I have a wheat intolerance'. I had just about heard of coeliac disease before, but the others? What was that all about?

It was my first trip to the US; I was wide-eyed with wonder. No one else at the table seemed to think it in the least unusual so I decided that they were all neurotic over there! I just absorbed it all and when I came home I remember telling everyone about this episode and several others and dismissing it as people's imagination. Little did I know that within a few years many people in these islands would be displaying signs of not one, but in some cases multiple, food allergies.

This was not a subject we needed to address in any detail in the early years of the School when we had only an occasional coeliac or diabetic student, but in more recent years the number of students with food allergies and intolerances has increased dramatically. The main foods that people are allergic to are wheat, dairy, pork, chicken, oranges, mushrooms and now even celery and pine nuts.

From the mid-1980s we began to get requests at the Cookery School for a course on food with no dairy products, and an increasing number of requests for gluten-free food. In June 1991 we offered a No Butter, Cream or Booze course – ideal for anyone allergic to dairy. In 2000 we taught Delicious Food for Coeliacs, which was run as a longer course in 2002 and morphed into a course in Healthy Gluten-free Eating by 2006. This course, taught by one of our former students and teachers Rosemary Kearney, is a huge success. Rosemary has been a coeliac all her life and is a beautiful cook. Teaching these courses is especially touching; the participants are a mixture of coeliacs, some newly diagnosed and still in the process of adjusting, and others who a lifelong coeliacs desperately trying to find good food and convinced that they will never again be able to taste a delicious slice of cake or a pudding. Others are parents or partners of coeliacs who are trying to cook for them. They are blown away by the food and so grateful for simple recipes that work – one woman actually burst into tears when she tasted Rosemary's muffins. We run three Healthy Gluten-free Eating courses a year and the numbers continue to rise. All our 12-week students attend this course as well, because knowledge of cooking for food allergies is now an essential part of a chef's repertoire, as coeliacs and other allergy sufferers have increased in numbers. Direction on how to cope with, and cater for, people with food allergies and intolerances is an integral part of the courses. However, it also presents an opportunity for students to provide delicious food for coeliacs and to service the growing demand for 'free-from' food.

The most common allergies and intolerances seem to be connected to wheat, dairy and eggs, although many students discover that they can eat our organic free-range eggs without any ill-effect. We have also had students who have been diagnosed as dairy intolerant but who find that they can eat our organic yogurt and drink our raw milk. This leads to questions and debate over whether it is the raw product that's the problem or what's done to it in processing that is resulting in the increase in food allergy sufferers – it would be fascinating to have more research on this.

Recently the Food Safety Authority of Ireland (FSAI) issued a list of 14 foods that restaurant guests may be allergic to: nuts, gluten (including cereals containing gluten), milk, shellfish, eggs, celery, fish, milk, crustaceans, almonds, cashew nuts, peanuts, oats and wheat. Since the late 1990s we have asked our incoming students to make us aware of any food issues. The figures seem to be growing each term and those suffering from food allergies can now be in excess of 25 per cent of a class.

Approximately 1 per cent of the Irish population is affected by coeliac disease. It is a complex issue but there is unquestionably

a genetic element to the disease. For this book, I tried hard to get definite answers to the allergy queries, but it is difficult to get definitive data. Some contend that the numbers are significantly greater nowadays because diagnosis is better, which is unquestionably the case. Certainly there is a greater awareness of the problem but self-diagnosis can skew the figures.

Several major studies are underway, including an EU-funded multidisciplinary project involving 17 European member-states on the 'Prevalence, cost and basis of food allergy across Europe'. Some of the data is already available www.europrevall.org. The next big body of work being carried out is by the European Food Safety Authority (EFSA) as a result of a request by FSAI. They are due to publish a draft report in 2013, then put it out for consultation and publish a final opinion in 2014. The questions asked by FSAI, which the report will tackle are: the prevalence of each allergy in the European Union; recommendations for threshold concentrations of each allergen in food that would provide an acceptable level of protection for at-risk consumers; the suitability, or otherwise, of qualitative and quantitative DNA-based tests for the detection and quantification of food allergens in comparison with immunological or other methods.

The jury is definitely out, but in my observations over 30 years, the amount of people who say they have some type of food allergy or intolerance has increased dramatically. We have had to remove peanut oil from the School altogether, having had several students with a nut allergy who carry an adrenaline injection in case they suffer an extreme allergic reaction. Our staff, teachers and fellow students are briefed on how to deal with a crisis situation if we have a student with a severe allergy.

The whole issue has made people more aware of and concerned about what goes into our food, and I feel deeply saddened that we are increasingly in a situation where people are becoming uneasy, and in some cases paranoid, about their food, sadly with some justification. This was absolutely not the case when I was a child, in fact it is a growing phenomenon of the last 20 years.

Dairy-free is easier in many ways – for those who must eliminate all dairy products from the diet, vegetable or extra virgin olive oil can be substituted in many cases, and there are many excellent recipes for olive oil cakes, biscuits and ice creams.

Nowadays few people eat the food of their parish or local area. At Ballymaloe we've been not only advocating, but living the 'support local' message for well over 60 years, long before the Cookery School was started in 1983. Locally produced food, particularly

local honey, milk, free-range eggs and vegetables, are said to carry the antibodies of your area, so it's really important to incorporate as much local produce into our diets as possible. We're fortunate to live in the centre of an organic farm, but many people whose only option is to buy food in the usual retail channels, tell me they feel very vulnerable and helpless. Most of the food we consume comes from all over the world, containing bacteria and enzymes that we are unfamiliar with and that our ancestors were never subjected to – could this be a factor in the extraordinary growth in food allergies and intolerances? Hay fever sufferers often find relief if they consume really local honey made from the pollens of the plants in the area where they live, and the same could potentially be true of other allergies. We would love to have more research done in this area.

Left: A student on a short course deep in concentration during a hands-on cooking session. Students on the short courses wear civvies, while those on the 12-week courses wear full chef's whites. In the early days they used to wear a variety of traditional chef's hats, which have now been replaced with bandanas and baseball caps.
Above: The ever cheerful Gary Masterson, one of the tutors at the School. Here he is in the larder preparing for the afternoon cookery demonstration.

Debbie Shaw's Red Quinoa Tabbouleh with Toasted Pine Nuts and Pomegranate

Debbie Shaw, a teacher at the Ballymaloe Cookery School, is our in-house nutritionist. This is Debbie's version of the classic Middle Eastern salad tabbouleh. She uses quinoa (pronounced 'keenwah') instead of bulgar wheat. Quinoa is an ancient Inca grain and a nutritional powerhouse, with all the amino acids (proteins) the body needs and more calcium than milk. It is a great alternative source of calcium for anyone on a dairy-free diet. It is also wheat and gluten-free, easy to digest and very satisfying – everyone loves this salad.

Rinse the quinoa in a sieve under cold running water for 2–3 minutes to remove the natural bitter outer coating. Put the quinoa and salt in a saucepan with a tight-fitting lid and cover with the carefully measured cold water. Bring to the boil, reduce the heat to very low and cook for 12 minutes, covered, or until the grain is tender. Remove the pan from the heat, keeping the lid on the pan, and set aside to steam for a further 10 minutes to fluff up the quinoa.

To make the dressing, mix the olive oil, lemon juice and honey together in a jar and season to taste.

To serve, add the remaining ingredients to the warm quinoa and pour over the dressing. Mix well and season with freshly ground black pepper, and a little more salt if necessary. Serve with grilled fish or chicken, or add some cooked chickpeas for a vegetarian option.

Serves 8

225g (8oz) red quinoa
½ teaspoon salt
350ml (12fl oz) cold water
25g (1oz) freshly chopped flat-leaf parsley, stalks removed
25g (1oz) freshly chopped mint, stalks removed
    seeds of 1 pomegranate
110g (4oz) spring onions, white and green parts, chopped
75g (3oz) pine nuts, toasted in a dry frying pan with no oil over
    a medium heat until lightly browned – keep them moving
    or they will burn!
50g (2oz) dried cranberries
2 medium carrots, peeled and coarsely grated
1½ teaspoons ground cinnamon
1 scant teaspoon ground allspice

For the dressing
50ml (2fl oz) fruity extra virgin olive oil
juice of 1 lemon
1 teaspoon honey
sea salt and freshly ground black pepper

Carrot and Sweet Potato Soup with Coriander and Cashew Nut Pesto

For me soup is comfort food. This is a quick and easy, low fat, dairy-free and seriously tasty soup. It is also a winter immune super-booster. The carrots and sweet potatoes are high in beta-carotene, which is converted to vitamin A in the body, essential for fighting infection and maintaining strong immunity. The ginger and garlic offer potent antibacterial and antiviral protection.

Heat the olive oil in a large saucepan. Add the carrot, sweet potato, onion, chilli (if using), garlic and ginger and season with a good pinch of salt and pepper. Sweat the vegetables over a low heat until tender but not coloured. Add the stock and bring to the boil. Continue to cook until the vegetables are completely tender.

Meanwhile, make the pesto. Put all of the ingredients into a food processor and whizz together.

To serve, blend the soup with the fresh coriander and pour into soup bowls. Drizzle each one with a teaspoon of the Coriander and cashew Nut Pesto before serving. (Any leftover pesto can be stored in a glass jam jar in the fridge, covered with a little olive oil, for 2–3 months.)

Serves 4–6

2 tablespoons olive oil
6 carrots, peeled and diced
2 medium sweet potatoes (orange not white), peeled and diced
1 large onion, diced
1 red chilli, deseeded and finely chopped (optional)
3 large juicy garlic cloves, peeled and finely chopped
2.5cm (1in) piece of fresh root ginger, peeled and finely grated
850ml–1.2 litres (1½–2 pints) homemade chicken or vegetable stock
2 tablespoons freshly chopped coriander

For the Coriander and Cashew Nut Pesto
75g (3oz) fresh coriander (leaves and soft stems)
25g (1oz) flat-leaf parsley (leaves only)
¼ red chilli, deseeded and finely chopped
1 stick of lemongrass, tough outer stalk removed, very finely chopped
1 large garlic clove, peeled and finely chopped
1 tablespoon chopped cashew nuts
juice of ½ lime
100ml (3½fl oz) extra virgin olive oil
pinch of sea salt and freshly ground black pepper

Spiced Pear, Pecan and Ginger Crumble

This is a low fat, dairy-free and truly tasty dessert. We use coconut oil (which, in spite of its name, is solid not liquid) instead of butter in this humble crumble. Because of their grainy texture and high pectin content, pears are a natural diuretic and help de-toxify the body. Ginger is a super immune booster with potent expectorant and antiseptic properties. In addition its active compound gingerol improves circulation and soothes a nauseous stomach.

Serves 6–8

8 large ripe pears, peeled and cored and cut into 2.5cm (1in)
slices lengthwise
1 scant tablespoon dark brown muscovado sugar
1 tablespoon finely grated fresh root ginger
juice and finely grated zest of ½ lemon

For the crumble
75g (3oz) white spelt flour
4 tablespoons solid coconut oil (not extra virgin),
broken into 2.5cm (1in) pieces
1½ tablespoons dark brown sugar
1 teaspoon ground cinnamon
50g (2oz) oats
1 tablespoon maple syrup
2 tablespoons coarsely chopped pecan nuts

Preheat the oven to 180°C/350°F/gas 4.

First make the crumble topping. Put the flour in a bowl and mix in the coconut oil pieces using a fork until it resembles large breadcrumbs. Add the sugar, cinnamon, oats, maple syrup and chopped pecans, mix and chill in the fridge while you prepare the pears.

Peel and slice the pears. Toss the pears with the brown sugar, grated ginger, lemon zest and lemon juice and put them into an ovenproof dish. Sprinkle them loosely with the chilled crumble topping. Bake the crumble for 20–25 minutes or until the topping is toasted and the pears are tender. Serve warm.

Gluten-free Raspberry Muffins

A deliciously light muffin – good at any time of the day! Teeny weeny raspberry muffins baked in petit four cases are adorable to serve with coffee and have the bonus of being gluten free.

Makes 16 regular muffins (or 24 mini muffins)

175g (6oz) salted butter
75g (3oz) ground almonds
1½ tablespoons grated lemon zest
125g (4½oz) gluten-free icing sugar, sifted
2 tablespoons fine cornmeal, sifted
3 tablespoons cornflour, sifted
5 organic egg whites
175g (6oz) raspberries

Preheat the oven to 200°C/400°F/gas 6 and line 1–2 large muffin tins or 2 mini muffin tins with paper cases.

Melt the butter in a saucepan and cook until it turns pale golden in colour.

Mix together the ground almonds, lemon zest, icing sugar, cornmeal and cornflour in a large bowl and pour in the melted butter. Gently mix together.

In a separate bowl, lightly beat the egg whites until they are slightly frothy. Fold the egg whites into the almond and butter mixture. Divide the mixture between the paper cases and dot with the raspberries.

Bake the large muffins for 20–30 minutes or the smaller muffins for 15–20 minutes, or until golden and springy to touch. Set aside to cool on a wire rack.

Dust with gluten-free icing sugar just before serving.

Rory O'Connell

" Ink is what springs to mind when I think back to the early days when Darina and I founded Ballymaloe Cookery School. Not squid ink, but printing ink from the old machine we used for copying recipes for our students. How I hated that manually operated and monstrous piece of equipment that now would look positively antique. How I celebrated the arrival of our first photocopier where all of the ink was carefully sealed in a cartridge and which allowed me to print an entire week of recipes without looking like I had come off second best after an entanglement with the world's largest cephalopod. Spanking clean sheets of printed paper and stapled together too – life-changing stuff.

It was not all glamorous photoshoots and filming sessions in those days but a constant cycle of shopping, teaching, learning, growing, running, printing, testing, digging, cleaning, washing up, clearing up, chair moving and endlessly reacting to the needs of a new and quickly growing business.

There were surprises and the biggest one for me was that I not only could, but also really loved to teach. This was not the sort of teaching that prepared students for an exam in several months' time, but for a deadline with ingredients the following day. I knew pretty quickly if my words and actions had achieved the desired effect – it was there on the plates the very next day. It was fun though, great fun, and our teaching and the joy of sharing our love of food and where it comes from always seemed to be wrapped up in a large parcel of laughter.

There have been many stand-out memories of course – the pleasure of hearing news of the successes of past students with their own businesses, cookery books, television programmes or just becoming really good happy cooks for the nourishment and pleasure of themselves and their loved ones.

I was also learning myself and had the great honour of standing alongside and assisting visiting chefs and culinary icons such as Jane Grigson, Claudia Roden and Madhur Jaffrey. To be on their right or left with a view into their saucepans and bowls, to be within a whisper of their words, to see their hands bringing their writing to life was as thrilling, inspirational and educational for me as I suspect it was for the students in the audience.

Watching the gardens and farm progress has also been a joy. To see students growing and harvesting the food that they are about to cook or slipping their hands into silky cheese curds gained from milk from the farm's cows or churning butter from the same cow's cream has lifted what we do to an altogether different level. We are now getting to the nub of the matter. We are not just a cookery school that teaches recipes, we are a place of learning that truly focuses on the essence of the matter at hand. In our case, that essence is food. "

Left: Rachel Allen and Rory O'Connell, who have been a mainstay of the School with me for many years.

Above (top): Rory, me and Rachel in the Garden Café.
Bottom (left): Rory and me teaching in matching aprons in the early days of the Cookery School.

Middle: Rory and me teaching together after we had expanded the School in 1989.
Bottom (right): Rory taking a class watched by an avid group of students.

Rory's Moroccan Harira Soup

'Moroccan food can be wonderful. It is one of the great cuisines of the world and in the hands of the skilled and knowledgeable cook strikes a beautiful balance of sweetness, saltiness, sourness and heady aromatic flavours.

In Morocco this soup is traditionally served to break the fast during the holy month of Ramadan. There are thousands of different recipes, with each household adding their own particular twist to suit tastes and preferences. Chickpeas, lentils and sometimes beans, meat – either beef or lamb – vegetables, herbs and spices are the basic ingredients. The smell of this soup cooking in the kitchen transports me back to exotic and mysterious Tangier. I prefer to use lamb rather than beef and find a more balanced flavour is achieved. This is a purely personal preference and I don't think there is a right or a wrong combination of ingredients. You may find the addition of the rice at the end of cooking to be unusual but it gives a velvety finish to the soup. Sometimes the rice is replaced with tiny bits of pasta, like orzo. Claudia Roden, in her wonderful book, *Arabesque*, mentions how in some cases a sourdough batter is added to give the velvety consistency or just a simple mixture of flour and water. In any event, this addition of starch needs to be very close to the time of eating as otherwise the rice or pasta can become soft and flabby.

This soup is substantial, as you can imagine it would need to be after fasting from sundown to sunrise. I like to serve it with lots of freshly chopped coriander and a lemon wedge on the side. The warmer the weather, the more inclined I am to squeeze a little lemon juice into the soup.'

Rory O'Connell

Serves 8

100g (3½oz) dried chickpeas, soaked in cold water overnight
110g (4oz) puy lentils
450g (1lb) boneless lamb, trimmed of all fat and cut into
    1cm (½in) cubes
1 large onion, finely chopped
1 teaspoon ground turmeric
½ teaspoon ground cinnamon
¼ teaspoon each of ground ginger, saffron strands and paprika
50g (2oz) butter
100g (3½oz) long grain rice
4 large ripe tomatoes, skinned, deseeded and chopped
2 tablespoons freshly chopped coriander
4 tablespoons freshly chopped flat-leaf parsley
sea salt, freshly ground black pepper and sugar

To serve
lemon wedges

Drain the chickpeas, discarding the soaking water. Put in a large saucepan with the lentils. Add the diced lamb, onion, turmeric, cinnamon, ginger, saffron and paprika. Cover with 1.5 litres (2½ pints) water and stir gently to mix. Season lightly with salt and pepper. Bring to the boil and skim off any froth that rises to the surface. Add half the butter.

Reduce the heat, cover with a lid and simmer for 1–1½ hours or until the chickpeas are tender. Keep an eye on the level of liquid in the pan and add a little more water if necessary.

Towards the end of the cooking time, prepare the rice. Bring 850ml (1½ pints) of water to the boil in a saucepan. Add the rice, stir gently and cook until tender. Drain the rice, reserving the cooking liquor.

Cook the chopped tomatoes in 3 tablespoons of the reserved cooking liquor until they collapse. Season with salt, pepper and a pinch of sugar.

Add the cooked tomatoes to the soup along with the cooked rice and the remaining butter. Bring to the boil, stirring, and simmer for 5 minutes. Taste and correct the seasoning. If necessary, add some of the reserved rice cooking liquor to thin out the soup a little. Add the chopped coriander and parsley, ladle into bowls and serve with the lemon wedges on the side.

Slow Roast Shoulder of Lamb with Aioli and Salsa Verde

Rory is a thoughtful cook who makes beautiful food; he is also immensely creative, so his dishes always look tantalising and irresistible. He often cooks this lamb for the student farewell dinner in early summer.

Rory says of this recipe: 'A few years ago, butchers had some difficulty selling the shoulder of lamb as it was considered inferior to the leg and loin. Now all that has changed and the cooking world realises that the shoulder is every bit as good as the more "prime" cuts and in some ways actually better. The hard-working and muscular shoulder has marvellous flavour but needs long and slow cooking to gently tenderise it so that the flesh becomes sweetly succulent. The cooked lamb in this dish should be soft and melting and will be gently pulled apart for serving rather than being carved. This recipe needs time. You can't rush the cooking of a shoulder of lamb, but once it is in the oven, there is plenty of time to prepare sauces and vegetables to accompany it.

I suggest two sauces here, the first a garlicky mayonnaise that is thinned with some of the lamb cooking juices and a fresh tasting and piquant herb salsa. The two combine really well with the soft flavoursome meat.

Shoulder of lamb is easily available and here the shoulder is cooked whole with just a sprinkle of sea salt and freshly ground black pepper. If the shoulder is excessively fatty, as may be the case later on in the lamb season, trim some of it off, or ask your butcher to do it for you.

The aioli to serve with the lamb is based on mayonnaise. I urge you to make your own mayonnaise either by hand or in a food mixer or processor. Good mayonnaise is one of the cornerstones in any good cook's repertoire.

Salsa verde has become something of a cliché in the last few years and as a result the quality has suffered. That doesn't mean that when made with fresh herbs and good ingredients, it can't be as exciting as the first time any of us tasted it. It is a wonderful refreshing foil for the sweet lamb and rich aioli. Search out best quality anchovies and capers for the salsa, they vary enormously in quality, so what seems like a bargain when you are buying them, may disappoint at a later stage.'

Preheat the oven to 180°C/ 350°F/gas 4. Put the lamb shoulder in a wide roasting tin or oven tray, skin-side up. Score the skin several times to encourage the fat to run out during the cooking and to crisp up the skin. Season with salt and pepper. Roast in the oven for 30 minutes, then reduce the temperature to 160°C/325°F/gas 3 and continue to cook for a further 3½ hours or until the meat is falling off the bone.

While the lamb is cooking, make the salsa verde. Remove the stalks from the rocket and herbs and discard. Chop the leaves to a texture halfway between coarse and fine, so that the individual flavours of the herbs stand out in the finished sauce. Put the chopped herbs in a small bowl and stir in the remaining ingredients for the salsa. It is unlikely that the salsa will need salt, because the anchovies are already quite salty, but very occasionally a pinch might be needed. Taste and correct the seasoning if necessary, adding a little lemon juice if the salsa needs sharpening up. Chill until ready to serve.

The crushed garlic can be mixed into the mayonnaise for the aioli, however this sauce cannot be finished until you have the juices from the cooked lamb.

To test if the lamb is cooked to a melting tenderness, pull the shank bone: if it is ready, some of the meat should come away easily from the bone. When the lamb is cooked, remove it from the oven and transfer it to a serving plate, covered with foil, to keep warm in a low oven (120°C/250°F/gas ½). There will be plenty of fatty cooking juices in the roasting tin. Strain these through a sieve into a glass bowl or measuring jug and set aside for a few minutes until the fat has risen to the surface. Skim off the fat carefully and thoroughly with a large spoon.

To finish the aioli, add 4–6 tablespoons of the degreased cooking juices to the garlicky mayonnaise and stir well to achieve a consistency similar to softly whipped cream – the mayonnaise should now just lightly coat the back of a spoon. Taste and correct the seasoning if necessary.

Pour the remaining degreased cooking juices into a small pan, bring to the boil and season to taste.

To serve the lamb, remove the meat from the bone in largish pieces using a pair of tongs or a serving fork. Divide the meat between hot serving plates, drizzle over some of the hot cooking juices and accompany with the salsa verde and aioli.

Serves 8–10

1 whole shoulder of lamb on the bone, weighing approx. 3.6kg (7lb 15oz)
Maldon sea salt and freshly ground black pepper

For the Aioli
6 large tablespoons homemade mayonnaise (see page 72)
2 garlic cloves, peeled and crushed to a paste

For the Salsa Verde
1 bunch of rocket, approx. 100g
1 bunch of flat-leaf parsley, approx. 100g
6 large sprigs of mint
6 sprigs of tarragon
1 tablespoon capers, coarsely chopped
2 garlic cloves, peeled and crushed to a smooth paste
8 anchovies, very finely chopped
1 tablespoon Dijon mustard
225ml (8fl oz) olive oil
finely grated zest of 1 lemon and a little juice

Chocolate and Caramel Mousse with Dark Caramel Sauce

This rich and concentrated mousse is another of Rory's recipes. He likes the combination of the chocolate and the burnt sugar caramel and serves this with caramel sauce and thick pouring cream. He advises that it is important to use chocolate with 62 per cent or 70 per cent cocoa solids here to give the depth of chocolatey flavour needed to counteract the sugar in the caramel.

Put the chocolate and butter in a Pyrex bowl. Put the bowl over a saucepan of cold water, making sure the water is not touching the bottom of the bowl, and put over a medium heat. Bring the water to a simmer and immediately remove from the heat, allowing the butter and chocolate to melt gently in the bowl over the saucepan.

Separate the eggs, putting the whites into a spotlessly clean bowl for whisking later. Whisk the yolks to a pale mousse in a separate bowl.

To make the caramel, put the sugar and 125ml (4fl oz) of the water into a heavy-bottomed saucepan and put over a low heat. Stir occasionally to encourage the sugar to dissolve before the liquid comes to the boil. Once it boils and has become a syrup, remove the spoon and do not stir again. Continue to cook the syrup until it darkens to a deep chestnut-coloured caramel. If it is colouring unevenly in the saucepan, tilt the pan gently to and fro to get it to even out by running the dark caramel into the paler syrup. Do not be tempted to stir. If you put a cold spoon into the caramel, it will 'block' and go solid. Keep going until the caramel is a deep chestnut colour and almost burnt. (For safety, I usually put the saucepan in the dry sink before adding that 100ml (4fl oz) of water – this way, the spluttering caramel just splashes on to the sides of the sink rather than the work top.) Then immediately and quickly add the remaining 100ml (4fl oz) of water, hot if possible to reduce spluttering.

Now the caramel will look a bit odd, but once you return the saucepan to the heat it will cook out to a single consistency again. Cook the caramel until it thickens again: when you dip a spoon into the caramel and allow it to drop off the spoon, it should fall in a thickish thread. Slowly and carefully pour the hot caramel onto the whisked egg yolks, whisking all the time. A food mixer with the whisk attachment or a hand-held electric whisk will do this job perfectly. The mixture will whisk to a mousse in a matter of minutes.

Stir the melted chocolate and vanilla extract into the mousse.

Serves 6

225g (8oz) plain chocolate (approx. 62 per cent cocoa solids), chopped into 1cm (½in) pieces
50g (2oz) salted butter, diced
4 organic eggs
225g (8oz) granulated or caster sugar
225ml (8fl oz) water
1 teaspoon pure vanilla extract

For the Dark Caramel Sauce
225g (8oz) granulated sugar
75ml (3fl oz) cold water
225ml (8fl oz) hot water

To serve
thick pouring cream
raspberries (optional)

You may need to be a little vigorous with the stirring.

Whisk the egg whites until stiff peaks form – do not allow them to overwhip and become grainy. Stir a quarter of the egg white into the mousse to soften the mixture, and then fold in the rest of the egg whites lightly yet thoroughly.

Pour the mixture into a shallow serving dish or six individual serving dishes. There will not be a lot of mousse, but it is rich so the servings should be small. Transfer to the fridge to chill for 4 hours.

To make the Dark Caramel Sauce, dissolve the sugar in the cold water over a gentle heat. Stir until the sugar has dissolved, then remove the spoon and simmer until the syrup caramelises to a chestnut colour. If sugar crystals form during cooking, brush down the sides of the pan with a wet brush, but do not stir. Remove the pan from the heat, pour in the hot water and continue to cook until the caramel dissolves and the sauce is quite smooth. Leave to cool.

Serve the mousse with the dark caramel sauce and thick pouring cream. Perfectly ripe raspberries, particularly the autumn varieties, are delicious served with this mousse.

Cooking with Spices

When Rory and I started the School in 1983, virtually our whole repertoire consisted of much-loved recipes from Ballymaloe House and from the few short courses I had taught with Myrtle. But quite quickly we began to expand our collection by testing recipes. Sometimes it was a delicious dish adapted from a meal I ate in a restaurant, others were recipes inspired by reading cookbooks or magazines or ones I came across in my travels.

Guest chefs brought new recipes, techniques and ingredients, including a variety of spices and Asian flavours. Claudia Roden brought Moroccan and Mediterranean specialities, Sri Owen introduced us to Indonesian and Malaysian food, Deh-ta Hsiung to Chinese favourites, Madhur Jaffrey to Indian and later Thai, Vietnamese and other Far Eastern dishes. We became more and more adventurous.

In the early days of the School, even garlic still seemed exotic to many. Students would ask to omit it from a recipe because it didn't 'agree with them'. The same was true for many fresh herbs, as apart from parsley, thyme and chives, they were seen as peculiar and strange – rosemary, for example, and tarragon, marjoram and chervil even more so. Myrtle grew all of these and used them in her cooking, but for most people these herbs were unavailable and unfamiliar. So in the mid-1980s we added a 2½-day course called Cooking with Fresh Herbs to the School schedule. We also grew a huge variety of fresh herbs in pots and gave advice on herb combinations and on how to start your own herb garden.

Apart from the basics like thyme, parsley and chives, fresh herbs were not sold in supermarkets at that time. Basil was virtually unavailable, even the seed was difficult to come by, but I had developed a craving for basil after attending Marcella Hazan's course in Italy. We grew several different varieties in the greenhouses and made lots of pesto and Genovese basil oil for the winter.

Fresh chillies, too, were almost impossible to buy, except from specialist shops, until the late eighties, so once again we grew our own. One year, we had 15 varieties including Scotch Bonnets and habanero, which were so hot we could scarcely handle them. At

Left: In the early years of the School even garlic was exotic to many students.
Above: Dried red chillies.

first I would explain the basics to students: the smaller the chilli, the more wary you need to be; the seeds and placenta are the hottest part, so you should remove and discard those if you don't want too much heat. Red chillies are often hotter than green as they are riper. I teach students to be careful not to rub their eyes or any other sensitive part of the body when handling chillies.

At first students were just concerned about heat, but gradually they began to distinguish the different flavours of various types of chilli and started to use them accordingly, e.g. jalapeño and serrano chillies for Mexican dishes and Thai chillies for Asian food. Chillies are widely available in supermarkets now but the variety on offer is still very limited. Most common are the red and green Dutch chillies (also known as Holland finger) and the thin Thai chilli and tiny chillies, sometimes referred to as rat droppings. The latter really pack a punch and we refer to them as scud missiles. They are so tiny you can scarcely see them in a Thai beef salad but if you eat one unexpectedly it's rather like being paralysed – you turn bright red, are rendered speechless and your eyes bulge.

Spices have had a similar evolution over the past 30 years of the School. In the early 1980s, we all knew about a handful of spices: cloves for apple tart and hot whiskey, caraway seeds for seed cake, dried ginger for rhubarb jam and ground for gingerbread. There was pepper of course, but ground white pepper was still in use in most households and pepper mills were considered very posh, while whole black peppercorns had to be ordered specially.

Madhur Jaffrey, Sri Owen and Claudia Roden introduced us to the magic of a whole range of Indian and Asian spices and showed us how to tease up to five different flavours out of each spice, depending on how one used it and when it was added to a dish.

At first it was quite difficult to source a wide variety of fresh spices, but as Irish people have gradually become exposed to spicy food, both here in Ireland and on their travels, they cannot get enough of it. In 2004 we started to put on a range of Cooking with Spices courses. We choose 8–10 spices and use many of our favourite recipes to illustrate how to cook with them. Everyone loves the food and leaves with the skills and confidence to experiment with them at home.

In 2006, Anglo-Indian past student Arun Kapil, started to import spices from his family's spice garden in South India. We were thrilled to be able to get superb quality, really fresh spices. Nowadays, spices, chilli and fresh herbs are a central component of much of our food, and our students get ever more adventurous.

Above: Jars of a huge number of spices line the shelves at the Cookery School as we try to introduce students to a diverse range of flavours from a variety of international cuisines.
Right: Over the past 30 years of the School the number of spices that students are familiar with has greatly increased, partly due to the food and spice markets, such as this one, that they encounter on their travels.

Sri Owen's Beef Rendang

Sri Owen was one of our earliest guest chefs in July 1989. Sri was born in West Sumatra and lived in Indonesia until moving to England in 1964. She introduced us to many gems including this rendang, a wonderful slow-cooked dish from Malaysia, Indonesia and Sumatra usually served for feasts and celebrations. It should be chunky and dry, yet succulent.

Serves 8

1.5kg (3lb 5oz) beef brisket or good stewing steak
5 shallots, chopped
4 garlic cloves, peeled and chopped
3cm (1¼in) piece of fresh root ginger, roughly chopped
4 red chillies, deseeded and roughly chopped (or 2 teaspoons chilli powder)
1 bay leaf
1 stick of lemongrass, bruised
1 teaspoon ground turmeric
1.8 litres (3 pints) coconut milk
sea salt and freshly ground black pepper

To serve
a handful of fresh mint leaves (optional)
lime wedges

Cut the meat into 4cm (1½in) cubes. Purée the shallots, garlic, ginger and chillies (or chilli powder) in a food processor. Scoop the purée into a wide sauté pan or wok, add the bay leaf, lemongrass, turmeric, salt and meat and pour in coconut milk. Bring to the boil, stirring, over a medium heat. Reduce the heat and bubble away gently for 3 hours, stirring from occasionally. After this time, the sauce should be quite thick.

Continue to cook, stirring frequently, until the coconut milk starts to go oily and then keep stirring until all of the oil has been absorbed by the meat. Taste and add more salt if necessary.

Serve hot with a bowl of fluffy rice. Sri likes to serve some fresh mint leaves and segments of lime with the rendang.

Note: Rendang keeps well in the fridge and reheats perfectly.

Spiced Cauliflower and Tomato with Parsley

This recipe comes from Chhatra Sagar in Rajasthan, where we have eaten some of the most delicious food in India.

Serves 6–8

1 dessertspoon extra virgin olive oil
1 bay leaf
2 cloves
5cm (2in) cinnamon stick
2 black cardamom pods
110g (4oz) onions, sliced
2–3 teaspoons finely grated fresh root ginger
1 large garlic clove, peeled and crushed
2 fresh chillies, chopped
2 teaspoons ground cumin
2 teaspoons ground coriander
900g (2lb) very ripe tomatoes, or 2 x 400g (14oz) cans of chopped tomatoes
2 tablespoons freshly chopped coriander
900g (2lb) cauliflower florets
110g (4oz) French beans
sea salt, freshly ground black pepper and sugar

To serve
2 tablespoons flat-leaf parsley

Heat the oil in a stainless-steel saucepan. Add the bay leaf, cloves, cinnamon stick and cardamom. Stir and sizzle for 30 seconds. Add the onions, ginger, garlic, chilli, cumin and coriander and toss until coated in oil. Cover and sweat over a gentle heat until completely soft but not coloured – approx. 10 minutes.

Remove the hard core from the tomatoes. If using fresh tomatoes, put them in a deep bowl and cover with boiling water for 10 seconds. Then remove and peel off the skins. Slice the tomatoes and add to the onions. Season with salt, black pepper and sugar to taste. Add the coriander and cook for a further 10–20 minutes or until the tomato softens.

Meanwhile, blanch the cauliflower florets in lightly salted water for 2–3 minutes. Drain, refresh under cold water and drain again. Blanch and refresh the beans in the same way, but for 1 minute only.

When the tomatoes are soft, add the cauliflower and beans. Taste and correct the seasoning if necessary. Scatter with flat-leaf parsley and serve.

Pears Poached in a Saffron Syrup

Most exotic of all the fruit compotes, pears cooked this way turn a wonderful deep golden colour and are delicately infused with the flavours of saffron and cardamom, two of the world's most precious spices. We use Conference and Doyenne du Comice pears. This compote is rich and intensely sweet and best served well chilled. (Be careful not to use too much saffron or the pears will be too strong.) The juice is delicious so serve lots with the pears. If there is some left over, set with gelatine to make delicious pear and saffron jellies. Use 3 teaspoons of powdered gelatine to 600ml (1 pint) of juice.

Serves 4

200g (7oz) granulated sugar
425ml (15fl oz) water
6 whole cardamom pods, lightly crushed
¼ teaspoon good-quality saffron threads
3 tablespoons freshly squeezed lemon juice
4 firm pears

Put the sugar, water, cardamom pods, saffron and lemon juice into a shallow, wide pan: we use a stainless-steel sauté pan. Stir to dissolve the sugar and bring to a simmer.

Meanwhile, peel the pears, cut them in half and remove the cores. As you prepare each pear, drop it straight into the simmering syrup, cut-side up.

Cover the pan with a circle of greaseproof paper and put the lid on the pan as well. Simmer away gently until the pears are tender, approx. 20–30 minutes, spooning the syrup over them every now and then.

Once the pears are cooked, carefully lift them out of the pan and arrange them in a single layer, cut-side down, in a serving dish. Pour the syrup over the pears. Alternatively, you can reduce the syrup first so that it thickens slightly. (For a more concentrated flavour, the syrup may be reduced a little after the pears have been removed to a serving dish. Be careful not to cook it for too long, or the syrup will caramelise.) Serve chilled.

Note: This compote keeps for several weeks, covered, in the fridge.

Variations

Poached Pears
Omit the saffron, cardamom pods and 3 tablespoons of lemon juice and simply add the thinly pared rind and juice of 1 lemon instead.

Poached Pears with Sweet Geranium Leaves
Omit the saffron and cardamom pods and add 3–4 large sweet-scented geranium leaves instead.

Poached Pears with Lemon Verbena Leaves
Omit the saffron and cardamom pods and add 4–6 lemon verbena leaves instead.

Poached Pears with Grated Ginger
Omit the saffron and cardamom pods and add a 2.5cm (1in) piece of peeled and thinly sliced fresh root ginger instead.

Keeping Chickens

I don't ever remember a time when we didn't have hens. When I was a child Mummy always kept a flock of Rhode Island Reds crossed with Leghorn. The hens had a large patch of grass at the far end of the vegetable garden, fenced in with chicken wire. The food scraps from the house were mixed with soaked 'presto' (rolled corn/maize) and some Layers Mash and fed to the hens every day. As children we took turns at feeding the hens and freshly laid eggs were part of our life. When the weather turned cold and wet the hens laid less but we had an abundance of eggs from around Easter throughout the summer. From Easter onwards, Mummy preserved

Above: A free-roaming Ballymaloe chicken, strutting her stuff in front of the Cookery School.
Right: We have 6–7 different traditional breeds of hens at Ballymaloe, which are all suited to free-range production. Hens are naturally forestial so they enjoy being able to shelter from the sun and perch on the branches of the trees. (Sussex white hens are pictured.)

some of this glut in buckets of Isinglass, also known as Waterglass, a substance derived from the swim bladders of fish and a form of collagen. It was sold in a tin and mixed with water in a bucket and used as a preservative for eggs. The eggs were carefully layered in this solution in the bucket and covered. They were kept in a cool place and used mainly for baking in winter when the hens virtually stopped laying and their fresh eggs were too scarce to be used for baking. They kept well for a few months and were very precious, even though they had an odd taste.

When Tim and I got married in 1970, I immediately thought of getting a few hens for Ballymaloe. Frank Walsh, who had worked on the farm for over 60 years, cleared out a little toolshed in the farmyard for my half a dozen birds. They were free-range but went indoors at night to roost.

When we started the School in 1983 we increased the flock in order to have enough eggs to use in the classes. Later when our yellow Transit van conked out, we converted it into a larger hen house, much to the amusement of the students. Now we have about 300 organic hens divided into three flocks, a mixture of traditional breeds: Maran, Rhode Island Red, Light Sussex, Leghorn and Ancona. I prefer the traditional breeds for the flavour and quality of the eggs, plus they are more suited to free-range production.

Apart from the Speckledy and Hebden Blacks, we've got quite a collection of rare breeds, which I'd love to add to even further – we have Silkies, Cochins, Buff Orpingtons, Marans, Pekin, Hamburgs, Araucanas, Campines and Welsummers. Some lay brown speckledy eggs, others, like the Anconas, almost blue, so beautiful. In fact, if I had to choose my last meal it would be a delicious boiled free-range egg with little soldiers of Timmy's soda bread – a forgotten flavour for most people nowadays. I was convinced that absolutely everyone knew about boiled eggs, but recently, to our astonishment, we met not one but two people who had never eaten a boiled egg before, so we delighted in introducing them to the most fundamental gourmet experience by collecting a few eggs from the nest underneath the rosemary bush outside our

kitchen door, boiling them gently so the yolk was still soft and the white just set. We showed them how to top them and enjoy with sea salt, freshly ground pepper and soldiers of hot toast smothered with homemade butter.

On the 12-week certificate courses the students feed the hens on a rota basis as part of their duties. The scraps from the morning's cooking that don't qualify for the stockpot, e.g. some vegetable peelings, scorched offerings, overcooked bread and other culinary mistakes, are relegated to the hens' bucket. It's an integral part of the students' education on how food is produced. They understand the wonderfully holistic system, where the leftover food scraps get fed to the hens, who reward us with beautiful fresh eggs a few days later. No waste, and we don't have to pay the local council to dispose of the garbage in landfill.

The system we operate is dual purpose. In each hen run, we have a builders' skip beside the gate. The hens now associate it with food so when we tip the bucket of food scraps in, the hens hop up and gobble up the tasty morsels. We scatter a layer of straw over the top in the evening. Usually the skip is full by the end of the week. It's a perfect combination of straw, some vegetable matter and chicken manure, which activates the compost. This is taken down on the front loader to the compost area and tipped onto a compost bay. The students understand the cycle and know that the compost will be returned to the ground to enrich and enhance the fertility of the soil when it is spread out on the land about nine months later.

The eggs from the grass-fed free-ranging hens are an essential part of our cooking and baking. Because they are allowed to forage and peck around in different areas with access to a variety of grasses, weeds and worms, the birds are healthy and the eggs totally delicious.

The students learn how to keep hens and many can't wait to get a little flock of their own. Having tasted and cooked with these beautiful eggs they realise the phenomenal difference that eggs of this quality make to the finished product. Some students love the hens and are intrigued by their antics, others are actually scared of them. One girl was so terrified when she saw the hens running towards her, she dropped the buckets and ran. Now we explain that the hens are not remotely interested in the person, just the food!

We had a student a few years ago who really enjoyed feeding the hens and regularly offered to feed them for his classmates. He was always amused when the hens ran towards him and joked that they were the only appreciative females he ever met!

Visitors to the School love to see the fancy fowl pecking around

Left: Michael Dwane, who has been working with us part-time on the farm for many years.
Above: This Barnevelder hen hatched out a duck egg, which Eileen O'Donovan's mother had given me as a present. The hen was delighted but a bit puzzled by her achievement, especially when the little duckling found the pond and swam merrily away as the hen pranced up and down on the bank squawking in alarm!

Above (top): One of our 'fancy fowl' – the heirloom varieties we have a Ballymaloe – perched on the garden seat for a siesta.
Above (middle): A Maran made a nest and hatched out a clutch of chicks on the top of the wall close to the courtyard barn.
Above (bottom): A chicken chorus line, on top of the wall.
Right: My daughter Lydia's painted illustration on the chick house, where we transfer the baby chicks after hatching them in the incubator. They then graduate to the Palais des Poulets next door when they reach about five months old.

by the Palais des Poulets – this is a rather grand name for a simple stone farm building with white-washed walls and a chandelier hanging rather incongruously from the ceiling.

We regularly got requests for advice on how to keep a few hens, so in May 2005 we offered our first How to Keep a Few Chickens in the Garden course. Such was the interest that almost 80 people signed up. We have continued to offer these courses as a part of our Forgotten Skills series, and it is heartening to see that there has been a phenomenal increase in the number of people keeping hens, both in urban and rural areas, in recent years. I was recently in New York and guess what the coolest new hobbies were – keeping chickens in your backyard and bees on your roof, can you imagine? Public demand is such that the by-laws have changed in many areas to enable people to keep their own fowl. At one dinner party in Brooklyn, guests spent over half an hour comparing notes on how to keep chickens!

At the farmers' market in Union Square they were selling eggs from several different rare breeds of hens, the beautiful blue-green eggs of the Araucanas were selling at several dollars a dozen more than the others and at Dean & DeLuca in Manhattan; beautiful duck eggs sell individually for two or three dollars each.

Eggs were starring on restaurant menus too; at The Green Table in Chelsea Market I had a beautiful plate of devilled eggs on a bed of red watercress, with crusty bread from Amy's Bakery next door. Scotch eggs were everywhere with even quail's eggs wrapped in a succulent mix of heritage pork sausage meat. At Buvette, a chic little French café on Grove St in the West Village I had a bowl of slow-cooked kale topped with a poached eggs and some grilled bread with crumbly pecorino for breakfast and 'ino in Bedford Street served Truffled egg on toast that were worth flying over for.

Like many people who keep their own hens, I'm frightfully fussy about eating eggs away from home, but nowadays in New York there are actually places where you can trust the quality of the eggs – they may even come from someone's backyard or a roof garden in the neighbourhood.

In 2006 we bought an incubator. We also keep some breeding pairs of traditional and rarer poultry in chicken arks (mobile miniature hen houses) in the orchard, so we have fertilised eggs for hatching. The problem is the fancier the breed, the less inclined they are to lay – sort of 'too posh to push!' They strut around being decorative rather than functional, but I love them nonetheless. Every term when we put eggs into the incubator and we demonstrate this to both the Cookery School students and the

children from the local school (9–12 years old) who are part of the East Cork Slow Food Educational Project. Twenty-one days later the chicks start to hatch out of the shells – you can't imagine the excitement from 'children' of all ages, another lesson in how food is produced. After several hours they fluff up and get perky enough to be moved out under the infra-red lamp in the Palais des Poulets. They remain warm and cosy under an infra-red lamp in the chicken shed for at least another month until they are hardy enough to go outdoors. After a few weeks they grow pin feathers and eventually proper plumage. We have to wait to see which birds grow little tails: those will grow into fine cockerels and the others will mature into hens. We fatten up the cockerels for the pot and the hens keep us supplied with beautiful eggs. In many countries there is a tradition of dyeing and painting eggs to be given as presents at Easter, a tradition that we very much foster in our family and in fact our clever hens actually lay coloured eggs with children's names on them on Easter Sunday!

Research has shown that organic, free-range eggs are considerably lower in cholesterol than eggs from intensive production systems. Hens lay a maximum of one a day, on average five days a week, depending on season or weather. Five or six hens will provide plenty of eggs for an average household. You don't need much space to keep a couple of hens, unlike cattle, sheep or pigs which need much more space and are a totally different proposition. They also generate a supply of nitrogen and phosphate-rich manure that will turn into a rich compost for your garden. They are brilliant for pest and weed control; we let the hens into the vegetable garden in the winter to gobble up slugs and insects. From a cook's point of view, the quality of an egg hugely affects the flavour and texture of food. The best mayonnaise, béarnaise and hollandaise sauce is made from fresh free-range eggs.

If students or visitors want to get a little flock of their own, I always advise first checking the planning regulations in their area. Usually regulations do not expressly forbid keeping livestock in your garden, so long as they are for family use rather than business purposes. Chickens are sometimes sold as livestock marts, farmers' markets or after summer agricultural shows. Buy from a reputable supplier and ask for a certificate to prove they are disease-free.

Eggs Bhurji

Geoffrey Dobbs owns several of the most beautiful hotels in Sri Lanka, I love the food he serves and have made several return trips. I have cooked several dinners there and always have some cookery classes from the Sri Lankan chefs in the kitchens. Even breakfast is a feast with freshly cut, perfectly ripe fruit, curd and jaggery, Ceylon tea, chilli eggs, stringhoppers (a Sri Lankan noodle speciality) or Eggs Bhurji – a memorable breakfast dish and easy to reproduce in less exotic climes.

Serves 2

25g (1oz) butter
1 teaspoon mustard seeds
a few small fresh curry leaves
2 spring onions, finely sliced
½ teaspoon grated fresh root ginger
½ hot green chilli, deseeded and thinly sliced
pinch of ground turmeric
½ teaspoon ground cumin
1 tomato, skinned and diced
4 organic eggs, beaten

To serve
toast or fried bread

Melt the butter in a frying pan over a medium heat. Add the mustard seeds, stir once, then add the curry leaves and spring onion. Stir and cook over a low to medium heat until the onions are soft. Add the ginger, chilli, turmeric, cumin and diced tomato and fry gently for a couple of minutes, stirring regularly.

Add the beaten eggs and continue to stir over a low heat until the eggs are softly scrambled. Serve on warm plates, accompanied by hot toast or fried bread.

Kuku Kadoo – Persian Courgette Omelette

This is the Persian version of a Spanish tortilla, Italian frittata or an Arabic eggah (also known as ajjah). There are myriad versions and some use baking powder instead of bicarbonate of soda. Traditionally this is cooked in a frying pan and flipped over but it also works very well in the oven. Kuku Kadoo is one of my favourites.

Serves 6–8

2 tablespoons extra virgin olive oil, plus extra for greasing
450g (1lb) onions, finely chopped
3 garlic cloves, peeled and crushed
¼ teaspoon grated fresh root ginger
6 small courgettes, halved lengthways and cut into thin slices
8 organic eggs
1 teaspoon ground turmeric
3 tablespoons plain flour
½ teaspoon bicarbonate of soda
sea salt and freshly ground black pepper

To serve
flat-leaf parsley sprigs and sumac

Preheat the oven to 180°C/350°F/gas 4 and grease a 25cm (10in) gratin dish with a little oil.

Heat the oil in a frying pan over a medium heat. Add the onion, garlic and ginger, cover with a lid and sweat for 6–8 minutes until soft but not coloured. Add the courgettes, season with salt and pepper and cook for 6–8 minutes, stirring.

Whisk the eggs in a large mixing bowl with the turmeric, flour and bicarbonate of soda. Add the cooked courgette mixture to the eggs and stir well. Pour into the greased gratin dish and bake for 25–30 minutes until just set. Serve sprinkled with parsley sprigs and sumac.

Asian Soy and Five-Spice Chicken Breasts with Cucumber, Radish and Mint Salad

The free-range chickens on Dan Aherne's organic farm in East Cork are reared for a minimum of 80 days, sometimes longer, so the breasts can be so large we just use four and divide each into two pieces.

Preheat the oven to 180°C/350°F/gas 4. Mix the flour and five-spice powder in a shallow bowl with a good pinch of sea salt and some freshly ground black pepper.

Heat a wok or frying pan over a high heat. Add the oil and heat until it is just starting to smoke. Meanwhile, toss the chicken breasts one at a time into the seasoned flour. Deep-fry the chicken breasts in the hot oil, a couple at a time, until the skin is crispy – approx. 3–5 minutes. Drain on kitchen paper and set aside, reserving the oil in the pan.

Arrange the lemon slices on a baking tray and lay the crispy chicken breasts on top. Roast in the hot oven until fully cooked, approx. 10–12 minutes depending on size.

To make the salad, cut the cucumber in half lengthways, then in half again. Cut into 1cm (½in dice) and transfer to a bowl. Trim the radishes and cut into similar-sized pieces and mix with the cucumber. Season with salt and freshly ground black pepper. Drizzle with the extra virgin olive oil and freshly squeezed lemon juice. Toss gently, add the herbs and mix. Taste again and correct the seasoning if necessary.

To finish the chicken, pour away all but 2 tablespoons of the oil in the wok or pan. Return the pan to the heat and add the finely grated ginger, honey, soy sauce, lemon juice and soft brown sugar. Bring to the boil and simmer for 3–4 minutes until the sauce starts to thicken. Add the cooked chicken pieces back to the pan and coat them with the sauce.

To serve, transfer the chicken and sauce to a serving dish. Accompany with noodles (or fettuccine) and the Cucumber, Radish and Mint Salad.

Serves 8

4 tablespoons plain white flour
1½ teaspoons Chinese five-spice powder
100ml (3½fl oz) sunflower oil, for deep-frying
8 organic chicken breasts (skin on)
1 lemon, cut into 8 slices
3cm (1¼in) piece of fresh root ginger, peeled and grated
75ml (3fl oz) honey
75ml (3fl oz) dark soy sauce
freshly squeezed juice of 2 lemons
2 tablespoons soft brown sugar
sea salt and freshly ground black pepper

For the Cucumber, Radish and Mint Salad
1 fresh cucumber
18–24 radishes, trimmed and quartered
sea salt and freshly ground black pepper
3 tablespoons extra virgin olive oil
1 tablespoon freshly squeezed lemon juice
a handful of fresh mint leaves
a handful of fresh flat-leaf parsley

Salad of Smoked Chicken with Parsnip Crisps and Myrtle Berries

We've got two *Myrtus ugni* planted in large terracotta pots on the balcony outside the kitchens. The bittersweet wine-coloured berries are delicious in winter salads, particularly with game, guinea fowl or smoked chicken, as in this recipe.

First make the parsnip crisps. Heat the oil to 150°C (300°F) in a deep-fryer.

Scrub and peel the parsnips. Either slice into wafter-thin rounds or peel off long slivers lengthways with a swivel-top peeler. Leave to dry on kitchen paper.

Drop a few of the parsnip rounds or slivers at a time into the hot oil; they colour and crisp up very quickly. Drain on kitchen paper and sprinkle lightly with salt. Keep warm in a low oven (approx. 110°C/225°F/gas ¼).

To make the French dressing, put all the ingredients into a blender and run at medium speed for approx. 1 minute. Set aside.

Put the salad leaves into a bowl. Sprinkle with a little French dressing and toss until the leaves are nicely coated. Taste and divide the salad between four large places.

Slice the chicken breast thinly and arrange upwards around the salad. Put a clump of warm parsnip crisps on top. Sprinkle some myrtle berries around the salad. Garnish with chervil or flat-leaf parsley and serve immediately.

Serves 4

a selection of mixed salad leaves such as Oak Leaf, Little Gem or lamb's lettuce, rocket, finely sliced Savoy cabbage, claytonia (winter purslane), Pennywort and Purslane
2 smoked chicken breasts
olive oil
approx. 100g myrtle berries
sea salt and freshly ground black pepper

For the Parsnip Crisps
sunflower or peanut oil
1 large parsnip
sea salt

For the French Dressing (Makes 225ml (8fl oz))
50ml (2 fl oz) wine vinegar
175ml (6fl oz) extra virgin olive oil
1 level teaspoon Dijon or English mustard
1 large garlic clove
1 spring onion
a sprig of flat-leaf parsley
a sprig of watercress
1 level teaspoon salt
few grinds of black pepper

To serve
chervil or flat-leaf parsley

Blathnaid's Chocolate Cake

We have about ten chocolate cakes in our repertoire, from Cynthia's Chocolate Cake made with cocoa and buttermilk, to the decadently rich Ballymaloe Chocolate Cake made with the very best chocolate money can buy, lots of ground almonds and a silky chocolate icing. But if I had to choose just one, it might have to be this recipe given to me by my sister Blathnaid Bergin. It is deliciously chocolatey, yet light and rich at the same time. You can serve it very simply with the chocolate ganache poured over the top or tart it up for a celebration cake.

Preheat the oven to 180°C/350°F/gas 4. Grease two 20cm (8in) cake tins with melted butter, dust with flour and line the base of each one with a circle of greaseproof paper.

To make the cake, put the milk and chopped chocolate into a saucepan and warm gently over a low heat until the chocolate melts. Set aside to cool.

Sift the flour, salt, bicarbonate of soda and baking power into a bowl. In a separate bowl, cream the butter and sugar until light and fluffy. Beat the eggs with the vanilla extract in another bowl and beat them into the creamed mixture a little at a time, adding 1 tablespoon of the flour with each addition. Fold in the cooled chocolate mixture, followed by the remaining flour. Divide between the two prepared tins and bake for 30–35 minutes or until the cakes have begun to shrink in slightly from the sides of the tin. Set aside to cool in their tins for a few minutes, and then turn them out carefully and transfer to a wire rack to cool completely.

Meanwhile, make the filling. Melt the chocolate in a heatproof bowl over a saucepan of hot water. Set aside to cool slightly. In a large mixing bowl, cream the butter for at least 10 minutes at high speed until pale and fluffy. Add the egg yolks and icing sugar and contine to beat vigorously for a further 5 minutes. Once the butter mixture is thoroughly mixed, remove 2 tablespoons and stir it into the cooled, melted chocolate. Then slowly pour the melted chocolate down the side of the mixing bowl into the butter mixture and fold it in quickly and gently until fully combined and smooth.

Once the cakes are cold you can start making the chocolate ganache. Put the chocolate in a large bowl. Heat the cream to boiling point, pour it over the chocolate and stir until it melts; set aside to cool. Whisk the cooled chocolate cream until it barely forms soft peaks, taking care not to overwhisk it or it will become too stiff to

Serves 10–12

150g (5oz) butter, plus extra for greasing
225g (8oz) plain white flour, plus extra for dusting
225ml (8fl oz) milk
75g (3oz) plain chocolate (approx. 52 per cent cocoa solids), chopped
pinch of salt
½ teaspoon bicarbonate of soda
2 level teaspoons baking power
275g (10oz) soft light brown sugar
3 organic eggs
1 teaspoon pure vanilla extract

For the chocolate filling
200g (7oz) plain chocolate (approx. 52 per cent cocoa solids), chopped
250g (9oz) butter, softened
4 organic egg yolks
150g (5oz) icing sugar, sifted

For the chocolate ganache
150g (5oz) plain chocolate (approx. 52 per cent cocoa solids), chopped
300ml (10fl oz) double cream

To decorate
chocolate curls
unsweetened cocoa powder and icing sugar, to dust

spread and may turn into chocolate butter. (Use as soon as possible, otherwise it will become too stiff to spread.)

To assemble the cake, split the cakes in half horizontally with a sharp serrated knife. Spread the chocolate filling onto each layer and sandwich the four layers together. Ice the cake with the chocolate ganache and decorate as you wish – we like to use chocolate curls, dredging them with unsweetened cocoa and icing sugar.

Butchery

There was great excitement in October 2005 when Hugh Fearnley-Whittingstall and his butcher at River Cottage, Ray Mears, came to teach a Cutting Up a Pig in a Day course at the School. Our local butcher, Frank Murphy, slaughtered a couple of our Saddleback pigs for them to butcher. Using these pigs, which had been hung for several days, Ray began by butchering the carcass and then continued on to explain the different cuts and how they can be used. Hugh and Ray demonstrated how to brine a leg to make a ham, then how to dry-cure bacon and salt pork belly. They used the head and trotters to make brawn and the liver and some pork belly were minced to make Ray's Rich Liver Pâté. They made delicious juicy sausages, chorizo and salami. The tenderloin was stuffed and roasted and the kidneys were devilled; not a scrap was wasted. Both the teachers and students were agog with excitement. Hugh is an inspirational teacher and he and Ray made a brilliant duo.

In 2005 my youngest daughter Emily brought her German boyfriend, Philip Dennhardt, home from New York with her. (He and Emily married down by the pond in the garden in 2011.) Philip is a master butcher from a long line of craft butchers who have passed their skills from generation to generation. He immediately started to teach some of the Forgotten Skills courses at the School, including Butchering; How to Cure a Pig in a Day and Use Every Morsel; How to Build a Smoker and Smoke Your Own Food; Butchery, Charcuterie and Sausage Making; Hands-on Pork Butchery, as well as tutoring bespoke courses for those who wanted hands-on butchery classes.

The first of these was in October 2006 when we ran a Pig in a Day course and a Basic Home Butchery Course. We now offer these courses every year and they are extremely popular. Participants learn how to butcher a side of pork like a professional and transform it into a full range of fresh and cured hams, succulent sausages and perfect charcuterie. They are instructed in how to produce air-dried ham, brine-cured ham, brawn, bacon, sausages, chorizos, salamis and country pâtés and terrines. Every morsel of the pig is put to good use.

Students who have a particular interest in doing their own in-house butchery have the option to learn more when Philip butchers our beef and occasional carcasses of lamb. We buy all our poultry whole and teach the students how to joint a chicken, duck, guinea fowl, quail or rabbit in a matter of minutes and then show them how to put every single scrap to delicious use and make a fine pot of stock or broth from the carcass and giblets.

Almost every term, Haulie Walsh, our Farm Manager, who has been with us since he was in his teens, takes one of our prime cattle to the local butcher to be slaughtered, so we also have our own dry-aged, well-hung beef for burgers and meat for prime-rib roasts, stews and casseroles. We show the students how to cut their own steaks and short ribs and explain how to buy and judge good meat. We urge them to build up a relationship with their local butcher, to inquire about the breed and feed, and to seek out dry-aged meat, rather than vacuum-packed meat joints. They also learn about hanging times. We encourage them to ask their butcher about the different cuts that are available and how best to cook them; you can learn something new every time you shop.

Left: Hugh Fearnley-Whittingstall and his River Cottage butcher,
Ray Mears, when they came to Ballymaloe in October 2005.
As well as butchering the carcasses of two of our Saddleback pigs,
they got students involved in making sausages.
Above: Our black Berkshire cross sow with her motley collection
of piglets snuffling around in the paddock.

The rise in interest in home-butchery has been phenomenal over the past decade. Both male and female students want to learn how to butcher, cure meat and make charcuterie. There's great excitement when we get one of our pigs back from our local butcher. Even though it's an extra-curricular activity on the 12-week course, there's always a queue of students who want to learn about the various meat cuts and discover how to butcher the carcass. We get a wide range of nationalities, but all seem to be fascinated. This trend is reflected in the proliferation of butchery classes everywhere from The Ginger Pig in London to The Meat Hook in Brooklyn – all are over-subscribed.

There's also a resurgence of interest in nose to tail eating for a variety of reasons, not least economic. Chefs such Fergus Henderson of St John in London have blazed a trail and put marrow bones, faggots, pigs' ears and scrag end back on their menus and reminded us how delicious the lesser-known cuts can be. The skill of cooking the cheaper cuts was all but lost until a combination of food trends and necessity forced us to re-evaluate. Now there's a realisation that anyone can slap a steak into a pan, but it takes greater skill and patience to coax a more muscular cut to melting tenderness and the added bonus is the sensational flavour. We now incorporate an increased number of slow-cooked dishes and offal into our menus at the School and the reaction is overwhelmingly positive.

There are other changes afoot, as dieticians regularly remind us that too much red meat can be detrimental to our hearts. Recent

food scares like the horsemeat scandal have highlighted the dangers of cheap meat and consequently more people seem to be deciding to eat less, but better quality free-range and organic meat.

The notion of eating less meat, but sourcing heritage breeds from small, less intensive production systems is gathering momentum. The general public have become more aware and concerned about animal welfare issues and sustainability. In the US and further afield, the idea of a meat-free Monday has started to gain credence for health, environmental and ethical reasons. It received a boost in 2009 when Sir Paul McCartney and his daughters Stella and Mary launched their Meat Free Monday campaign. In April 2010 Mario Batali launched Meat Free Monday menus in all 14 of his restaurants and many other high profile chefs including Wolfgang Puck have followed suit.

The Food and Agriculture Organization of the United Nations (FAO) estimates that livestock production is responsible for up to 18 per cent of global greenhouse gas emissions. Some estimates put the figure even higher. Global meat production also uses massive amounts of water. However, here in Ireland our animals are predominantly grass-fed and we are certainly not short of water thus far, but who knows what lies in store with global warming. Another good reason for Meat Free Monday is the growing body of research that indicates that meat- and dairy-heavy diets can play a role in obesity, which increases people's risk of developing many chronic diseases including cancer, heart disease and stroke.

Slow Food also promotes the idea that responsible meat consumption means eating less meat and only eating meat from animals that have been raised with a high quality of life. They try to teach people to pay a fair price for meat, on that reflects the true cost of production that respects animal welfare. Slow Food's consumer guide, Too Much at Steak, outlines good practice that can be applied to everyday life, when shopping and eating at home or in restaurants.

Above: Student Emily Ashworth making sausages with Philip Dennhardt on the 12-week course.
Right: Preparing a leg of lamb for roasting – I have removed the chine bone and am about to trim the knuckle. I really enjoy butchering; at Ballymaloe we buy all our joints of meat unprepared so that we can teach students this skill.

Dawn Chorus

Dennis O'Sullivan has worked with us as a painter, plasterer, slater and glazier for over 40 years and has been involved in the process of converting many of the farm buildings into the cottages where the students reside when they are at the School. Dennis's absorbing hobby is birdwatching. It is fantastic to have an almost resident ornithologist on site. He's extraordinarily knowledgeable and observant and can always tell us where there's a nesting pair of this or that species on the farm or in the local area.

In 2006 Dennis offered to do a bird survey of the farm and he has been doing it brilliantly ever since. It's been a very interesting exercise and Dennis has been fascinated to discover the biodiversity of species on our 100 acres. There are 46 different bird species at present, much higher than the average, but consistent with Soil Association surveys that show increased biodiversity on organic farms.

The farm is rich in trees and hedgerows and we have always resisted the temptation to chop hedges as is the common practice in modern farming. My father-in-law Ivan Allen had a lifelong interest in birds and was made a fellow of The Royal Society for the Protection of Birds (RSPB) in the late 1980s. Even though he was a progressive conventional farmer for most of his life, he always created and protected the bird habitats on the farm, sometimes delaying or mowing around nests in the grass so as not to disturb the nesting birds.

I'm not sure why it took me so long to think to ask Dennis to take the students on a Dawn Chorus walk. We introduced it in 2008 and it's been a regular facet of the summer courses ever since; more recently Dennis has introduced Dusk Chorus walks as well. The students love them, as do we, and they greatly enhance our enjoyment of the environment we are fortunate enough to live in.

Slow-cooked Shin of Beef

This slow-cooked shin of beef is fantastic winter food. Gillian Hegarty, who teaches at the School and worked at the River Café, loves to cook this dish, one of Rose and Ruthie's favourites. It takes 12 hours of gentle simmering to reduce the shin to a rich, melting tenderness but it is so worth it. The beef is wonderful served with polenta but we also love it with potato and rosemary gratin and a good green salad.

Serves 6–8

1 shin of beef on the bone, weighing approx. 3kg (6lb 8oz)
75cl bottle of Chianti Classico (or more)
50 garlic cloves, peeled
8 thyme sprigs
3 tablespoons freshly ground black pepper
sea salt

To serve
½ loaf of sourdough bread, sliced and toasted
freshly grated Parmesan (optional)
extra virgin olive oil, for drizzling

Preheat the oven to 160°C/325°F/gas 3. If necessary, ask your butcher to cut the shin of beef from knuckle to knuckle into shorter lengths, approx. 18cm (7in) long.

Put the shin of beef into a large casserole or saucepan with a good tight-fitting lid. Cover with the wine. Add the garlic, thyme, pepper and a little salt and slowly bring to the boil. Cover with a greaseproof-paper lid and the lid of the saucepan. Cook gently in the preheated oven for 12 hours. Check every 3–4 hours and add more wine if the beef is uncovered. You may need to use more than one bottle of wine.

To serve, put the toasted sourdough bread in a bowl and the meat and juices on top. Sprinkle with Parmesan, if using, and a good drizzle of extra virgin olive oil. This dish can also be served with soft polenta.

Grilled Bavette or Hanger Steak with Shallots

A touch chewy but juicy and packed with flavour, this cut is a lot cheaper than fillet or sirloin steak, but probably not for long as a growing number of chefs have discovered this secret butcher's cut, which the French call Bavette.

Serves 4–6

50ml (2fl oz) extra virgin olive oil
2 garlic cloves, peeled and crushed
2 teaspoons freshly ground black pepper
700–900g (1½– 2lb) Bavette or Hanger steak
20g (¾oz) butter
6–10 shallots, finely sliced
1–2 tablespoons red wine vinegar
Maldon sea salt

To serve
freshly chopped flat-leaf parsley

First marinate the steaks. Mix the olive oil, garlic and cracked pepper together in a shallow dish, add the steaks and turn a couple of times. Cover with clingfilm and set aside to marinate in the fridge for at least 4 hours. Remove the steaks from the marinade and pat dry on kitchen paper.

Preheat a griddle pan over a high heat. Season the beef generously with sea salt and freshly ground black pepper. Sear well on all sides, reduce the heat and cook until rare (52°C/125°F) or medium (54°C/130°F). Remove the steaks from the pan and set aside to rest, covered with an upturned plate, while you deglaze the pan.

Melt the butter in the pan, add the shallots and sweat gently for 3–4 minutes until soft and slightly coloured. Increase the heat, add the vinegar and bring to the boil. Reduce the heat and stir well with a wooden spoon to scrape all the nice caramelised bits from the bottom of the pan.

To serve, cut the steaks into thin slices across the grain and sprinkle with the shallots and some freshly chopped parsley. They are delicious accompanied with a béarnaise sauce and lots of chips or sautéed potatoes.

Ham Hocks with Haricot Bean and Tomato Stew

Ham hocks are delicious with so many things – bean stew, cabbage and champ, lentils, shredded into a broth with diced vegetables or in a split pea soup. We also love to add chunks of quartered cabbages to the cooking water approx. 30 minutes before the end of cooking. Ham hocks are excellent value for money, one will easily feed two people or more when added to a chunky bean or lentil soup.

Soak the beans overnight in plenty of cold water.

Put the ham hocks into a deep saucepan, add the vegetables and seasonings. Cover with cold water, bring to the boil and simmer for 2–2½ hours or until the meat is virtually falling off the bones.

While the ham hocks are cooking, strain the beans, put in a saucepan and cover with fresh cold water. Add the bouquet garni, carrot and onion, cover and simmer until the beans are soft but not mushy – anything from 30–60 minutes. Just before the end of the cooking time add a pinch of salt. Remove the bouquet garni and vegetables and discard.

Meanwhile, sweat the chopped onion gently in olive oil in a wide saucepan until soft but not coloured, approx. 7–8 minutes. Add the garlic and cook for a further 1–2 minutes, then add the chopped tomatoes and their juice and cook for 6–8 minutes. Add the cooked beans and rosemary and cook for a further 5 minutes.

Remove the meat from the ham hocks, including the skin, and add to the bean stew. Simmer for 3–4 minutes, adding some of the bean liquid if necessary, and season well with salt, freshly ground black pepper and sugar. The mixture should be juicy but not swimming in liquid.

Sprinkle with lots of flat-leaf parsley and garnish with a sprig of rosemary to serve.

To make Ham Hock and Bean Soup, add 1.2 litres (2 pints) of chicken stock and some bean water to the stew for a deliciously robust soup.

Serves 4

2 fresh or smoked ham hocks
1 onion
4 garlic cloves
1 carrot, thickly sliced
2 celery sticks, chopped
1 bay leaf
1 teaspoon black peppercorns

For the Haricot Bean and Tomato Stew
200g (7oz) dried haricot beans
bouquet garni
1 whole carrot
1 whole onion
3 tablespoons olive oil
175g (6oz) chopped onion
4 large garlic cloves, crushed
1 x 400g (14oz) can of chopped tomatoes
1–2 tablespoons freshly chopped rosemary
sea salt, freshly ground black pepper and sugar

To serve
lots of flat-leaf parsley
a sprig of rosemary

Self-sufficiency

During the Celtic Tiger period between 1995–2008 there was rapid economic growth in Ireland with a building boom and a lot of immigrant labour. The country became quite wealthy and a lot of people had much more disposable income than they had been used to. Many lost a grip on reality and there was a frenzy of consumerism. Why bother to sow or grow or cook? If it could be bought, it was bought. But the music suddenly stopped in September 2008 when there was a serious banking crisis and Ireland, along with many other European countries, went into recession. Many people lost their jobs and were unable to pay mortgages on property they had bought during the 'good times' when property was over-valued. A period of serious austerity followed and people were forced to come down to earth and face a somewhat unpalatable reality. It took a while for people to adjust but quite soon many began to see the value of a degree of self-sufficiency.

As a result, the interest in re-learning almost forgotten skills has really gathered momentum in recent years. Many of our series of Forgotten Skills courses at the School were started in response to queries or requests from people who had never learned to make do and now needed to make their money stretch much further. These courses teach techniques such as preserving, pickling, smoking as well as how to keep your own chickens to show people how to make the most of their food and also produce their own. A course on How to Make Homemade Butter, Yogurt and Several Cheeses was first run in May 2006 to encourage people to make some dairy products at home or to add value to their produce on the farm. From day one it got an enthusiastic response; participants are given the option to arrive early to help bring in the cows and watch them being milked and they love it.

The class starts by separating the cream from the milk in the electric separator. The cream is churned into rich yellow butter and the milk is transformed into a variety of dairy products, from thick yogurt and labne to paneer, cottage cheese and a myriad of other cheeses. The whey is used to make beautiful tender ricotta (meaning re-cooked). The average Holstein Friesian milk produces

4–4.5 per cent butterfat (or milkfat), but our Jersey milk produces up to 6–7 per cent butterfat, depending on the time of year. The thick yellow cream is sublime with anything from porridge to coffee granita. This simple course takes the mystery out of these basic skills and gives people the confidence they need to experiment at home.

In 2008 we converted the hen house below the School into a milking parlour and dairy. Tim and Eileen O'Donovan started to make the Jersey milk into delicious, smooth yogurt and, buoyed on by this success, began to experiment with making a semi-hard cheese in 2009. The 12-week students were fascinated and soon became involved in making their own cheese. Now cheese is made several times a week and any students who wish to can make their own cheese, care for it during the term and take it home when they leave. Students who make cheese later in the term often come back to collect their cheese, which normally takes 12 weeks to mature.

The apple orchards in Kinoith were first planted by my father-in-law Ivan Allen in about 1935–1936 and there were beehives scattered through the orchards to enhance pollination. He grew about 15 varieties of apple in total, a mixture of cookers and eaters (dessert apples). Grenadier were ripe for using in September for compotes and apple pies, Bramley's Seedling matured later and could be stored through the winter in several cold stores in the farmyard, several of which have now been converted into student cottages. The 13 or more dessert apple varieties including Beauty of Bath, Lady Sudeley, James Grieve, Worcester Pearmain and Cox's Orange Pippin were chosen for flavour and keeping quality. The apples were sold from the apple-packing shed (now the Cookery School) and to wholesalers and a supermarket in Cork for a brief period in the late 1970s. Each year the price decreased and when we learned that thousands of acres of apples were being planted in Chile, we realised that the writing was on the wall for a small apple production unit such as ours.

We therefore made the decision to grub out most of the apple orchards but kept the orchard in the front of our house with a mixture of Worcester Pearmain, Grenadier, Bramley's Seeding and a few Cox's Orange Pippin. This, plus the new heirloom varieties that

Left: The students' cheeses with their names and details of the process on each label. Each one will taste slightly different depending on the way each person has handled it and interpreted the cheesemaking process. Right: Cheese going into the smoker. Emer Fitzgerald, a long-term teacher at the School, has a particular passion for the forgotten skills of foraging, pickling and smoking. Students love to experiment with smoking all different types of food, as well as the more traditional fish.

we have planted in recent years behind the Shell House, provides us with apples for the School and Ballymaloe House. We carefully store the Bramley's Seedling for winter use and in good years manage to have cooking apples until late February or early March.

Left: We are fortunate to be situated in the middle of a farm as we can grow most of our own produce. Some crops are seasonal but with onions, for example, we try to grow enough to provide us throughout the year as they can be dried and preserved for use over the winter.
Above: My daughter Emily picking potatoes.
Right: We preserve food throughout the seasons in a variety of ways, starting with marmalade during the citrus fruit season when the Seville and Malaga oranges reach the shops just after Christmas. As well as teaching preserving on the 12-week course we also run shorter pickling, preserving and fermentation courses, and have recently been inspired by Sandor Ellix Katz, the fermentation revivalist, after he visited Ballymaloe for the inaugural Literary Festival of Food and Wine in 2013.

Beekeeping

Up until the late 1970s our orchardist Sean Mullane also managed to look after the beehives situated throughout the orchards. We extracted the honey in the late summer and mainly apple blossom honey was much sought-after. It was extracted cold and the raw honey re-crystallised in the jars. It was truly delicious – a taste of Ballymaloe containing the antibodies of the area.

For many years we had no bees but we now have several hives back in the orchard. Initially they were looked after by our son Toby, but he became allergic to bee stings and so was forced to stop in 2008. A local beekeeper, Gary O'Keeffe, now cares for the bees and we purchase the honey from him in return for looking after the apiary. The students are fascinated and some want to learn how to keep bees and manage a beehive. We teach them about the crisis in bees around the world as more colonies are decimated by disease. Given the importance of bees in the ecosystem and the food chain, plus the multiple services they provide to humans, their survival is essential. The European Food Safety Authority (EFSA) has the mandate to improve EU food safety and to ensure a high level of consumer protection, so has an important role to play in protecting the survival of bees. The EFSA has completed a review of neonicotinoids (some of the most widely used insecticides in the world) as part of ongoing activities related to bees, and further research is conituning. Other studies have shown that exposure to neonicotinoids at sub-lethal doses can have significant effects on bee health and bee colonies; even doses that are not fatal may have damaging effects. So it was very welcome news when it was announced in April 2013 that the EU has imposed a two-year ban on the use of three neonicotinoid pesticides.

We try to keep students up-to-date on the latest research on the effect of neonicotinoids and other factors on bee colonies. Varroa, a parasitic mite, which attacks honey bees, and foulbrood, which also attacks bee colonies, have both had serious effects on the bee population.

Many students have gone on to keep bees at home on the roofs or balconies of their buildings as well as on farms and in gardens. In 2000 I gave my four children a present of a beehive for Christmas – it was no problem getting a beehive but it's really tough to get a nook of bees!

Above: A bee collecting pollen from a Nicotiana plant in the gardens at Ballymaloe.
Right: Delicious honey, rich in antibodies.
Far right: Our beekeeper Gary O'Keeffe checking the beehives.
We were all thrilled and relieved in the summer of 2013 to discover that we had not lost any of our bees in a year when most beekeepers were happy if 50 per cent of their bees had survived the winter. This created considerable interest from beekeepers and some think it could be linked to the biodiversity on the farm.

Bee Bedlam

In the summer of 2009 we had a young guy mowing the lawns who
fancied himself as Stirling Moss; despite lots of warnings he rode the
ride-on mower like a racing car and of course collided with a couple of
beehives. The irate bees tumbled out and he made a quick getaway on
the mower, but several garden visitors were forced to make a run for it
and the gardens had to be closed for the afternoon!

Pickled Vegetables

We are crazy about pickled vegetables and find all sorts of ways to serve them. I first came across lightly pickled vegetables at Momofuku in New York.

Makes approx. 1 litre (1¾ pints)

prepared fruit or vegetables of your choice (see right)

For the brine
450ml (16fl oz) hot water
225ml (8fl oz) rice vinegar
9 tablespoons sugar
4½ teaspoons dairy salt

Put all the ingredients for the brine into a bowl. Stir until the sugar and salt have dissolved. Tightly pack the vegetables or fruit into a 1.5 litre (2½ pints) sterilised Kilner jar, pressing them down well. Cover with the brine and fasten the lid.

Transfer the jar to the fridge to cure. Most pickled vegetables will keep for approx. 1 month. They can be eaten immediately, however they are best kept for at least 2–3 days before opening.

Pickled Carrots

900g (2lb) baby carrots, well scrubbed, peeled and trimmed

If very fresh, leave a little of the green stalks attached but wash well. Pack tightly into jars and cover with the brine. Refrigerate and mature for 2–3 days before eating.

Pickled Fennel

900g (2lb) fennel, cut into quarters and then sliced thinly lengthways
1 teaspoon coriander seeds

Pack tightly into jars and cover with the brine. Refrigerate and mature for 2–3 days before eating.

Pickled Beetroot

900g (2lb) small young beetroots, peeled and thinly sliced into discs or half-moons

Pack tightly into jars and cover with the brine. Refrigerate and mature for 2–3 days before eating.

Pickled Cherries

1kg (2¼lb) cherries

Halve and destone the cherries, keeping the pips. Crush the pips in a pestle and mortar, tip into a muslin bag and tie.

Place the bag of pips in a saucepan along with the ingredients for the brine (omitting the salt). Bring to the boil. Pack the cherries into a jar and pour over the hot brine. Cool and refrigerate. Mature for 2–3 days before eating with goat's cheese or duck.

Pickling and other types of preserving have changed from something that we do out of necessity into a real trend. Many restaurants are now lined with jars of pickles and jams made in-house from scratch by the chefs.

Ballymaloe Homemade Yogurt

Yogurt can be made from fresh milk but it must be brought to 90°C (194°F) to pasteurise first, then allowed to cool to a lukewarm 42°C (107.6°F) before use. Boiling destroys unwanted bacteria in the milk, which could interfere with the good bacterial action of *bacillus*.

600ml (1 pint) fresh whole milk
2–3 teaspoons natural 'live' yogurt

Heat the milk to 90°C (194°F) and allow to cool to 42°C (107.6°F). Stir in the live yogurt. Pour into a deep bowl, cover and set aside in a warm, draught-free place until set. This usually takes approx. 14 hours. The cooler the temperature, the longer the yogurt will take to set, but too high a temperature will kill the *bacillus* and the yogurt will not form.

Yogurt can be set in a warm airing cupboard or boiler room, a vacuum flask with a wide neck or an insulated ice bucket. Alternatively, an earthenware pot with a lid, wrapped up in a thick towel or blanket and put near a radiator, will also do the job. The simple aim is to provide steady, even warmth to allow the *bacillus* to grow.

Remember to keep back 2 tablespoons of yogurt as the starter for the next batch. After two or three batches you may need to use a fresh starter. Special yogurt starters can be purchased online.

Yogurt with Honey and Dates

unsweetened natural yogurt, very cold
fresh Medjool dates
thick cream
local honey
fresh almonds or lightly toasted almonds
fresh mint leaves, to garnish

Half-fill a pudding bowl or glass with yogurt. Stone and roughly chop the dates. Put a few on the top of each helping of yogurt. Spoon a good dollop of thick cream over the top and then trickle over 1 teaspoon of runny honey. Scatter a few almonds and a couple of shredded mint leaves on top and serve.

Penny's Kraut-Chi (Sauerkraut)

Sandor Ellix Katz, the fermenatation revivalist from the US, has a global cult following and came to Ireland for the Ballymaloe Literary Festival of Food and Wine in 2013. We are all fans, including my daughter-in-law Penny, who has been experimenting with all manner of fermented foods. This is her recipe, which keeps for three months or more and is delicious served with cold meats, cheese, salads or toasted sourdough sandwiches.

Makes 1 x 1.5 litre (2½ pint) jar

300g (10oz) cabbage (red or green), thinly sliced
300g (10oz) carrots, scrubbed then grated
200g (7oz) onion, thinly sliced
3 large garlic cloves, peeled and coarsely chopped
400g (14oz) beetroot, scrubbed then grated
½ level tablespoon salt
½–1 teaspoon chilli flakes

Scrub and wash your vegetables well. Don't peel the carrots or the beetroot – the skin contains the highest density of microbes to get fermentation off to a good start.

Put all the ingredients, except the chilli, into a large bowl and mix thoroughly. Squeeze between your hands as much as possible to get the juices coming out of the vegetables. Add the chilli.

After a few minutes' mixing, pack the vegetables very tightly into a sterilised 1.5 litre (2½ pint) Kilner jar. Weigh down the top of the vegetables with something heavy (e.g. a sterilised jar filled with water). The vegetables should be totally submerged under a layer of their own juices. Fermentation happens anaerobically to produce the beneficial bacteria that you want.

Keep the jar out of the fridge for approx. 5 days until it reaches the desired level of sourness – it may take a little longer if you like it sour. Many people then transfer the pickled vegetables to the fridge, but they will keep stored outside of the fridge indefinitely as long as they are covered in a layer of the juices. Penny eats this dish with everything – it can be an acquired taste to start with, but, as Penny has discovered, it is one that you can become completely hooked on. She enjoys it with her own homemade buckwheat bread and occasionally with a sweet chutney for a particularly appealing mix of sweet and sour flavours.

Sustainable Fishing

Above: Fishing nets at Ballycotton harbour with the famous Ballycotton lifeboats in the background.

Ballymaloe Cookery School is situated within minutes of Shanagarry Strand and the little fishing village of Ballycotton. In January or February it is sometimes difficult to predict when the herrings will come in but if we are really lucky we get a bucket or two of sprats. When the sprats are in, the herrings chase them right to the shore and it's easy to scoop them up, but you must be there. We cook them whole right away, dipped in well-seasoned flour and deep-fried (they are delicious with almost any kind of mayonnaise-based sauce) and we always eat the lot, which takes some courage for the non-initiated, but they soon become addicted. They are also delicious served simply with aioli or soused with tomatoes and mustard seeds. Whitebait come in late summer and are cooked in a similar way, served with a few rocket leaves and chilli crème fraîche or made into whitebait fritters, with a wedge of lemon on the side.

As the years pass, despite our proximity to the sea, it becomes increasingly difficult to source really fresh day-boat fish. As the stocks become scarcer, due to a combination of overfishing and the discard policy, many of the fishermen have to go further afield for their catch and some boats are at sea for up to five days. Landed landed fish may therefore vary from 0–5 days old and the carbon footprint of the process has increased appreciably by using vessels that can stay offshore for so long. The fish is iced down to preserve it in prime condition but still, wherever possible our preference, both for the Cookery School and the restaurant at Ballymaloe House, is for day-boat fish caught by smaller, day-tripper boats that land their catch when it has only been out of the water for a few hours. Most chefs acknowledge that fish landed in this way is the greatest quality, with the best flavour and it is therefore much sought-after, although sadly, these days, quite hard to come by.

I first became aware of the sustainable seafood issue in the early noughties at a Slow Food Conference in Turin (Slow Food have been running a Slow Fish conference every year since 2003). I was shocked by the statistics. For example, the International Council for Exploration of the Seas (ICES) estimated in 2005 that 95 per cent of assessed EU fish stocks were overfished. Whilst that figure

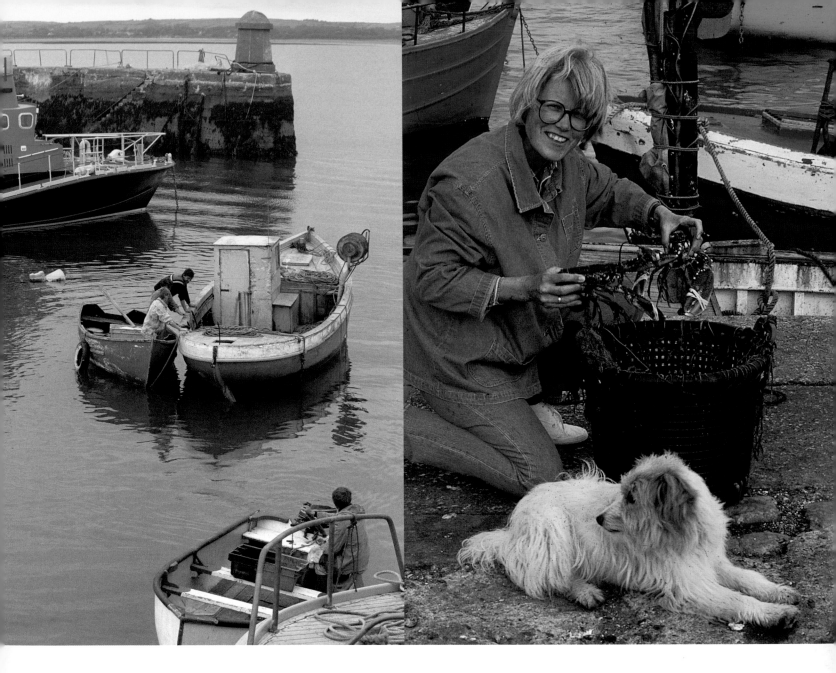

Above (left): Even though Ballycotton harbour is small with a few day boats and a couple of larger vessels, a huge variety of fish and seafood is landed there throughout the year.

Above (right): Collecting lobster directly from the boats at Ballycotton. We only serve lobster when we can get them directly from Ballycotton as we don't like to keep them in tanks. In 2008 I was awarded the Chef of the Year Award at the Conservation Leadership Awards at the Monterey Bay Aquarium, California. I collected my award and met Julie Packard, Executive Director and Vice Chair of the Aquarium's Board of Trustees, who is committed to advancing ocean conservation. I returned home even more determined to spread the word about the impact of our food choices on the environment.

has fallen to 40 per cent in 2013, the EU Commission estimate that 20 per cent of the wild fish consumed across the world has been caught and landed by ships operating on the high seas outside any sort of official supervision. Such statistics ensured I immediately resolved to try to heighten awareness of the issue.

'Sustainable' is a widely used term but it is not a straightforward concept. In the context of food production it means that we can interact with the environment and the creatures with which we share it to harvest food and provide for the needs of today, without damaging the ability of that environment to provide for the needs of tomorrow and future generations. Sustainable fishing of wild-caught sea fish includes measures to ensure that enough fish are allowed to breed in order to maintain the population at viable

levels, but it also includes the wider environmental footprint of this form of food production, e.g. fossil-fuel usage of boats and their impact on the ocean floor ecosystem. It is therefore unwise or even foolhardy to regard a particular species as truly sustainable. For just one species of fish there exists differences in its 'sustainability' depending on which stock it comes from, the catch area or catch methods. Conversely, for highly migratory fish stocks, e.g. blue-fin tuna, they may be managed sustainably in one region yet the same fish may be over-exploited in another area. There exist entire bureaucratic and regulatory strictures limiting what fishermen can do in the interests of sustainability, but these have to date failed in balancing society's competing desires for cheap, constantly available seafood, vibrant fishing industries, habitat protection and sustainable fish stocks. We teach the students that the best we as consumers can do is to make informed choices and understand where our seafood comes from, how it was caught, transported and landed; where our spend goes. Those who fish responsibly are usually proud to impart their passion and deserve our support.

We therefore put a Sustainable Seafood course on the Cookery School programme in 2006 (we had been offering a Seafood Course since the early years of the School), emphasising the importance of not buying or serving endangered species such as eel, skate or shark, or fish from stocks that are under threat such as Irish Sea cod, sole or plaice. We educate the students about alternative species that can be substituted for some of the threatened species, for example rather than using cod or hake to get flaky white fish meat, pollock or coley (saithe) may be a good alternative. We give both the students on the Sustainable Seafood course and the 12-week students a pocket fish guide to take away with them so that they have an accessible reference to check which species are endangered and what substitutes they can use.

Most people who don't live within sight of the sea will probably buy their fish in a supermarket, but we tell students who are fortunate to have a good fishmonger close by to build up a relationship with them in the same way as with a local butcher, and to ask lots of questions to increase their fish knowledge – the different species, when they are in season and how to cook them.

Shoaling fish, such as mackerel or herring, tend to be particularly good at recovering from commercial exploitation so we encourage students to use these species. The Northern Ireland Pelagic Sustainability Group (NIPSG) Irish Sea herring fishery entered into Marine Stewardship Council (MSC) assessment in 2013. The MSC is a commercial company that examines individual fisheries

and accredits the acceptable exploitation of that fishery by boats that are members of the group that pay the accreditation fee. It is a concept that only applies to 'clean' fisheries where a fisherman can have a reasonable target and only catch a particular fish type. The blue MSC logo appears on fish that have been caught at one of its certified fisheries and is a quick shorthand to buying sustainable fish. However, because of its assessment methods, MSC certification is not applicable to a mixed bottom-trawl or beam-trawl fishery where the various bottom-dwelling species are caught in proportion to the mixture on the sea-floor. In other words, the absence of MSC-labelling is not necessarily the absence of a responsible approach.

Hugh Fearnley-Whittingstall has done trojan work to try to influence changes to the EU fisheries policy with regard to discards, which includes the wasteful practice of throwing overboard fish that fishermen have caught without a quota. However, discards only arise if fishermen use a fishing method that catches those fish. And it only happens repeatedly if fishermen frequently return to an area and continually use that fishing method, which will therefore catch fish for which the fishermen do not have a quota. Discards also arise when fishermen catch undersize fish or when they try to boost the value of their fishing trip and available quota by throwing out smaller, but perfectly legal, fish in order to only retain onboard higher-value larger fish and therefore maximise their return on a limited quota. Thankfully there has been a EU policy initiative to address this entire area, which will broadly consist of measures to minimise discards, such as quota allocation proportionate to fish presence, technical gear modifications to target specific fish, plus an obligation to land all catches regardless of marketability and value.

It is important to conserve fish so it is available as a food choice, particularly as it has many health benefits. Packed with vitamins and minerals, and a major source of omega-3 fatty acids, fish can help to protect against a range of diseases from cancer to heart disease and depression to arthritis. We need to ensure that the rich and complex ecosystem of our seas is maintained for future generations so that they too can enjoy the advantages of fish.

Left: Beautiful fresh trout.
Right (top): There is a skill in picking up lobsters so you don't get nipped.
Right (middle): The late Tommy Sliney, who used to sell fish from his donkey and cart on the pier in Ballycotton, where he would fillet your purchase for you.
Right (bottom): Tommy Sliney bringing in a box of fish. I dedicated my Simply Delicious Fish book to him – he gave away more fish than he ever sold!

Deep-fried Squid with Aioli and Tomato and Chilli Jam

One of my favourite squid recipes is from Gillian Hegarty, a past student and now head chef at Ballymaloe House. Squid can be a bit intimidating for some people to cook, but you should cook it either for seconds, so it turns from translucent to white, or for a long time, otherwise it can become tough and rubbery.

First make the Tomato and Chilli Jam. Preheat the oven to 200°C/400°F/gas 6. Arrange the tomatoes in a roasting tin in a single layer and roast in the hot oven for approx. 30 minutes.

Meanwhile, put the sugar in a heavy-bottomed saucepan and dissolve over a low heat. Once the sugar has dissolved, increase the heat and continue to cook until the sugar caramelises to a pale golden brown. Tip in the roasted tomatoes, along with the cooking juices, and add the remaining ingredients for the jam. Bring to the boil and reduce by half. Liquidise until really fine and smooth. Set aside.

To make the Aioli, put all the ingredients, except the olive oil, in a food processor and blitz until smooth. Keeping the motor running, add the olive oil in a slow, steady trickle through the feeder tube until emulsified. Set aside.

Prepare the squid flour by mixing together the rice flour, potato flour and milk powder in a shallow dish. Season with the salt and white pepper.

Cut each squid in half and open out. Score the flesh deeply at an angle, and then cut each piece into 4cm (1½in) squares. Pour the milk into a shallow bowl.

Preheat the oil in a deep-fat fryer to 180°C (350°F). Dip the squid in the milk and shake off any excess. Coat in the flour mixture and deep-fry in the hot oil until golden brown (don't overcrowd the deep-fryer). Season with a sprinkle of cayenne pepper and extra salt if needed. Serve with the Aioli and the Tomato and Chilli Jam.

Any leftover jam can be stored in an airtight jar in the fridge. Serve with goat's cheese and cold meats and use in sandwiches.

Serves 8

2 large squid
600ml (1 pint) milk
sunflower oil, for deep-frying
cayenne pepper, for dusting

For the squid flour
250g (9oz) rice flour
250g (9oz) potato flour
1 tablespoon rice milk powder
1 tablespoon salt
½ tablespoon ground white pepper

For the Aioli
4 organic egg yolks
1 teaspoon Dijon mustard
½ tablespoon ground turmeric
4 garlic cloves, peeled
freshly squeezed juice of 1 lemon
450ml (16fl oz) extra virgin olive oil
sea salt and freshly ground black pepper

For the Tomato and Chilli Jam
500g (18oz) very ripe tomatoes, halved
310g (11oz) golden caster sugar
4 red chillies, bashed with a rolling pin
4 garlic cloves, peeled and roughly crushed
5cm (2in) piece of fresh root ginger, peeled and roughly chopped
1 tablespoon fish sauce (nam pla)
100ml (3½fl oz) red wine vinegar

Crab and Asparagus with Thai Mayonnaise on Sourdough

There is no shortage of common crabs to be had from the fishermen in Ballycotton nowadays, a big change from when I first came to Ballymaloe 40 years ago. Myrtle and Ivan were still trying to coax the fishermen to bring in crab so we could serve it on the menu. We had to promise to take the entire catch, be it four or 40, so it was a feast or a famine. Myrtle would never accept crab claws, for fear of encouraging the practice of harvesting the claws and throwing the crabs back into the sea, preferring instead to buy whole crabs so she could use both the flaky white meat and the creamy brown meat from the body in her repertoire of Ballymaloe recipes. This is one of the rare recipes where we use just white meat.

Bring some water to the boil in an oval casserole or saucepan that will fit the asparagus spears. Season with 1 teaspoon salt per 600ml (1 pint) water. Prepare the asparagus spears by snapping off the tough end where it breaks naturally. Lay the asparagus in the boiling water and cook for 2–4 minutes depending on the thickness. The asparagus should still be crisp and al dente for this recipe. Remove the asparagus with a slotted spoon and plunge immediately into cold water. Refresh under cold running water and drain thoroughly.

To make the Thai Mayonnaise, stir the garlic, chilli, lime zest, fish sauce and chopped coriander into the mayonnaise. Taste and correct the seasoning if necessary. Mix in the crabmeat and set aside.

To serve, toast or chargrill the bread. Drizzle with a little extra virgin olive oil and scatter a few rocket leaves over each slice. Pile the crab mixture on top. Toss the cold asparagus spears in a little extra virgin olive oil and split each spear in half lengthways. Arrange the asparagus over the crabmeat and serve immediately.

Serves 4

6 asparagus spears
225g (8oz) white crabmeat
4 slices of sourdough bread (see page 172), thinly sliced
   no more than 8mm (1/3in) thick)
extra virgin olive oil, for drizzling
a handful of rocket leaves
sea salt

For the Thai Mayonnaise
4 tablespoons homemade mayonnaise (see page 72)
1 garlic clove, peeled and crushed
½ red chilli, deseeded and finely diced
freshly grated zest of ½ lime
3 scant tablespoons fish sauce (nam pla)
2 teaspoons freshly chopped coriander

Salmon with Tomato, Ginger and Fresh Coriander

Claudia Roden first introduced me to Salmon with Ginger and Coriander; it sounds like an extraordinary combination but try it, it's delicious hot or cold. For the past couple of years we have had a few beautiful wild salmon from the Blackwater river, less than an hour's drive from Shanagarry, and have appreciated every precious mouthful.

Put the olive oil in a wide, stainless-steel sauté pan, add the garlic and tomatoes and cook over a medium heat until the tomatoes soften and break down, approx. 10–15 minutes. Add the grated ginger and cook for a further 5 minutes. Season with salt, pepper and sugar. Remove from the heat and set aside.

Cook the salmon gently in a little butter in a wide frying pan for approx. 3 minutes each side. (Alternatively put the salmon into the sauce, cover and cook gently in the sauce.)

Remove the salmon fillets from the pan and arrange on hot serving plates. Just before serving add the coriander and spoon the sauce over the salmon. Serve immediately.

Serves 6

1 teaspoon olive oil
2–4 garlic cloves, peeled and finely chopped
8 very ripe tomatoes, peeled and chopped
1 tablespoon freshly grated root ginger
butter, for frying
6 x 110g (4oz) fresh wild salmon fillets
2 tablespoons freshly chopped coriander leaves, plus extra to garnish
sea salt, freshly ground black pepper and sugar

Salmon was one of the first victims of overfishing and so fishing was restricted for a number of years to allow the stocks to build up again. Anglers feel that the proliferation of salmon farms around the coast has also affected salmon stocks and argue that escapees from such farms have bred with the wild salmon to the latter's detriment.

Roast Fish with Dill Butter and Courgettes

The fish can be cooked whole or cut into portions.
Allow 110g (4oz) for a starter, 175g (6oz) for a main course.
This is a brilliantly easy way to cook fish – haddock, hake,
grey sea mullet or wild salmon can all be used.

Preheat the oven to 240°C/475°F/gas 9. Gut the fish and descale
it if necessary.

Line a roasting tin with foil or greaseproof paper, put the fish on
top and brush all over with the melted butter and oil. Season well
with salt and freshly ground pepper.

Bake the fish for approx. 5–8 minutes, depending on the
thickness of the fish. The fish is cooked when the flesh changes
from transparent to opaque.

Meanwhile, prepare the courgettes. Top and tail the courgettes
and cut them into 5mm (¼in) thick slices. Melt the butter or olive
oil in a frying pan, toss in the courgettes and coat well. Cook until
barely tender, approx. 4–5 minutes. Add the chopped marjoram,
season with salt and freshly ground black pepper and tip into a hot
serving dish. It is vital that the courgettes are undercooked as they
will continue to cook after they have been removed from the heat.

To make the Dill Butter, melt the butter in a small pan and stir
in the freshly chopped dill.

To serve, carefully transfer the fish onto a serving dish. Spoon
a little of the dill butter over the hot fish and serve the remainder
separately. Garnish with the chervil sprigs and accompany with
the hot courgettes.

Serves 4–6

1 whole fresh fish fillet, such as grey mullet or wild salmon
25g (1oz) butter, melted
25g (1oz) extra virgin oil
sea salt and freshly ground black pepper

For the Courgettes
450g (1lb) courgettes, no larger than 12.5cm (5in) in length
25g (1oz) butter or 2 tablespoons extra virgin olive oil
1 tablespoon freshly chopped marjoram

For the Dill Butter
110g (4oz) butter
2–4 tablespoons freshly chopped dill

To serve
sprigs of chervil

Thomasina Miers

" I had never been to Ireland before I left for Ballymaloe. I was 25 years old and deeply depressed by life and my own inability to find a career that I could stick at; I was in serious need of inspiration. If there is anything that Ballymaloe does unfailingly it is to inspire. From the moment I drove off the ferry from Holyhead and set foot on Irish soil I had an inkling that I was finally on the right track.

I was right. From the beautiful cottages with their roaring log fires, to the chickens (and their wonderful eggs) that ate the scraps of delicious food from our cooking; the greenhouses that provided the mustard, rocket, mizuna and baby bull that made those delicious salads we had every day for lunch; the wild sea on our doorstep that produced the mackerel and mussels and Carrageen moss that we learned to prepare. These were some of the tangible things that I remember with nostalgia, reinforced by the knowledge that for the Allens this is their normal everyday way of life.

Less tangible but just as vivid for me were the lessons we learned. Lessons in bread making and the magic of sourdough from Timmy, lessons in it-didn't-matter-what from Rory O'Connell, so skilful and elegant was his cooking and way with words. Then there was the whole story of food from Darina – where it came from, how it was grown, what impact its growing and our eating had on the planet, how terroir affected flavour, how love and passion for food inspired a whole gallery of producers to make cheeses, cured meats, smoked fish and other delicacies up and down the country. Nuggets of information from the mighty Myrtle Allen that I gleaned whilst earning my keep as a trolley-dolly at Ballymaloe House only deepened my thirst for knowledge.

It doesn't harm the School that it is tucked away in one of the prettiest parts of the world, or that this corner of Ireland is full of Ballymaloe alumni cooking fresh local ingredients with tested skills and enormous vim. It doesn't hurt that the local pubs were brimming with gnarled and vibrant characters who could have stepped out of the radio and who treated you like a long-lost cousin within days of meeting. In my memory there seemed to be a jam happening every other night with wild boys in wild bands who

Left: Thomasina Miers at the Ballymaloe Literary Festival of Food and Wine in 2013.

Right (top): Thomasina Miers with the instantly recognisable Pamela Black, a senior teacher at the School. Thomasina has returned to the School several times to teach guest chef courses on Mexican food, which has become her passion and the focus of her chain of Wahaca restaurants.

Right (bottom): Thomasina Miers demonstrating with Stevie Parle, her fellow classmate at Ballymaloe on the 12-week course in January 2002, and Rachel Allen – some of the new young voices in food.

played intoxicatingly beautiful Irish ballads in houses found down winding country lanes.

Darina has spawned generations of cooks who have scattered across the globe to weave their own food stories in their own particular way, but all with her maxims ringing in their ears. If I close my eyes today, all these years later, I can see her clearly in the classroom rubbing her hands together, eyes shining brightly with the fun of the recipe.

You go to Ballymaloe not solely to learn to become a chef, but to learn an approach to food that is inextricably bound up in the pleasure gained from preparing and eating food, a pleasure that is ingeniously intensified when shared with either family or friends. You learn along the way skills such as boiling an egg, making the perfect meringue, sweating vegetables, clarifying stock or deglazing a pan, but you never forget that the most important aspect is the simple joy of making good food. **"**

Oaxacan Chicken Soup

Mexico and Mexican food most definitely have a special place in my heart, a passion that I share with Thomasina Miers. I particularly love Oaxaca, a colourful colonial town in the Sierra Nevada Valley, where this soup comes from. Adding extra bits to a bowl of soup always adds to the enjoyment for me.

Serves 6

1.8 litres (3 pints) well-flavoured chicken stock, well skimmed
225g (8oz) shredded chicken (cooked or raw)
sea salt and freshly ground black pepper

To serve
2–3 ripe Hass avocados, cut into 5mm (¼in) dice
6 medium tomatoes, cut into 5mm (¼in) dice
2 medium red onions, cut into 5mm (¼in) dice
3 green serrano or jalapeño chillies, thinly sliced
4–6 tablespoons freshly chopped coriander leaves
3 limes, cut into wedges

Put the chicken stock into a wide saucepan and bring to the boil. Taste and season – it should have a full rich flavour, otherwise the soup with be bland and insipid.

Add the shredded chicken – I sometimes use scraps from the chicken carcass from the stockpot, however you can use raw or cooked chicken. Cooked chicken just needs to be reheated in the broth. Raw white meat will take a few minutes to cook and brown meat a little longer. Poach it gently so it doesn't toughen. Taste again and correct the seasoning if necessary.

To serve, ladle the soup into bowls. Provide each guest with a side plate containing some diced avocado, tomato, red onions, thinly sliced green chilli, chopped coriander and lime segments to add to the soup as they choose.

Chilaquiles Verdes o Rojos

Mexico, like many other cultures, has many ways of using up leftovers and a tradition that it is sinful and unlucky to waste even a scrap of tortilla. Chilaquiles are one of the many ways to use up tortillas deliciously.

Many of the chickens in Mexico are corn fed so the skin is a rich golden colour. One chicken produces a mound of shredded meat when it is pulled apart along the natural grain.

Preheat the over to 230°C/450°F/gas 8.

First poach the chicken breast. Put it in a small saucepan, cover with the chicken stock and simmer gently until cooked, approx. 15–18 minutes depending on size. Shred the flesh and set aside, reserving the poaching liquid.

Meanwhile, cut each tortilla into eight pieces. If they are moist and floppy, dry them out in a moderate oven for a few minutes; they are best stale and leathery for this dish.

Preheat the oil in a deep-fat fryer and cook the tortilla pieces in batches until crisp and lightly golden. Drain on kitchen paper.

To make the salsa, peel off the husks from the tomatillos and discard. Put them into a saucepan with the chillies and cover with cold water. Bring to the boil and cook until soft, approx. 10 minutes. Drain through a sieve, discarding the cooking liquor, and transfer the cooked tomatoes and chillies to a food processor. Add the onion, garlic, coriander, salt and water this and blitz for several minutes. Taste and correct the seasoning if necessary.

To assemble the dish, arrange half of the tortillas over the base of a deep-sided 20 x 10cm (8 x 5in) ovenproof dish. Scatter the shreddedchicken over the top and season with some salt and freshly ground black pepper. Top with the remaining tortillas. Thin out the tomatillo sauce with a little of the chicken broth if necessary and pour over the tortillas. Sprinkle over a little grated cheese and bake for 5–10 minutes until hot and bubbling.

Serve immediately with the soured cream and cheese and scattered with the sliced onions (if using) and fresh coriander.

Serves 4

1 large chicken breast
approx. 225ml (8fl oz) chicken broth
6–8 corn tortillas (stale is fine)
sunflower oil, for deep-frying
sea salt and freshly ground black pepper

For the Tomatillo Salsa
6 tomatillos (green tomatoes covered with a papery husk),
    weighing approx. 500g (18oz)
4 serrano chillies
1 heaped tablespoon chopped onion
1 small garlic clove, peeled
a handful of fresh coriander (leaves and soft stems)
½ teaspoon salt
2 tablespoons water

To serve
2–4 tablespoons soured cream
4–8 tablespoons crumbled Queso Fresco (or grated mozzarella
    and Cheddar cheese mixed together)
1 onion, thinly sliced (optional)
fresh coriander leaves

Hoja Santa Quesadilla

Hoja santa is an aromatic South American herb with a very particular flavour and its name means 'sacred leaf' in Spanish. You can get a plant from several specialist garden centres in the UK, but it will need to be looked after with tender loving care in a greenhouse. However, it is totally worth it for the magical flavour it adds to so many dishes. If hoja santa is not available, any number of other fresh herbs would be good here – wild garlic, even spring onion and some chopped chilli, a little diced chorizo or some tapenade.

Serves 1

2–3 white corn tortillas
1 hoja santa leaf (*Piper auritum*), approx. 20cm (8in) across
Oaxaca string cheese (or a mixture of grated mozzarella cheese and mature Cheddar cheese)
pinch of salt

To serve
Tomatillo Salsa (see left)

Lay a tortilla on a chopping board. Tear off a few pieces of fresh hoja santa leaf and scatter over the tortilla. Sprinkle with the cheese and season with a pinch of salt.

Heat a griddle pan or heavy frying pan over a medium heat. Cook the tortilla for a couple of minutes. As soon as the cheese starts to melt, fold over and cook the other side until slightly crisp on both sides. Serve with the Tomatillo Salsa.

The Soft Fruit Garden

Above: An early crop of raspberries.
Right: A selection of soft fruits from our berry and currant garden.

For many years we were able to get beautiful summer berries and currants for the Cookery School, such as raspberries, tayberries, loganberries, and black, white and redcurrants from Sunnyside Farm near Fermoy. But John Howard eventually gave up growing berries in 2009, defeated by inclement weather and new labour laws, which made it difficult to get fruit pickers at opportune times. Sourcing consistent supplies of organic fruit in any significant quantity had become problematic, so in 2010 we decided to plant a currant and berry garden next to the Celtic Maze to have our own supply of organic fruit.

This approximately half-acre fruit garden is planted in straight rows interspersed with grass paths. Clumps of lavender, chives and other edible flowers are planted at the end of each row to attract bees, butterflies and beneficial insects into the gardens to help with pollination. We grow a variety of soft fruits including strawberries, raspberries, blackcurrants, redcurrants, whitecurrants, tayberries and gooseberries. Blackcurrants are one of the first fruits to come into leaf in spring. Green gooseberries are ready in May and, even though they are still hard and green, this is when they are best for pies, compotes and fools and are particularly delicious with elderflower, which is in full bloom at that time. Next come strawberries in June, followed by raspberries and all the currants in July, then loganberries, tayberries and boysenberries in August. Autumn raspberries ripen in September and October – they are a more mellow and flavoursome crop than the summer raspberries. The fruit is picked daily by hand and is used to make jams, cakes, desserts, popsicles and ice cream by our students and by Julija Makejeva, who cooks for the Ballymaloe stall at Midleton Farmers' Market.

In 2012 we added a blueberry patch for the joy of being able to pick our own, having first added lots of acid components to our naturally limey soil, as blueberries need acid soil to flourish. The birds really love blueberries, so we've built a protective cage over the plants to stop the birds eating them. My husband Tim also bought two scary inflatable 'men' from an English farm website,

who leap up at irregular intervals and scare both garden visitors and the birds – very effective.

As well as supplying the School with delicious produce to cook with, the fruit garden is also used as a teaching garden. The students, many for the first time, see how fruit grows and learn how to pick it directly off the bushes. They are excited to learn that they can also use some of the young leaves for cordials and granita; blackcurrant leaf sorbet is particularly delicious. We tell them raspberry leaf tea is supposed to induce labour, information they can store up for another time!

The berry and currant garden forms part of the larger farm and gardens to provide an ever-changing outdoor classroom where students can observe the changing seasons and learn how to judge when the vegetables, fruit and herbs are perfect for picking. The fact that fruit and vegetables are not all identical in size and perfectly shaped comes as quite a shock to many people who buy only from the supermarket shelves. We teach them about the phenomenal amount of waste resulting from customers' demands for perfect produce – farmers reckon they have done well if 40–50 per cent of a crop reaches the supermarket shelves; the remainder is wasted or ploughed back into the ground. A shocking realisation at any time, but particularly in Ireland today, where just one of the charities in Cork, Penny Dinners, is feeding 900–1,000 people a week. (Hearing this, some of the students are moved to volunteer to help this charity at weekends.)

When the students pick and taste the fresh fruit and vegetables directly from the plants and bushes, the flavour can be a revelation, so they are less interested in buying imported produce in the winter when it is out of season and much more expensive. We also discuss air miles and the challenge of reducing our carbon footprint, something we can do by buying fruits from local suppliers in season rather than strawberries in the middle of winter, when they will have to have been flown in from halfway across the world.

We also teach the students how to use up gluts of fruit and vegetables and to have fun pickling and preserving.

In addition the School offers a variety of gardening courses on Designing a Herbaceous Border, Creating a Fruit Garden and Winter Pruning. These are taught by Susan Turner, our consultant head gardener, who was previously head gardener at Yalding Organic Gardens in the UK.

Above: Loganberries growing in the currant and berry garden. You need to resist picking them until they are dark red, otherwise they taste bitter and unappealing. We never seem to have enough of them as their bittersweet flavour makes super pies, jams, ice creams and fools. If ever we do have a surplus, they also freeze well. They are well worth growing as, unlike raspberries, they can be difficult to source from the shops.

Mike Butt Award

In 2010 I was honoured by the Restaurants Association of Ireland (RAI) for my contribution to the Irish Restaurant Industry and the Food Movement. When I accepted this award in Dublin, I spoke of my concerns about the loss of basic skills among chefs, at a time when an increasing number of restaurants were just opting for 'catalogue cooking'. Some are choosing this option for economic reasons and others because it is the path of least resistance from the food hygiene and food safety perspective. If the food arrives pre-packaged in plastic or polystyrene trays, it has the seal of approval of the FSA (Food Safety Authority). All chefs need to do is pop the food portion in a microwave or water bath, and slit open the top of the packet. Fish is filleted, poultry is jointed, racks of lamb are French trimmed, sauces are already made, perfect tartlets come waiting to be filled and chocolate curls ready to be popped onto ice creams or mousses.

It is all terrifically convenient and very tempting, and indeed it can be very impressive, but the price of this compromise (to convenience), is a sameness in menus all over the country. What is even more serious is that many chefs are becoming increasingly de-skilled, for in many kitchens they no longer need to be able to make a loaf of bread, whip up a bowl of mayonnaise or produce buttery feather-light puff pastry, not to mention a pot of jam.

I encouraged the inclusion of a module in the curriculum in the catering colleges, or Institutes of Technology as they are now called, to encourage sourcing and to introduce artisan food producers to the students. I got a resounding round of applause from the audience, many of whom were restaurant owners and head chefs who were having to cope with the precise difficulties I had outlined. I also encouraged the colleges to consider planting vegetable, herb and fruit gardens in their extensive grounds, so students could learn how to grow and harvest.

❧

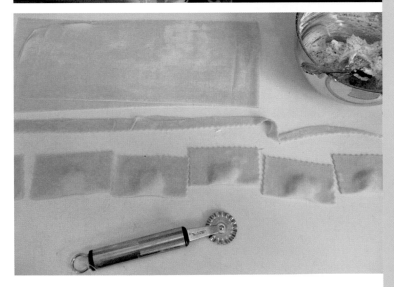

Above: Students making pasta from scratch at the Ballymaloe Cookery School.

Pan-grilled Summer Mackerel with Green Gooseberry Sauce

We only eat mackerel when they come into Ballycotton Bay from early summer and become more plentiful towards the end of August. There have recently been concerns over the sustainability of mackerel, but it is worth checking in your area or with your local fisheries board as the stocks vary from place to place. This is a master recipe for pan-grilling fish. The simplest and possibly the most delicious way to cook really fresh mackerel.

First make the Green Gooseberry Sauce. Top and tail the gooseberries, put them into a stainless-steel saucepan and barely cover with the stock syrup. Bring to the boil and simmer until the fruit bursts. Taste. Stir in a small knob of butter if you like, but it is very good without it.

Preheat a griddle pan. Dip each fish fillet into seasoned flour and shake off any excess. Spread a little softened butter over the flesh side of each fillet, as though you were buttering a slice of bread rather meanly. When the griddle is quite hot, but not smoking, put the fish fillets, butter-side down, in the pan; they should sizzle as soon as they touch the pan. Reduce the heat slightly. Cook the fillets for 4–5 minutes on the first side, then turn over and cook on the skin side until crisp and golden. Serve on a hot plate, accompanied by the warm gooseberry sauce and lemon wedges.

Serves 1–2

2–4 fillets of very fresh mackerel (allow 175g (6oz) fish per person as a main course, or 75g (3oz) as a starter)
seasoned flour
small knob of butter, softened

For the Green Gooseberry Sauce
275g (10oz) fresh green gooseberries
approx. 175ml (6fl oz) stock syrup (see page 284), to cover
knob of butter (optional)

To serve
lemon wedges

Blackcurrant Popsicles

We use all the summer fruits to make ice lollies – raspberries, strawberries and blackcurrants – with combinations like blackberry and sweet geranium, redcurrant and strawberry, peach and raspberry, or raspberry and basil. In winter we make a variety of citrus popsicles, including blood orange and tangerine. They are loved not just by children but people of all ages, and I particularly enjoy serving them at the end of a dinner party.

Makes 6

450g (1lb) blackcurrants
225–300ml (8–10fl oz) stock syrup (see below)

Put the blackcurrants in a medium saucepan, pour over the syrup and bring to the boil. Cook for 3–5 minutes until the blackcurrants burst, and then liquidise. Strain through a nylon sieve and set aside to cool.

Taste and add a little more syrup if necessary. It needs to taste sweeter than you would like because the freezing dulls the sweetness. Pour into popsicle moulds, cover, insert a stick and freeze until needed. These are best eaten within a few days.

Stock Syrup

Makes 825ml (28fl oz)

450g (1lb) granulated sugar
600ml (1 pint) water

Dissolve the sugar in the water over a low heat. Bring to the boil and boil hard for 2 minutes. Set aside to cool. Any leftover syrup can be stored in a sealed container in the fridge for approx. 1 month.

Camilla's Strawberry and Rose Petal Jam

When my friend Camilla Plum, Danish cook, farmer and cookery writer, comes to stay, she wanders through the farm, gardens and greenhouses, picking and collecting fresh ingredients and cooking non-stop. Last summer, she filled her apron with rose petals from the scented old roses – she tossed them into a saucepan with some fresh strawberries and made this exquisite jam. We also made rose syrup and crystallised the petals to decorate desserts and cakes.

Makes 2–3 x 370g jars (13oz)

450g (1lb) granulated sugar
1kg (2¼lb) fresh strawberries
1 litre (1¾ pints) rose petals from fragrant old roses
juice of 1 lemon

Preheat the oven to 130°C/275°F/gas 1. Pour the sugar into an ovenproof dish lined with baking parchment and warm it in the low oven for 20 minutes.

Meanwhile, put the strawberries in a wide, heavy-bottomed stainless-steel saucepan and cook over a brisk heat until the juices run and the fruit breaks down. Add the rose petals and the warmed sugar and stir until the sugar has dissolved. Bring to the boil and continue to cook for 5–8 minutes until a set is reached. To test for a set, spoon a teaspoon of the hot jam onto a cold plate and set aside for a few minutes in a cool place. If setting point has been reached the jam should wrinkle when pressed with a finger. (If the jam isn't set, return the pan to the heat and boil for a few minutes longer.) Stir in the freshly squeezed lemon juice, remove from the heat and pour into sterilised jars with non-reactive lids. Fasten the lids. Store in a cool, dark place and in the fridge once opened.

Rachel Allen

" Of course I'd seen Darina on television before, but never in real life. I was a teenager when she first appeared on our screens in Ireland with her bright red glasses, long linen skirts and her no-fuss approach to food. At that stage I was toying with the idea of becoming a fashion designer, a shoe designer or maybe even an actress. So when my sister and parents encouraged me to leave Dublin to go down to Ballymaloe to learn how to cook at the age of 18, I really didn't know what to expect.

Darina came racing into the demonstration kitchen on the first morning of the 12-week certificate course (I was soon to learn that she never goes anywhere slowly!) and began to speak to us about food. She was talking about provenance, sustainability, seasonality and something called organic growing. This was January 1990 and food was in a very different place back then. The big trend was 'vertical food'; one thing sitting on top of another and then another and then topped with a turned carrot or something similar. So why on earth was this woman talking passionately about the soil, keeping chickens and growing vegetables without chemicals or pesticides? I thought I had come here to learn how to cook?

It took a few hours of fervent and tireless talk where Darina also spoke about her mother-in-law, Myrtle Allen, and the radically integrated approach here at Ballymaloe before I finally clicked. To get great food, we need great produce – and to get great produce, we need great soil.

Over the next 12 weeks I was to learn a tremendous amount from Darina and her brother, the equally extraordinary Rory O'Connell. Each has their own distinctive style of teaching, yet both share the same passion for great food, drive to eliminate food waste and an unwavering commitment to their extremely high standards. It is an ethos that runs throughout the School and is practised by the many, many people who work here, each with their crucial part to play in making Ballymaloe what it is.

I was so encouraged by the approach to food here that I decided to stay around for a while and got a job working in the restaurant kitchen at Ballymaloe House (though Darina tells me now that she

Left: Rachel and me enjoying a cup of tea in a moment's rest outside the Cookery School.
Above (top): Rachel and me at the School in the mid-1990s.
Above (bottom): Claire Cullinane, Breda Murphy and Rachel O'Neill, later to be Rachel Allen. I wish I knew what had attracted their attention.

Left: Rachel and me posing together for a piece in Observer Food Monthly on 'What's it like to run a restaurant with your family?'.
Below (top): Myrtle Allen, Rachel and me in the Blue Dining Room of the Cookery School with my grandson Joshua.
Below (bottom): Rachel chatting to Triana and Sue Cullinane as they prepare for a long-table dinner with Rory O'Connell in the background.
Right: Rachel and me demonstrating together at the Ballymaloe Cookery School. Rachel teaches regularly at the School and we occasionally demonstrate together. The afternoon demonstrations throughout the year, such as this one, are open to the public, but demand is usually high so it's always wise to book ahead.

knew only too well that it was the lure of her eldest son that kept me here!)

At Ballymaloe House the ethos was no different to that of the School. The menu there changes every day and is dictated by what's growing at the time and what fish is available that day. Myrtle, or Mrs Allen as everyone calls her, is another unbelievably impressive woman and, like her daughter-in-law, is indefatigable.

After cooking and learning so much at Ballymaloe House, I eventually went back to the Cookery School to teach. I was drawn to the electric atmosphere of so many learning minds. I continue to be inspired each day by the School, especially when a student masters a new technique or discovers a love of some new dish.

When I'm writing a cookery book I always think of my teaching at the School. It is at the core of all my work and I feel an immense privilege to be a part of the School. I get the same thrill whenever I see a new group of students arriving. Often from as many as 15 different countries, they begin their journey at Ballymaloe. They learn at once about the fundamental relationship between growing good food and cooking good food. They become a part of the harvest and the dairy. Then of course there are the kitchens, where countless people have received the tools and knowledge to go on either to great professional achievement or simply better quality home-cooked meals. Whatever they do and wherever they go, Ballymaloe can always be credited with instilling in its students a lifelong passion and enthusiasm for growing, cooking and sharing great food. **"**

Long-table Dinners

Since 2010, we have organised a feast in the greenhouses to celebrate the work of the gardeners and farmers. As soon as the early potatoes are harvested we plant a lawn in one of the greenhouse bays. By July we have a lush green carpet. We lay a long table with starched white-linen tablecloths in the midst of the scarlet runner beans, tomatoes and edible flowers. All the meat and vegetables comes from the farm and gardens and the fish and shellfish from nearby Ballycotton. When the tickets go on sale, they sell out within a matter of days and many people come back year after year. Some travel from the US, UK and Holland.

We welcome the guests in mid-afternoon with a glass of Prosecco and some freshly grilled sourdough bread from Arbutus artisan bakery, simply drizzled with Capezzana extra virgin olive oil and a few flakes of sea salt, as well as heirloom tomatoes and a little basil, or scattered wild chanterelles foraged by Melissa Odendahl or topped with a chunky purée of broad beans. After a little talk we divide into two or three groups to walk through the farm, gardens and orchards, stopping on the way to visit the milking parlour, where our small herd of Jersey cows are milked every morning, and the dairy, where we separate the milk from the cream to make butter, cheese and yogurt. Then through the fruit garden, past the Palais des Poulets, through the little wood into the kitchen garden where the willow scarecrows keep guard over the vegetables. It's then across the courtyard and into Lydia's Garden, pausing to look at the summerhouse floor made from broken china

by the Quaker Strangman sisters. It incorporates the shamrock, rose and thistle, the emblem of these islands, and the date it was made – 1912. Those who would like to have a bird's eye view of the herb garden climb up on to the treehouse, while others walk through the arches in the beech hedge into the formal herb garden with its boxwood hedges and limestone sundial. Then it's on down into the pleasure garden, to the pond, past the walnuts, nut trees and ancient magnolia.

The ducks and geese glide past the classical folly and chase each other around the fountain. Further on we pass the happy, lazy pigs snoozing in the field – Saddlebacks and Gloucester Old Spots blissfully unaware that their slow-roasted sibling is on the menu in the greenhouse close by. From there we walk under the bridal arch created for our daughter Emily and her husband Philip's wedding, and on through the herbaceous borders to the Shell House, an octagonal folly with a seashell-crusted interior created by Blott Kerr Wilson in 1995 to celebrate our 25th wedding anniversary. The currant and berry garden is over to the left, close to the Celtic maze where the latest Petal Folly, designed by Jeremy Williams, peeps up over the hornbeam, yew and beech hedges. The interior was richly embellished with exotic birds and flowers by Michael Dillon in 2012. Then on through the wildflower meadow, through the field vegetables, such as asparagus, seakale and Jerusalem artichokes, and into the greenhouse. There my son-in-law, Rupert Hugh-Jones, and his friends are playing a mix of traditional, classical and hip-hop music.

In mid-July there is an abundance of produce interspersed with flowers, so it makes a breathtaking scene. My brother Rory, his ace team of teachers and our housekeepers beaver away in the field kitchen they have set up in the bay of the greenhouses next to the long table. The 100 guests take their places at the table. In 2013 many were drawn down to the end of the greenhouse where, just outside the door, Adam O'Connor and my grandson Joshua were working on a huge graffiti piece of pesky birds, snails and insects about to attack the organic produce. The feast begins with one delicious dish after another. I cannot imagine how they create such delicious food. In 2013, Baroness Julia Neuberger, a Jewish rabbi friend, said grace and we all gave thanks for the bounty of the earth and celebrated the work of those who produce our beautiful, nourishing food.

My daughter Lydia creates a hand-drawn, watercolour menu

for each guest and these are now becoming collector's items. (She also creates these menus for the Farewell dinners that the 12-week students have at the end of every course, as well as for other special celebrations we have at the School.)

The proceeds of the long-table dinners go to support the East Cork Slow Food Educational Project, which links in with nine local schools to teach the children how to grow, cook and keep hens.

In 2011 the Outstanding in the Field team came to Ballymaloe with their founder, Jim Denevan, whose brainchild it was to have long-table dinners on farms and vineyards, in apple orchards and community gardens, and on mountain tops and beaches right across the US and Canada. The event came about after my daughter Emily met Leif Hedendal in a pub in California. He told her how he and his friends had been organising these dinners, which had been a phenomenal success, and their next stop was Europe. They were scouting for a venue in Ireland, the UK, France, Spain or Denmark. Did she know of anywhere? Emily explained that a dinner in a field in Ireland was a risky business, but how about a greenhouse? And so a plan was hatched.

We had already had several long-table dinners in the greenhouses to celebrate the work of the farmers and gardeners, so had had some practice. The School farm and garden gang snipped and clipped for several weeks to have the whole place looking its best for the event. The weather forecast was for rain and gale force winds. We all held our breath and pleaded with our friends who had a direct line to the Holy Ghost to intercede on our behalf. We'd be happy with just one drizzle-free hour to walk through the farm. And so it was.

People travelled from the US, Mexico, Holland and the UK to join the Irish guests. We invited some of the Irish artisan producers whose food we were serving, so it was a wonderfully convivial event, enjoying and celebrating their delicious produce.

Left: The guests sit down to a long-table dinner in the greenhouse.
Right (top): The beautifully laid long table, covered with crisp white linen, before the guests arrive.
Right (middle): Rory O'Connell with petit fours for the guests to finish off their dinner.
Right (bottom): The band providing musical entertainment in the greenhouse.

Sumac Lamb Chops with Tomato and Cucumber Salad

Sumac is a Middle Eastern berry that is crushed up and sold as a red spice powder. The flavour is quite distinctive, delivering a uniquely sour taste. You can get hold of sumac in specialist food shops and some big supermarkets.

Put a large griddle pan or frying pan over a high heat and allow it to get quite hot. As the pan heats up, drizzle 1 teaspoon of olive oil over each lamb chop and rub in well on both sides. Season each chop with ½ teaspoon of sumac and plenty of salt and pepper, rubbing in the spice and seasoning with your fingers.

Put the chops in the hot pan and fry for 2–4 minutes on each side, depending on the thickness of the chops and how pink you like them.

As the lamb chops cook, mix together the ingredients for the salad in a bowl and season with salt and pepper. Divide the lamb chops and salad between plates and sprinkle each one with a pinch of sumac to serve.

Serves 4

8 lamb chops, each weighing approx. 175–225g (6–8oz)
8 teaspoons olive oil
4 teaspoons sumac, plus extra to serve
sea salt and freshly ground black pepper

For the Tomato and Cucumber salad
2 tomatoes, cut into 1cm (½in) dice
300g (10½oz) cucumber, cut into 1cm (½in) dice
150ml (5fl oz) natural yogurt

Roasted Vegetable Coconut Curry

The creamy coconut milk and myriad spices grant these vegetables both elegance and luxury. Roasting the vegetables in the paste really brings out their sweetness. Making your own curry paste takes minutes and the complex depth of flavour means it's always worth doing. Chana masala is made up of equal quantities of ground coriander seeds, cumin seeds and turmeric.

Preheat the oven to 160°C/325°F/gas 3. First make the curry paste. Put a small frying pan over a medium heat and add the coriander seeds, cumin seeds and chana masala. Cook, tossing frequently, for approx. 1 minute or until they start to pop. Tip into a spice grinder or pestle and mortar and crush to a fine powder.

Put the ginger, garlic, chillies, onions and vegetable oil in a food processor and whizz for 2–3 minutes or until smooth. Pour this mixture into a large saucepan or casserole dish and stir in the freshly ground spices, along with the turmeric, sugar and salt. Set over a medium to low heat and cook, stirring occasionally, for approx. 5 minutes or until the mixture has reduced slightly.

Remove the curry paste from the heat and pour half of the mixture into a large bowl. Keep the remaining paste in the pan and stir in the coconut milk and stock, mixing well until combined.

Add the yogurt to the spice paste in the bowl and stir well, then add the root vegetables and onions. Stir well until the vegetables are thoroughly coated and then divide the contents of the bowl between two roasting tins. Cook in the preheated oven until the vegetables are lightly browned, approx. 1 hour.

Remove the vegetables from the oven and tip them into the saucepan or casserole dish with the coconut milk mixture. Put over a medium heat for a few minutes to warm through, and then stir in the spinach. Cook for a few minutes until the spinach has wilted.

To serve, spoon the curried vegetables into serving bowls and sprinkle with the fresh coriander and a scattering of toasted cashew nuts. Drizzle a spoonful of yogurt or crème fraîche over each portion.

Serves 8–10

2 x 400ml (14fl oz) cans of coconut milk
600ml (1 pint) vegetable stock
400ml (14fl oz) natural yogurt
4 large carrots, peeled and cut into 2cm (¾in) cubes
6 parsnips, peeled, cores removed and flesh cut into 2cm (¾in) cubes
700g (1½lb) sweet potatoes, peeled and cut into 2cm (¾in) cubes
4 onions, peeled and cut into eighths
150g spinach (any large stalks removed before weighing), chopped

For the curry paste
1 tablespoon coriander seeds
2 teaspoons cumin seeds
2 teaspoons chana masala
50g (2oz) fresh root ginger, peeled and roughly chopped
12 garlic cloves, peeled
4 red chillies, deseeded and roughly chopped
200g (7oz) onions, peeled and quartered
50ml (2fl oz) vegetable oil
1 tablespoon ground turmeric
2 teaspoons caster sugar
2 teaspoons sea salt

To serve
large bunch of coriander, freshly chopped
100g (3½oz) cashew nuts, toasted and chopped
200ml (7fl oz) natural yogurt or crème fraîche

White Chocolate Mendiants with Dried Cranberries, Cherries and Pistachios

Mendiants are a traditional French treat. They are unbelievably fast and easy to make, yet they look so elegant served at the end of a meal. The French would use different nuts and dried fruits to represent the four mendicant or monastic orders of the Dominicans (raisins), Augustians (hazelnuts), Franciscans (dried figs) and Carmelites (almonds). These can be made a few days in advance; make sure to store them somewhere cool, but preferably not the fridge as they will 'sweat'.

Makes 28

110g (4oz) white chocolate (we use Valrhona)
10g (½oz) dried cranberries or cherries
10g (½oz) shelled pistachios, coarsely chopped
50g (2oz) dark chocolate
edible gold leaf (optional)

Line two baking trays with baking parchment.

Put the white chocolate into a Pyrex bowl and set over a saucepan of hot water, making sure that the bottom of the bowl doesn't touch the water. Bring the water to the boil, then immediately remove from the heat and set aside until the chocolate has melted.

Put teaspoons of the melted white chocolate, spaced a little apart, onto the parchment paper. Shake gently to level, then quickly dot them with a few dried cranberries or cherries and some coarsely chopped pistachios. Allow to set.

Meanwhile, melt and cool the dark chocolate. Peel the medallions of white chocolate off the paper and brush the bases with the dark chocolate. Arrange the mendiants upside down on the baking parchment and leave to set. These look wonderfully festive scattered with edible gold leaf or served on a gold doily on a chilled plate.

The New Nordic Movement

A table at Noma restaurant in Copenhagen is one of the hottest, most sought-after meals in the world. In 2012 Noma was named best restaurant in the world by *Restaurant* magazine in their influential World's Best 50 list for the third consecutive year. Curious chefs and food lovers from around the globe fly into Copenhagen to eat at this simple establishment, which has defined the gastronomy of a whole nation and generated a flow of food tourism that benefits not only Noma but a growing number of restaurants in Copenhagen and the hinterland. So why is Noma causing such a sensation? Well, chef René Redzepi and his team cook and serve Nordic ingredients proudly. The food is fresh and seasonal, and much is foraged from the wild. It is incredibly delicious. But Noma is not just about the food; the whole experience challenged many of our concepts of how it should taste and be served.

In just a few short years, the centre of the gastronomic world has moved from Spain to the Nordic countries. Ferran Adrià, a genius whose food I have enjoyed many times, is unique. He and his acolytes concentrate on transforming textures and flavours, often to stunning effect, but even though I listened hard, one never heard the words 'fresh' or 'seasonal' and there was no discussion about breeds, feed or tradition. The new culinary movement, spearheaded by René Redzepi and Magnus Nilsson, is flowing not from Spain, France, Italy or the Mediterranean, but from Copenhagen and Stockholm, and as far north as Lapland. It began in 2004 when prominent chefs from the region, including Redzepi and Claus Meyer, signed a Kitchen Manifesto emphasising the need for purity, simplicity and freshness in their cooking, and for increased use of seasonal foods. Restaurants were encouraged to develop traditional dishes making use of ingredients benefiting from their local region's specific climate, water and soil. Just as many chefs began investing in water baths, siphons, gels and expensive kitchen gadgets, it became clear that the huge wave of technical cooking was on its way out. Instead what is catching young chefs' imaginations is the New Nordic or authentic cuisine. This new movement, honouring nature and the seasons, resonates much more with me.

To quote Julia Moskin in *The New York Times*, this style of cooking is 'earthy and refined, ancient and modern, both playful and deeply serious. Instead of the new (techniques, stabilisers, ingredients), it emphasises the old (drying, smoking, pickling, curing), with a larger goal of returning balance to the earth itself'. Challenging in the extreme Nordic climate where chefs say goodbye to fresh ingredients at the beginning of October and don't see them again until they welcome their re-emergence in April. Food is presented on plates in the midst of rocks and shells, moss, twigs and bark, lichen, hay and pine, in a recreation of its natural environment.

On arrival at Noma, a converted herring warehouse, you walk down three or four steps – the kitchen is directly ahead – and are greeted by several of the chefs and shown to your table. The room is simple yet incredibly sophisticated. And then the feast begins. Lots of little snacks arrive in quick succession, then the pace slows down and the dishes become slightly larger. Virtually all are vegetarian. In an exquisite meal of almost 20 courses, we had meat just twice: tiny medallions of bone marrow in one dish and paper thin slices of duck breast in another. I hadn't even noticed the absence of meat until someone mentioned it in passing. It was a beautiful celebration of vegetables and wild foods. At Noma the chefs not only plate the food in the kitchen but also help to serve it to the guests – such a simple yet brilliant concept. The chefs, normally hidden behind closed doors, get to experience the guests' reaction to their food. Noma has simply one of the best dining experiences I've ever had.

There were three Irish chefs in the Noma kitchen, one of whom is a past student of the Ballymaloe Cookery School. Louise Bannon, who did the 12-week course in 2002, baked the bread and produced many of the tempting desserts on our visit. The bread was mouthwatering, served warm in a little felt nest with the most incredibly delicious butter I have ever tasted. It's made by a Swedish couple who have just five goats. They stop the butter just when the cream is starting to split, drain and wash it then serve the curdled butter fat at that stage – completely delicious.

Noma alone is worth the trip to Copenhagen, but one can have many memorable breakfasts, brunches, lunches, afternoon teas and dinners there, although there never seems to be enough time to enjoy them all. At Nimb Herman in Tivoli we had a fantastically good lunch. The first 'course' was two pieces of oysterleaf (also known as oysterplant) served on a little mound of empty oyster shells. This intriguing little plant, *Mertensia maritima*, tastes distantly of oysters, a little teaser at the beginning of the meal. The next three courses were oyster-related. A cushion of oyster-flavoured foam was served on a flat pebble, with instructions to allow it to slide off the pebble into your mouth. It dissolved into a little pool of briny deliciousness. This was followed by a couple of oysters with smoked olive oil, and then a pine-flavoured granita served on a plate of seaweed and rocks with little sprigs of pine tucked in here and there. Next up, oyster, veal and soured cream, served in a marrow bone – sublime – and on it went. We enjoyed a plate of Danish farmhouse cheeses: Red Christian from Jutland, Trope Need Krondil, a hay cheese, and a blue cheese from Fyn, served with a little loaf of warm walnut bread with rose hip marmalade and chutney. Several puddings and three cheeky petit fours signalled the end of the meal. I forgot to count the courses, each was tiny and perfectly pitched, a celebration of Nordic seasonal ingredients with a mischevious, fun element running throughout.

Denmark is not the only Scandinavian country producing food fitting the tenets of the New Nordic movment. I've been lucky enough to visit Jukka Oresto, a past student, in his homeland to taste traditional Finnish foods, visit the markets and bake bread in a wood-burning stove on a farm in Karppala, north of Tampere. Eila Haapaniemi, her daughter Eija and her daughter-in-law Sari, lovingly taught me how to make some of the traditional Finnish breads passed down from generation to generation. We ate Pullo, a sweet bread flavoured with anise and topped with crunchy sugar, straight from the oven with glasses of cold milk. I tasted elk for the first time and was greatly surprised to discover that it was not at all strong, but juicy and succulent. The meal incorporated many Finnish specialities – herring dishes, Finnish pancakes and a particularly distinctive Finnish potato dish called rosolli.

The market in any country provides a peephole into the food and lifestyle of the people. Helsinki's neat and tidy covered markets gave a fascinating insight into the traditional food of the Finns. A tantalising array of smoked fish, several types of gravlax, Finnish cheese, wonderful breads (rye, barley and wheat), a variety of crispbreads, plus a special dark bread to serve with reindeer, pleated

Karelian pasties and sugar Possu with different fillings were all on offer. It is these traditional foods that the Nordic movement is keen on using, promoting and preserving.

We've also brought Scandinavian food trends to the School, with multiple visits from guest chef Camilla Plum. She came from Fuglebjerggaard in Denmark to stay in 2012 and showed me how to make beautiful herb salts and preserve tomatoes using Maldon sea salt or Sel de Guérande – she's a totally natural cook. Camilla sprinkled chopped verbena salt over and into a chicken, which we roasted several hours later and ate accompanied by roast potatoes with lemon and bay leaves. It is one of the best things I have ever eaten and her simple salt transformed the chicken. I now teach the students how to make these delicious salts.

The whole ethos of the New Nordic movement excites me in a way that molecular gastronomy didn't. I love the honouring of tradition and find myself searching in the deepest recesses of my memory to try to recollect forgotten skills, such as how Pa made vegetable pits in our kitchen garden in Cullohill years ago to store root vegetables and Bramley apples for use over the winter.

Above: Camilla Plum, Danish organic cook, farmer and cookbook author, during the Ballymaloe Literary Festival of Food and Wine in 2013.

Thanksgiving

Since the second year of the School we have had American students on virtually every course. For them, Thanksgiving is the big celebration of the year. If they are at the School when Thanksgiving falls, they often decide to cook a huge dinner for all their class. The centrepiece is a fine free-range turkey from Nora Aherne who has been supplying poultry to the School since the beginning. However, many have never cooked a Thanksgiving dinner before and rely on childhood memories rather than experience to guide them.

So, in November 2012 we decided to add a Thanksgiving Course to our brochure. It proved to be a resounding success. We invited all of our American students to tell us about their favourite Thanksgiving meal. Several wanted to share a recipe; some sounded a little strange to us, but Sweet Potato and Marshmallows is definitely a favourite. A version from Jared Batson, one of our American students, got a terrific reaction. Several others talked about Green Beans and Mushrooms. I enquired about how it was made. There was much giggling and then they told me: 'Take a couple of cans of green beans, top with a can of mushroom soup, sprinkle with sliced crispy onion and put into the oven'. Definitely a step too far for me, so we decided to try a more homemade version with the last of the season's French beans, blanched and refreshed, mushroom a la crème, crispy onion and flaked almonds. It was sooo good, everyone fought over the last morsel. Pumpkin Pie is another Thanksgiving favourite. The American version is made with canned Libby's pumpkin purée, but Eoin Cluskey, a student from Dublin, made this pie with finely chopped fresh pumpkin flesh, by far the best anyone had ever eaten. We made three stuffings with the turkey: chestnut and sausage, oyster stuffing and our own special buttery, herby bread stuffing, which seemed to be the favourite.

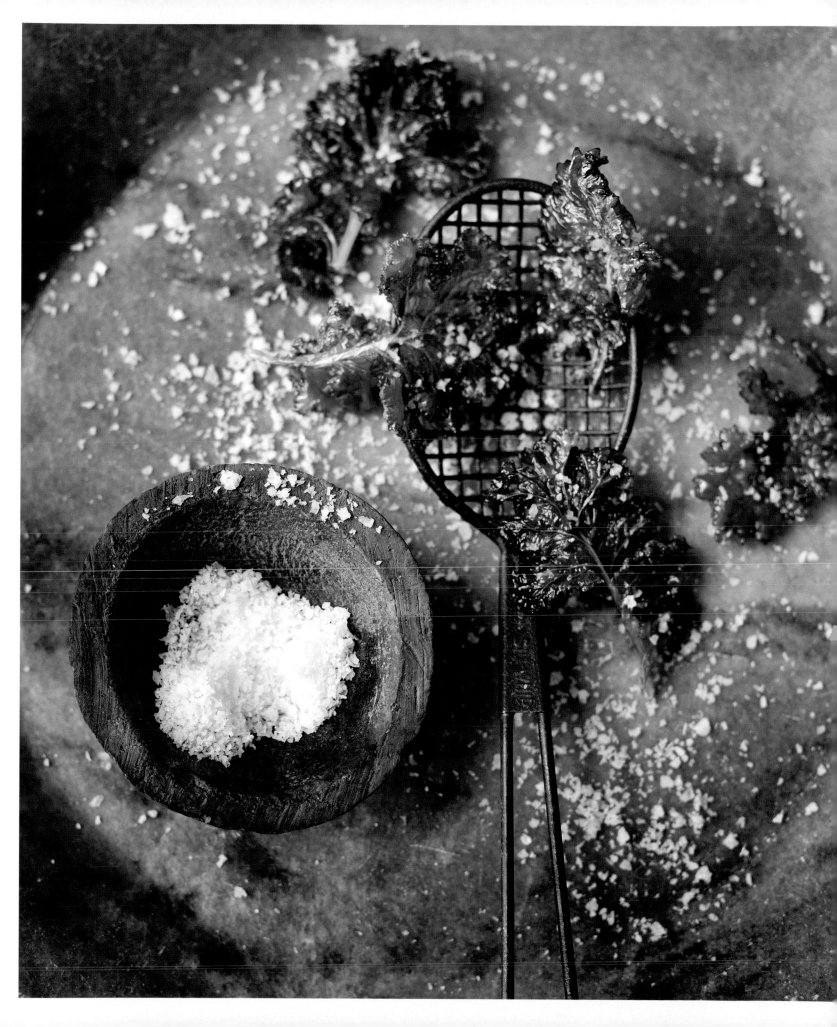

Kale Crisps

Suddenly Kale is the coolest ingredient – it's all over the place, on restaurant menus, at farmers' markets, even on supermarket shelves, and kale crisps are the snack of the moment. I'm not complaining as I love kale – it's super nutritious and we grow four different varieties here at the School – Red Russian, Ragged Jack, asparagus and curly kale. I find the latter works best for this recipe.

A couple of years ago we invested in a dehydrator – it's not a must-have bit of kitchen equipment, but if you do decide to buy one you can have fun experimenting. It's brilliant for drying fresh herbs, tomatoes and wild mushrooms – in a good mushroom season it will pay for itself in no time. Kale crisps will only take approx. 3–4 hours in a dehydrator at 57°C (135°F).

Makes lots

250g (9oz) curly kale
2 tablespoons extra virgin olive oil
sea salt and sugar

Preheat the oven to 150°C/300°F/gas 2. Strip the leaves off the kale, tear into bite-sized pieces and put in a bowl. Sprinkle with extra virgin olive oil, a little salt and a pinch of sugar and toss well. Spread out in a single layer on two baking trays.

Bake in the preheated oven for approx. 20 minutes until crisp. Transfer to a wire rack to cool and crisp further. Enjoy.

Yannick and Louise's Banana Shallots with Anchovy Crème Fraîche

Yannick Van Aeken and Louise Bannon both spent five years in the kitchen at Noma in Copenhagen. In November 2012 they gave a pop-up dinner in the Garden Café at Ballymaloe using ingredients that they gathered from the hedgerows, seashore and the farm. This recipe is one they cooked when they returned to do a further pop-up at the Ballymaloe Literary Festival of Food and Wine in May 2013.

Makes approx. 40 crisps

4 banana shallots
sunflower oil or duck fat, to cover

For the Anchovy Crème Fraîche
100g (3½oz) anchovy fillets
250g (9oz) crème fraîche

Preheat the oven to 120°C/250°F/gas ½ and line two baking trays with baking parchment.

Cut the banana shallots in half lengthways. Put them in a saucepan or sauté pan, cover them with the sunflower oil or duck fat and simmer over a low heat until they are beginning to soften, approx. 20 minutes. Set aside to cool. Drain the shallots, reserving the oil. (The shallot-infused oil can be used for salad dressings or roast potatoes. It has a light shallot-confit flavour. Store in a glass jam jar in the fridge.)

Remove the skins from the cooled shallots and carefully separate the layers one by one. Arrange them on the prepared baking trays in a single layer and cover them with another layer of baking parchment. Lay another baking tray on top of each to flatten the shallots completely.

Cook for 1 hour or until the shallots are dark brown and caramelised. Remove and drain on kitchen paper.

To make the anchovy cream, blitz the anchovies with the crème fraîche and spoon into a little dish.

Serve the shallot crisps in a little bowl, accompanied by the anchovy crème fraîche.

Oysterleaf and Sea Urchins

We had a wonderful lunch in 2012 at Nimb Herman in Tivoli Gardens in Copenhagen. The first 'course' was just two leaves presented on a flat stone. The waiter was mightily impressed when I recognised them as oysterleaf, which we have been growing here in the greenhouses from a plant given to me by Giana Ferguson of Gubbeen. Oysterleaf tastes distinctly of oysters even if you are blindfolded.

If you can get flat, smooth beach stones to serve the sea urchins and oysterleaf on it makes a lovely presentation. If not, just use small plates. Seawater adds an extra dimension to this dish but if you do not have access to fresh seawater then just leave it out.

Serves 4

4 sea urchins
8 pieces of oysterleaf (*Mertensia maritima*)
4 tablespoons seawater

Open the sea urchins carefully and remove the corals. Check to make sure they are free of the urchin spines or shell.

For each serving, put two oysterleaves and the corals from a sea urchin on each plate. Drizzle over a little seawater and serve immediately.

Shrimps in the Shell with Bacon Mayonnaise

This is another recipe that Louise Bannon and Yannick Van Aeken cooked at their pop-up restaurant in the Garden Café at the Cookery School. We get wonderful fresh shrimps directly from the boats in Ballycotton for a good part of the year and Yannick and Louise showed us how to deep-fry them whole in the shell. They were unbelievably delicious and we have been cooking them this way ever since.

Start with the mayonnaise. Preheat the oven to 160°C/325°F/gas 3.

Scatter the diced bacon in a roasting tin and cook for 20 minutes. Remove from the oven and set aside to cool. Pour the vegetable oil into a sterilised 1 litre (1¾ pint) jar and add the bacon. Leave to infuse in the oil overnight.

The following morning, drain the oil through a sieve, discarding the bacon. In a bowl, whisk the egg yolks, white wine vinegar, mustard and sea salt together. Holding the bacon-infused oil in one hand and the whisk in the other, gradually add the oil in a steady stream, whisking all the time until the mayonnaise is thick and smooth. (If the mayonnaise starts to split, just add a little hot water to re-emulsify.) Taste and correct the seasoning if necessary.

Preheat the sunflower oil in a deep-fat fryer. Toss the whole shrimps, a few at a time, in the seasoned flour. Shake off the excess and fry in batches in the hot oil for 1–2 minutes or until crisp. Drain on kitchen paper.

Serve the shrimps with a bowl of the Bacon Mayonnaise. Eat the lot, shells and all – they will be crunchy and delicious – the best flavour comes from the heads, so it's a must to eat everything.

Serves 16 as a canapé or 8 as a starter

sunflower oil, for deep-frying
1kg (2¼lb) whole fresh raw shrimps in the shell
seasoned flour

For the Bacon Mayonnaise
200g (7oz) smoked streaky bacon, diced
1 litre (1¾ pints) vegetable oil
12 organic egg yolks
40g (1½oz) white wine vinegar
40g (1½oz) Dijon mustard
big pinch of Irish sea salt, ground

The Students

Over the past 30 years we've had students from Ireland, Great Britain, Sweden, Norway, Finland, Denmark, Holland, Austria, Germany, Alaska, USA, Mexico, Chile, Italy, France, Belgium, Sicily, Japan, India, Malaysia, Sri Lanka, Singapore, Hong Kong and mainland China, Dubai, Latvia, Cyprus, Poland, Switzerland, Russia, Korea, Lithuania, Australia, New Zealand, South Africa, Kenya, Peru, Zimbabwe and Zambia. Fourteen nationalities in one group was our most diverse so far, and we've had a wide range of ages from officially 18 (but there have been several highly-motivated 16-year-olds) to 69. One lovely American celebrated his 70th birthday while he was with us and achieved his lifelong ambition of being able to cook.

So our little village of Shanagarry becomes very cosmopolitan with students from all over the world mingling with the local community in the pubs and restaurants. Local shopkeepers also tell me that the school greatly enhances the economy and atmosphere of the village. You can also imagine how tempting it is to have so many beautiful young people in the area for months at a time. We've had lots of romances and several weddings, so we've been instrumental in bringing 'new blood' into the area! Needless to say even a whisper of a party or a celebration at the Cookery School causes a flurry of excitement and I've been known to chase away 'likely lads' with six packs from the School on several occasions in the middle of the night, until they get the message that 'the old bat' will appear out in her nightie. They have now reluctantly realised that the Cookery School, with all its tempting morsels, is out of bounds for all non-students.

Even though we do stress it in the brochure, the intensity of the 12-week course invariably comes as a surprise to the students. For those who have already gone to university, the fact that they must turn up for every class sometimes comes as a shock – it's not an optional extra and a 'hangover' is not a legitimate excuse, as many a groggy student has discovered when they wake up to find me peering down at them, giving them the option of going to the doctor (50 euros) or putting on their whites!

Left: At Ballymaloe Cookery School we use the gardens and farm as an outdoor classroom and the School as indoor classroom. I show the students our Egremont Russet heritage variety of apples, which has a lovely, full crop every year and grows outside the Blue Dining Room. Above: A busy hands-on session in Kitchen Two during a 12-week course in the early days of the School.

Sounds like gastro-boot-camp, but we really want everyone who comes to not only get value for money, but much, much more.

Past students tell us that the Ballymaloe Cookery School is not just about learning to cook, it's an introduction to a particular way of life. In the cottages, students quickly learn many life skills including how to wash up and use an iron and a hoover; a first, and a shock, for many who have never before shared a house with anyone except their family.

I suppose it shouldn't come as a surprise in these days of central heating that so many young people don't know how to light an open fire or a stove. Even though the cottages are 'toasty warm', they love the comfort of an open fire, so we show them how to set a fire with newspaper, kindling, dried citrus peels and dry timber. A wheelbarrow always sits in the courtyard to encourage students to collect fallen twigs and miscellaneous bits of timber when they go for a walk in the garden or the woods. One student told me that the fire always feels warmer when she collects the timber herself!

Students enrol on the 12-week course for any number of reasons. Many are determined to be professional cooks or chefs and are here to gain the skills to earn their living from cooking. Others take a career break to fulfil a dream of learning to cook so they can cook and entertain their family and friends with confidence and panache. For some it's a chance to re-skill or change career, but the majority want to be able to earn a living from their cooking skills. They can travel all over the world and get a job. Being able to cook is one of the easiest ways to win friends and influence people and there

are a myriad of opportunities for those who can cook to use their new skills – in restaurant kitchens, catering businesses and farmers' markets; by food styling or food writing; cooking on boats, in ski chalets, on television or as personal chefs. If students are unsure of the opportunities, the deal is this: if they make me a pot of tea after class any day and produce a homemade biscuit I will explore the possibilities with them. Because I'm a member of the IACP, Slow Food, Euro-Toques, Guild of Food Writers in UK and Irish Food Writers' Guild, I am fortunate enough to have contacts all over the world, which I can share with them. Fortunately, many restaurants and food businesses love to have the Ballymaloe Cookery School students in their kitchens because of their passion for real food and their interest in sustainable food issues, and of course the skills they have learned from our 'everything from scratch' approach.

Students use their skills in a diverse range of ways. Ireland's Whitbread Round the World crew were the best fed crew in the 23-boat fleet according to a piece in *The Irish Times* in 1989, as Richard Gibson, from Baltimore USA, who did the 12-week certificate course in 1987, was the chef on board. He had a hugely challenging task; on a racing yacht the galley is tiny, with a limited number of pots and pans and storage space and a weight limit for provisions (only root vegetables qualify because they keep well). The food must be delicious and even, more importantly, nourishing to give the crew strength and keep them in good humour. During the course of the Whitbread race he provided approximately 13,770 meals to his crew mates with a batterie de cuisine of three pots, a chef's knife and a mixing bowl, using a four-ring cooker and one oven. Sadly their hopes were dashed after the yacht's boom broke halfway through the last leg, but Richard gave the despondent crew a treat he'd been saving for an occasion when they might need their spirits lifted – he produced some freshly baked cookies!

It's a few years ago now since a chap called Paddy Daly, a shoe polish salesman from Dublin, arrived to do a one-week Introductory Course at the Cookery School. When he arrived into the car park in his camper van it took him all the courage he could muster to actually walk into the School. Paddy, a man in his sixties, was going through a harrowing time, nursing his much-loved wife through a long illness. He was bereft and had lost his will to live.

Above: Students on the 12-week course wear chef's whites while students on the shorter courses wear their 'civvies'.
Right: Students relaxing in the courtyard after a busy day's cooking at the School.

She had been a wonderful cook – Paddy missed her delicious food so much and was becoming more and more despondent when he was unable to cook tasty, delicious food to cheer her up as her health deteriorated. In a concerted effort to provide new hope and enthusiasm in his life, his family had clubbed together to give him a present of a cooking course. Paddy himself wasn't at all keen, but he was dispatched to Cork and felt he had to make the effort in response to their generous gesture.

He eventually plucked up the courage to venture into the School and, somehow, the experience changed his life. It renewed his zest for living and the skills he learned enabled him to brighten his wife's last months, and have given both him and his family and friends endless pleasure ever since. He has made several return visits over the years. Paddy telephones us periodically and I was particularly touched by hearing how, on noticing that many other people are alone in his neighbourhood, he and some friends started something on the SOS – 'share our skills principle' – that is quietly making a difference to many people's lives. He invites and welcomes the person into his house and teaches them how to make a loaf of bread, a pot of stew and a soup, and then they sit down and eat it together and chat. The 'student' can then make it at home and pass on the skill to someone else. No money changes

hands. Paddy says the reward is in the sharing and the delight of the recipient. What a beautiful idea – those of us who have learned how to cook can make such a difference to people's lives by passing on our skills to those less fortunate.

Since 2005, two French horticultural colleges have been sending their students as interns. Both say that there is nowhere else in Europe where they can get such a range of experience, or the combination of farm, gardens, greenhouse, animals, poultry, dairy, cheesemaking and delicious food. The latter is certainly a big attraction, and we understand that there's huge competition to be chosen for a 'stage' at the Ballymaloe Cookery School Organic Farm and Gardens. We too love to have them with us and their presence enriches our lives. They come with a brilliant work ethic, eager to learn and properly equipped with all-weather clothes and footwear. Before they leave, as a little thank-you, many cook us a family dinner – we've had not only French, but also Ukrainian, Lithuanian, Russian and Croatian farewell meals.

Early in 2001, an executive from the Farm Apprenticeship Board telephoned to ask whether we could offer work experience on our farm to a young Ukrainian girl. She had been working on a dairy farm in the Midlands since her arrival in Ireland in November, milking 80 cows, and was ready for a change of scene. We arranged

to meet, and we chatted about the Ukraine and her family. Her grandmother had a farm, but Elena herself had studied economics at the Zhytomyr National Agroecological University and was highly educated and eager to travel and improve her languages. The Farm Apprenticeship Scheme gives her and many others like her this opportunity. When they come to Ireland, they get a warm welcome and are treated with respect and given comfortable accommodation and delicious food. Elena loved working here on the farm and in the gardens and enjoyed the food. Nonetheless, like so many travellers, she missed the food of her native country. For so many of us, foods are inextricably linked with happy memories of childhood.

I'm always fascinated to learn about other food cultures. Elena described the food of her region of Ukraine and then offered to cook some of her favourite dishes for us. She telephoned her mother and grandmother who really entered into the spirit, and not only gave her lots of advice but sent a huge can of caviar for our aperitif; it was delicious. We were spreading it sparingly on some thinly sliced white bread, but Elena said 'nonsense, we spread it like butter at home'. We invited some friends and Elena cooked a delicious meal for us.

Occasionally a past student comes back to the school to do a cookery demonstration for the students. In March 2013 Maria Cho from Korea, who did the 12-week course with us in September 2009, returned to teach us all the basics of Korean food through some of her favourite dishes. The students loved her food and were inspired by her stories about how, after a series of emails and letters had failed to get a response, she secured work experience in many of her favourite restaurants (such as Locanda Locatelli, Moro and Marcus Wareing in London, the sustainable food project at the American Academy in Rome – which was her favourite – and Boulette's Larder and Chez Panisse in the US), simply by turning up at the kitchen door and more or less refusing to go until they gave her a chance.

Far left: Sign welcoming students to the School.
Left: The Garden Café at the School, where the students eat the food they have cooked during a morning session for lunch alongside the teachers.
Above (left): The huge overhead mirror and TV monitors ensure that the students can see right into the saucepans during cookery demonstrations.
Above (middle): For students on the summer 12-week course the courtyard provides a lovely place to relax.
Above (right): 12-week students get the chance for some leisure activites during time off from cooking, such as exploring the surrounding local area by bike.

Arun Kapil's Garam Masala Cookies

Arun Kapil is an Anglo-Indian past student from the 12-week course in September 2004. He was previously a DJ but when he came to the Ballymaloe Cookery School he discovered his real passion was food. He realised there was an opportunity to import fresh spices, which he now does from his relatives' spice gardens in India. He sometimes includes recipes alongside the packets of spice mix that he sells.

Preheat the oven to 220°C/425°F/gas 7.

First make the cookie dough. Put the butter and sugar in the bowl of a food processor. Turn the food processor onto a high speed and cream the butter and sugar together for a few minutes until pale. (You may need to cream the butter by itself for a while before adding the sugar if it's straight out of the fridge.)

In a separate bowl, mix all the dry ingredients together: the flour, oats, baking powder and garam masala.

Reduce the speed of the food processor to slow and add the dry ingredients, a handful at a time to avoid clouds of flour engulfing you and your kitchen. Once the mixture has come together, turn off the food processor, take out the dough and put it on a lightly floured, clean surface.

Using your favourite rolling pin, roll out the dough to a thickness of approx. 2cm (¾in) – don't forget to keep rubbing flour onto your rolling pin to prevent the dough from sticking to it. Cut out the cookies using the cutter of your choice – the lid of an empty jam jar will do fine.

Put the cookie shapes onto a baking tray (there is no need to flour it, oil it or use any sort of baking parchment). Pop the tray onto the middle shelf of the oven. Bake the cookies for 10–15 minutes or until golden brown, then remove them from the oven and transfer to a wire rack to cool.

Wait until they've cooled down completely before serving.

Serve these excellent cookies with a pot of chai for an alternative, fragrant afternoon chill-out, with rhubarb fool or gooseberry fool, or crumbled up and used as an alternative base for a creamy cheesecake.

Makes 30–40 cookies, depending on the size of your cutter

110g (4oz) salted butter
75g (3oz) caster sugar
50g (2oz) plain flour, plus extra for dusting
150g (5oz) porridge oats
pinch of baking powder
3 teaspoons garam masala

Many students have shared recipes with us over the past 30 years and some become part of our repertoire, even making an appearance in some of my books!

Alison Heafey's Autumn Nut and Caramel Tart

This recipe comes from former student Alison Heafey, who got it from her friend Cindy Mushet, author of *The Art and Soul of Baking*. I always encourage students to share recipes as well as asking for recipes in restaurants; it's a great way to expand your culinary skills.

Preheat the oven to 180°C/350°F/gas 4.

First make the pastry. Put the flour, sugar and salt in a food processor fitted with the metal blade. Pulse five times to blend the ingredients. Add the butter and pulse 6–8 times until it is the size of large peas. In a small bowl, whisk together the egg yolks, vanilla extract and 1 teaspoon of water. Add to the food processor, then process until the dough begins to form small clumps. To test the dough, squeeze a handful of clumps – when you open your hand they should hold together. If they fall apart, sprinkle the remaining water over the dough and pulse several times. If necessary, add up to one further teaspoon of water to bring the dough together.

Remove the dough from the bowl and knead it gently 2–3 times, to bring the dough together. Shape it into a round disc approx. 15cm (6in) across. Set aside in the fridge to chill for 30 minutes.

Break the cold dough into 2.5–5cm (1–2in) pieces and scatter them evenly over the bottom of a 24cm (9½in) tart tin. Use the heel of your hand to press the dough flat, connecting the pieces in a smooth layer. Press from the centre of the tin outwards, building up some extra dough around the base at the edge of the tart. Using your thumbs, press this excess up the sides of the tin, making sure it is the same thickness as the dough on the bottom. Roll your thumb over the top edge of the tin to remove any excess dough (save this for patching any cracks that might form during baking). Chill for at least 30 minutes.

Bake 'blind' for 20–22 minutes or until the edges and centre are set. (If the shell is cracking and sticking to the baking parchment lining, replace it and continue to bake for a further 5–6 minutes.) Remove the baking parchment and beans and set aside to cool.

Once cooled, return the pastry shell to the oven and bake for a further 10–12 minutes or until the crust is a pale tan colour. Transfer to a rack and cool completely before adding the filling.

Meanwhile, make the frangipane filling. Put the almonds and sugar in the bowl of a food processor and process until finely ground. Add the butter and blend. Add the eggs, flour and almond extract and mix thoroughly. Pour the filling into the tart case and bake for 30–35 minutes, or until firm in the centre and lightly browned. Set aside to cool completely.

To make the topping, put the water, sugar and golden (or corn)

Serves 10–12

For the vanilla shortcrust pastry
175g (6oz) plain flour
50g (2oz) sugar
¼ teaspoon sea salt
110g (4oz) cold unsalted butter, cut into 1.5cm (½in) pieces
2 large organic egg yolks
2 teaspoons pure vanilla extract
1–2 teaspoons water

For the frangipane filling
110g (4oz) whole natural almonds, lightly toasted
100g (3½oz) caster sugar
50g (2oz) unsalted butter, softened
2 large organic eggs
2 tablespoons plain flour
½ teaspoon almond extract

For the nut and caramel topping
110g (4oz) water
300g (10½oz) granulated sugar
2 tablespoons golden or corn syrup
110g (4oz) unsalted butter, softened
110g (4oz) double cream, at room temperature
75g (3oz) whole unsalted almonds, lightly toasted
60g (2½oz) pecan halves, lightly toasted
50g (2oz) walnut halves, lightly toasted

syrup in a saucepan large enough to eventually hold all the nuts as well. Heat slowly until the sugar has dissolved and the liquid is clear. Then increase the heat to high and boil rapidly until the sugar darkens to a rich golden brown colour.

Remove the pan from the heat and immediately add the butter and cream (be careful, as the mixture will rise in the pan and splutter). Stir briefly with a wooden spoon to blend, then add the toasted nuts. Stir gently to coat the nuts in the caramel sauce, then immediately spoon the nuts over the cooled frangipane tart, reserving the caramel in the pan. Use two spoons, not your fingers, because the mixture will be very hot. Finish, if you like, by spooning some of the caramel sauce over the nuts. Set aside to cool.

Remove from the tin just before serving. Serve at room temperature.

Kaitlyn's Lemon Curd Meringue Cake

We love the way some of our students add their own creative touch to a basic recipe. Kaitlyn Brenner from Massachusetts, a student on the 12-week course in January 2012, served this at her exam.

Preheat the oven to 150°C/300°F/gas 2 and line a baking tray with baking parchment.

Start with the meringue kisses. Put the egg whites and sugar in the bowl of a mixer and whisk at high speed until the mixture forms stiff, dry peaks. Spoon into a piping bag fitted with a star nozzle and pipe approx. 30 rosettes onto the baking parchment, making each one approx. 4cm (1½in) in diameter. Bake immediately in the oven for 45–50 minutes or until crisp. Remove from the oven and set aside to cool.

Meanwhile, make the lemon curd. Beat together the whole eggs and egg yolks together in a bowl. Melt the butter in a saucepan over a very low heat. Add the caster sugar, lemon zest and juice, followed by the beaten eggs. Stir carefully over a gentle heat with a straight-ended wooden spatula until the mixture coats the back of it. Remove the lemon curd from the heat and set aside to cool.

Once the meringues are cooked, increase the oven temperature to 190°C/375°F/gas 5. Grease two 18cm (7in) cake tins with a little melted butter, put a round of baking parchment in the bottom of each tin and dust lightly with flour.

To make the sponge, cream the butter with the sugar and lemon zest until pale and fluffy. Beat in the eggs, one at a time, adding a tablespoon of flour with each addition. Beat very well, and then fold in the remaining flour. Divide the mixture evenly between the prepared tins and bake in the oven for 20–25 minutes or until the cakes are well risen, golden and feel spongy to the touch.

Remove the cakes from the oven and set aside to cool in the tins for a few minutes before turning them out onto a wire rack to cool completely.

Meanwhile, make the icing. Mix 8 tablespoons of the cooled lemon curd into the mascarpone and beat in the sifted icing sugar.

To serve, split the cakes in half horizontally with a sharp serrated knife. Sandwich the four layers together with the lemon curd and lemon mascarpone icing, reserving some of the icing for the top and sides of the cake. Put the cake on a stand and use a warm palette knife to spread the top and sides of the cake with the reserved icing. While the icing is still wet, stick the meringue kisses all over the cake and decorate with fresh or frosted lemon balm leaves, if using.

Serves 8–10

175g (6oz) butter, plus extra for greasing
175g (6oz) self-raising flour, plus extra for dusting
175g (6oz) caster sugar
grated zest of 2 lemons
3 organic eggs

For the meringue kisses
2 organic egg whites (reserve the yolks for the lemon curd)
110g (4oz) caster sugar

For the lemon curd
4 organic eggs, plus 2 organic egg yolks
110g (4oz) butter
225g (8oz) caster sugar
grated zest and juice of 4 lemons

For the lemon mascarpone icing
8 tablespoons lemon curd (see above)
225ml (8fl oz) mascarpone
4 tablespoons icing sugar, sifted

To decorate
fresh or frosted lemon balm leaves (optional)

Madhulika's Grandmother's Pork Masala

Madhulika Sundaram came from Chennai in South India to do the 12-week certificate course in April 2013. She showed us how to cook several of her family recipes, including this delicious Pork Masala. You can reduce the amount of chillies in this recipe if you like a milder flavour.

Serves 6

100g (3½oz) sunflower oil
25g (1oz) brown mustard seeds
1 rounded tablespoon cumin seeds
500g (18oz) onion, finely chopped
1kg (2¼lb) pork shoulder, cut into 2.5cm (1in) dice
100g (3½oz) fresh root ginger, peeled and finely diced
100g (3½oz) garlic, peeled and finely chopped
1 level teaspoon ground turmeric
6–10 red chillies, sliced into rings
350–450ml (12–16fl oz) water
1 teaspoon soft brown sugar (optional)
sea salt

Put the oil in a saucepan over a high heat, when it begins to bubble, add the mustard seeds and cumin. As soon as the mustard seeds pop, add the onions and cook until light brown. Reduce the heat to medium and add the diced pork, ginger, garlic, turmeric and chillies to the pan. Stir well, cover and leave to cook over a medium heat for 15 minutes.

Add 350ml (12fl oz) of water, season lightly with salt and stir. Cover the pan and allow to cook gently for 40 minutes over a medium heat, stirring at regular intervals. The water should be almost fully reduced at this stage. Add half the sugar, stir well and add more if desired.

Serve in a warm bowl with rice and a fruit raita.

Coriander Kimchi

This simple kimchi works well with other Korean dishes, such as Bulgogi (see right).

200g (7oz) coriander leaves
1 tablespoon Korean soy sauce
1 tablespoon cider vinegar
⅓ tablespoon organic caster sugar
½ tablespoon chilli powder
1 teaspoon toasted sesame seed oil
1 teaspoon toasted sesame seeds

Wash or rinse the coriander leaves gently under cold water.

Mix the soy sauce and vinegar with the sugar and chilli powder in a small bowl. Just before serving, add the sesame oil and seeds. Serve with Bulgogi (see left) or steamed white rice.

Bulgogi

When past student Maria Cho from Korea returned to give a cookery demonstration at the School, the students went crazy for her food. Bulgogi is quite a mission to make, but so good it's certainly worth the efoort. Matganjang is a seasoned soy sauce and a very useful marinade that can be prepared ahead of time and used for many dishes. It will keep in the fridge for up to a month.

First make the matganjang. Put the soy sauce, sugar and water in a large saucepan and bring to the boil. Once boiling, add the mirin and sake or vermouth. Bring to the boil again, add the apple and lemon, then remove from the heat. Cover with a lid. Allow to cool completely, then return to the heat and bring to the boil.

Getting the meat for this dish can be tricky, but worth it. You need to ask your butcher for a fillet of beef and to freeze it for you, thus making it easier for him to slice it thinly for you.

To defrost the meat, put it in a sieve and leave it at room temperature, so the blood can drain out. Once defrosted, cut the meat into 7–8 x 1cm (½in) strips.

While the meat is defrosting, prepare the vegetables.

Drain the mushrooms and trim the stems off the mushrooms and discard. Slice the caps into 5mm (¼in) slivers.

Mix together the matganjang, crushed garlic, ginger paste, pear (if using) and a little pepper and pour over the vegetables and beef. Mix well with your hands. Then garnish with sesame oil and seeds. Leave to marinate for 20 minutes.

Fry off the mixture to heat through – approx. 5–6 minutes – and serve immediately with rice.

Serves 4–6

500g (18oz) beef, sliced (lean beef tenderloin roast, eye of round or sirloin)
100g (3½oz) onion, finely chopped into 3mm (⅛in) dice
50g (2oz) spring onion, chopped into 3cm (1¼in) batons
100g (3½oz) dried shiitake mushrooms, soaked in boiling water for 30 minutes
110ml (4fl oz) matganjang
1½ tablespoon and 1½ teaspoons crushed garlic
1 tablespoon ginger paste
1 pear, peeled and grated (optional)
freshly ground black pepper

For the matganjang
1.2 litres (2 pints) organic soy sauce
500g (18oz) organic sugar
110ml (4fl oz) water
110ml (4fl oz) mirin
110ml (4fl oz) sake or vermouth
½ apple, thinly sliced
½ lemon, thinly sliced

To serve
½ tablespoon sesame oil
1 tablespoon toasted sesame seeds

Index

~~❧~~

Picture Credits

*All photographs by Laura Edwards
except for the following:*

Tim Allen: 10 (bottom), 11,
12, 17, 18, 19, 20, 21, 22, 23,
24, 25, 27 (top), 28, 34, 35, 37,
42, 43 (top), 49, 50, 52, 63,
78, 81, 82, 92, 93, 101, 102,
104, 111, 116, 127 (left), 138,
139 (top), 143, 150, 151, 152,
153, 158, 164, 165, 177 (left),
180 (bottom), 188 (except bottom
right), 190, 191 (top), 192, 193,
194, 198, 199 (except bottom),
214, 215, 224, 233, 236 (except
bottom), 237, 244, 245, 252,
254 (top left and right), 255 (top
left and bottom right), 257 (top
to bottom right), 263 (left), 265,
273, 274, 287, 288 (middle
and bottom), 290, 291; **Peter
Cassidy**: 7, 32, 33, 60, 62, 69,
70, 72, 79, 88, 100, 109, 117
(bottom), 125, 128, 167, 177
(right), 200, 222, 254 (bottom
left), 255 (top right), 278, 299,
309 (left and middle); **Kevin
Dunne**: 13, 61, 305: **Cullen
Allen**: 16, 230; **Ray Main**: 26,
220, 247; **Joleen Cronin**: 43
(bottom), 199 (bottom), 297;
John Minihan: 149; **Melanie
Eclare**: 180 (top), 252, 263
(right); **Emily Ashworth**: 188
(bottom right), 191 (bottom), 236
(bottom), 246, 281, 308 (right),
309 (right); **Francine Lawrence**:
223; **Ray Roberts/Impact Photo
Library**: 225; **Cristian Barnett**:
257; **Diane Cusack**: 272; **Pål
Hansen**: 288 (top); **Susan
McKeown**: 306.

Newspaper articles: The Boston
Globe (p.14); The Irish Times
(p. 83); Guardian (p.141).

Acknowledgements

Where to start?! Thirty-plus years of thank yous would fill every page of this book. I must start with the late Mór Murnahan, kindly senior lecturer at the catering college in Cathal Brugha Street, Dublin, who stuffed a piece of paper into my hand in 1968 with a name and address on it and said 'write to her'. The name on the piece of paper was Myrtle Allen, who is now my mother-in-law. She and my late father-in-law Ivan Allen have been a lifelong inspiration and support – a heartfelt thank you to you both.

Special mention also for my brother Rory O'Connell, who started the School with me in 1983 and who has continued to support me and teach here at the School as well as organising all the events and celebrations with the Cookery School team.

To all the wonderful people, past and present, who have worked with us here in every area of the enterprise over the years. We owe each and every one of you a huge debt of gratitude for the way you welcome, care for, and so generously and enthusiastically pass on your knowledge to everyone who comes to the School. This book is also your celebration and achievement.

To Emer Fitzgerald, who patiently and meticulously tested recipes over and over for this book.

Then there's Haulie Walsh, Eileen O'Donovan, Susan Turner and their team: the gardeners and organic farmers, all our suppliers, artisan producers, fishermen and fishmongers, butchers, bakers, poultry producers, fish smokers, cheesemakers......Where would we be without you? We are enormously grateful to you all.

Some other long-standing members of staff have been with us for in some cases over 30 years: Adrienne Forbes; Doreen Costine; Evelyn Ryan; Florrie Cullinane; Joe Cronin; Mary Dewane; Maura Daly; Pam Black; Sharon Hogan and Sue Cullinane. Will Kenneally, Dennis O'Sullivan, Jimmy Lee and all the builders and decorators of the 'no problem team' were involved every step of the way.

A particular tribute to Aunt Florence, who welcomes and entertains everyone who visits the Cookery School.

A huge thanks also to the many students who shared their recipes with us and now with all of you.

We are also indebted to Colm McCan, consultant sommelier at Ballymaloe House, who takes the mystery out of wine and also enthuses the students with a passion for organic, biodynamic and natural wines. Over the years, he has enticed some of the most iconic winemakers in the world to the Ballymaloe Cookery School and The Grainstore as well as inspirational speakers such as Jancis Robinson and Nick Lander.

Kyle Cathie has published seven of my cookbooks, a huge thank you for your encouragement, support and patience. Special thanks also to my editor Vicky Orchard, for her guidance and astute editing. And to Catherine Ward, for copy editing the recipes; to Louise Leffler, for the beautiful design, Linda Tubby and Polly Webb-Wilson, the ace team who cooked, propped and styled my foods for the photographs.

To Laura Edwards for her beautiful photos of the food and Kinoith. And to Emily Ashworth for generously sharing her photographs of her time at the School.

To the photographers who kindly gave us permission to use their images: Peter Cassidy, Ray Main, Melanie Eclare, Kevin Dunne, Cullen Allen, Joleen Cronin, Diane Cusack, John Minihan, Pål Hansen, Susan McKeown, Cristian Barnett, Francine Lawrence and Ray Roberts.

A special acknowledgment also to Susan McKeown, for trawling through and collating old photos for weeks on end.

Rosalie Dunne, my PA of 24 years, came out of retirement to help with research. Her exceptional recall has been invaluable in piecing together the many wonderful memories of the last 30 years. I simply couldn't have put this book together without her input – a heartfelt thank you.

To Tim, for his constant support and for creating such a beautiful environment around the Cookery School. Last, but not least, our children: Isaac, Toby, Lydia and Emily and their partners Rachel, Penny, Rupert and Philip, all of whom contribute in a myriad significant ways. Finally our nine grandchildren: Joshua, Lucca, Scarlet, Willow, India, Amelia, Jasper, Ottilie and Zaiah, who will hopefully carry on the legacy that Ivan and Myrtle entrusted to us.

Guest Chefs

To the myriad guest chefs who have come to the Ballymaloe Cookery School since 1984 to share their knowledge with us. The list of names reads like a 'Who's Who' of the food world.

Deh-Ta Hsiung; John Desmond; Claudia Roden; Madhur Jaffrey; Ada Parasiliti; Lady Suzanne Mahon; Alicia Ríos; Sri Owen; Jane Grigson; Antony Worrall Thompson; Rose Gray & Ruth Rogers; Frances Bissell; Margaret Ryan; Anne Willan; Marcella Hazan; Sophie Grigson; Roger & Olivia Goodwillie; Alastair Little; Paul & Jeanne Rankin; Ursula Ferrigno; John Ash (Fetzer Vineyard); Seamus O'Connell; Rory O'Connell; Naranjan McCormack; Nina Simonds; Kevin Orbell-McSean; Rachel Allen; Rick Bayless; Julia Wight; Marie-José Sevilla; Sam Clark; George Gossip; Denis Cotter; Doris Lehnigk; Eric Treuille; Wasinee Soratee Beech; Paul Flynn; Maggie Beer; Merrilees Parker; Suzie McCully; Hugh Fearnley-Whittingstall; Peter Gordon; Skye Gyngell; Claire Ptak; Richard Corrigan; Thomasina Miers; Gerard Coleman; Yotam Ottolenghi & Sami Tamimi; Jean-Pierre Moullé; Philip Dennhardt; Debbie Shaw; Eddie O'Neill; Barny Haughton; Shermin Mustafa; Sunil Ghai; Gillian Hegarty; Pamela Black; Mary Jo McMillin; Jeremy Lee; Mickael Viljanen; Kitty Travers (La Grotta Ices); J.R. Ryall; Jacob Kenedy; Chad Robertson & Richard Hart (Tartine Bakery); Maria Cho; David Thompson; Stevie Parle; Camilla Plum; Bill Yosses; David Tanis; Yannick Van Aeken & Louise Bannon.

The Ballymaloe
Cookery School

Ballymaloe
Cookery
School